IMAGES
of America

Rural Life in Murray County

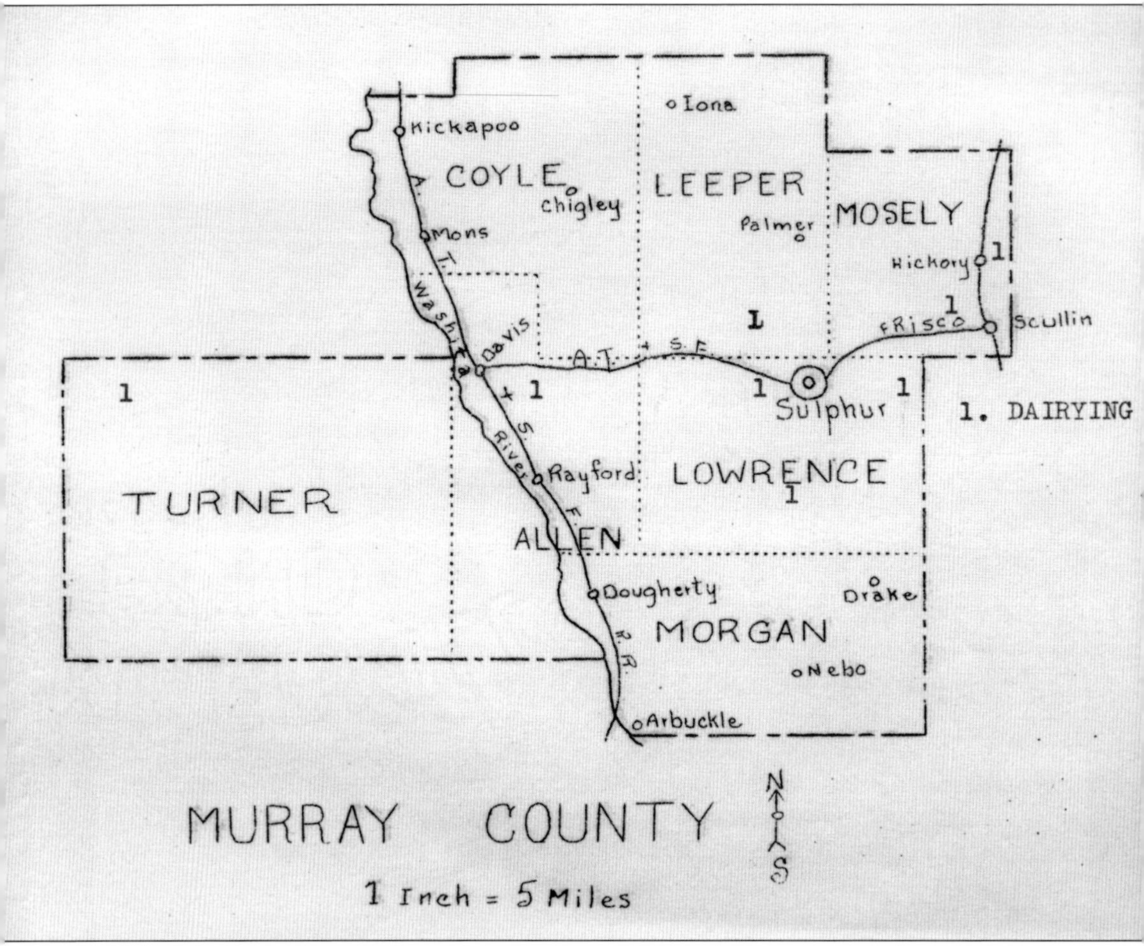

This hand-drawn map of Murray County is the first map found in extension records (1930). The agent used the "1" on the map to mark the largest dairies found in the county at that time. The record makes reference to over 20 farms with dairy cattle demonstrations and a total sale of $75,000 of butterfat sold in 1929–1930, more than the cash value of the cotton crop for the same time. During the time of this map, the agent was working to educate farmers on the use of the cooperative creamery and the importance of exchanging of bulls across the county to change dairy cattle blood lines in order to increase milk production. (Courtesy of the Murray County Extension Service.)

On the Cover: The state home demonstration agent, Norma Brumbaugh, is served the first cup of punch during a meeting of the Home Demonstration Club at the home of Mrs. C.E. Stockton. Mrs. Stockton's husband made the tea cart from scrap lumber, and the proud club hostess uses her best crock and teacups for serving. Her smile leads the viewer to believe she is very proud to be hosting such an important guest. (Courtesy of the Murray County Extension Service.)

IMAGES
of America

RURAL LIFE IN MURRAY COUNTY

Debbie Sharp

ARCADIA
PUBLISHING

ISBN 978-1-4671-1391-5

Published by Arcadia Publishing
Charleston, South Carolina

Printed in the United States of America

Library of Congress Control Number: 2015940335

For all general information, please contact Arcadia Publishing:
Telephone 843-853-2070
Fax 843-853-0044
E-mail sales@arcadiapublishing.com
For customer service and orders:
Toll-Free 1-888-313-2665

Visit us on the Internet at www.arcadiapublishing.com

This book is dedicated to the memory of Roland Earsom, a true Murray County historian who coined the phrase, "Yesterday's necessities are tomorrow's treasures, only if collected today," and to the early extension agents who truly were pioneers of rural education.

CONTENTS

Acknowledgments

This book was created with three goals in mind; first, to pay tribute to the early-day settlers of the rugged Arbuckle Mountains; to acknowledge the tremendous impact the Oklahoma A&M Cooperative Extension has had on the lives of Murray County citizens; and finally, to record for generations to come what we know about the county's people, communities, schools, and extension agents during the early 20th century.

Unless otherwise noted, the images appearing in this book are from the files of extension records. Other photographs have been borrowed from local families or other sources.

The Cooperative Extension Service continues today to meet the educational needs of both the rural and city dwellers of Murray County. The year 2014 marked the 100th birthday of Cooperative Extension Service work in America. Many countries from across the world study the Cooperative Extension Service model as well as the successes the work has accomplished. This is Murray County's personal story.

This book documents with photographs and captions the history of the families, communities, schools, and the lands of Murray County, as education and new practices were introduced and lives were changed for the better.

INTRODUCTION

Murray County, located in south central Oklahoma, is the state's third smallest county in land area and consists of rolling hills, large outcrops of rocks, and some of the world's most unusual rock formations as part of the Arbuckle Mountains. The county is the home of the state's largest waterfalls, 177-foot Turner Falls, and the nation's seventh oldest, and smallest national park, the original Platt National Park, established in 1904 and, later, renamed Chickasaw National Recreation Area in 1976.

The area was named in honor of William H. "Alfalfa Bill" Murray, president of the 1906 Oklahoma Constitutional Convention and, later, the ninth governor of the new state of Oklahoma, which entered the Union in 1907.

Present-day Murray County was once part of the land granted to the Choctaw Nation by the Treaty of Dancing Rabbit Creek in 1820. The Chickasaw Nation later received the area of land that makes up Murray County under the Treaty of Doaksville in 1838, and the area became part of the Chickasaw Nation in 1855.

In 1902, the Chickasaw Nation sold to the US government a 640-acre parcel of land, and Congress established the Sulphur Springs Reservation in an effort to protect 32 freshwater and mineral springs. The name was changed in 1904 to Platt National Park.

All land in Oklahoma, with the exception of the Panhandle, is surveyed from the "Initial Point," a location established in the Arbuckle Mountains in 1870, and is located in Murray County. The historic rock marker, from which surveying began, is located about one mile from the original Fort Arbuckle.

In an effort to truly appreciate the content of this book, one has to understand the humble beginnings of education of the rural populations across America. These hardworking people often received little public education because leaving school at an early age and working on their family farms was necessary in helping to provide for their families. Nationwide, this common practice kept families in poor living and economic conditions. With the passage of the Morrill Act of 1862, under the authority of Pres. Abraham Lincoln, the door to rural education opened slightly when the federal government issued the instruction for each state to set up a land-grant university for the purpose of teaching branches of learning related to agriculture and mechanical arts. In 1890, the territorial legislature established Oklahoma's land-grant college, naming the school Oklahoma Agricultural & Mechanical (A&M) College.

There was little outreach from the college for the first decade. There were the occasional off-campus lectures and an on-campus institute; time was needed for developing and growing, as well as introducing people to the roles of college and the need for higher education.

In 1914, Congress passed the Smith-Lever Act, which created a series of cooperative partnerships across the nation with the land-grant institutions, the individual states, and with the people of each county and parish. The mission of this partnership was to inform people about current developments in agriculture and home economics and to work with youth development, which became known as the 4-H Program. This partnership was known as the Cooperative Extension Work in Agriculture and Home Economics.

Before the arrival of Murray County's first agents, Oklahoma A&M College used farm agents to ride from farm to farm in a buggy or on horseback to share information; however, most of this work was in the northern and western parts of the state. Railroads were also used and proved to be the most reliable method of transportation, opening routes to the southern and eastern parts of the state. In 1913, the Santa Fe Railroad and the Oklahoma A&M College equipped and staffed an eight-car train that carried poultry and hogs along with agents who spoke on domestic science and boys' and girls' agriculture clubs. The train was then switched to the Frisco lines, which traveled the other directions, and records show the train made stops in Sulphur and Davis, the first introduction of agriculture education to Murray County citizens.

In 1929, the first county farm agent arrived in Murray County. This agent, S.E. Lewis, worked for eight months and was followed by agent L.I. Bennett. The first office was located in a creamery but was later moved to the courthouse where agents and a clerk shared office space with the county superintendent of schools.

In February 1929, Susie Baker arrived in Murray County to become the first county home demonstration agent. Prior to the arrival of these two agents, the county records reflect some type of youth work was organized around 1923, perhaps that of the Boy's Corn Club and the Girl's Tomato Club. After the arrival of these two agents, the youth work became recognized as the 4-H Club.

Rural life in Murray County was difficult when extension work began. There were poor roads, very poor living conditions, little running water or indoor plumbing, rugged mountain terrain, and land that had been over worked with the growing of cotton. The 1930s saw the most severe drought on record. Traditional farming practices, overgrazing, inappropriate farming practices, high winds, and the economic depression all led to the name "Dirty Thirties," which was a tough time to try to introduce new ideas and change the way of life, and thinking, for so many. The new agents had their work cut out for them.

In the county's earliest days (in 1929 records), the towns of Sulphur, Davis, Dougherty, Hickory, and Scullin were hubs of activity. There were five high schools located in Sulphur, Davis, Joy, Dougherty, Scullin, and Hickory and 15 two-room schools located at Palmer, Drake, Oak Grove, Fletcher, Big Canyon, Nebo, Buckhorn, Russell, Fair View, Chigley, Iona, Prices Chapel, Colbert, Rock Creek, and Koller. Three one-room schools were located at Moss, Sunshine, and Carr Chapel.

The county was connected with two state highways, Highway 18 running north and west and Highway 22 running south and east. There were 50 miles of graveled roads connecting Davis to Sulphur and Davis to the Carter County line; a good dirt and natural-gravel road connected Sulphur to Dougherty; and 25 miles of concrete road connected Davis and Wynnewood.

Principal crops were cotton, corn, Kaffir corn, oats, alfalfa, peanuts, and grain sorghum. Fruits, berries, and melons were grown, and some livestock was being raised, especially dairy cattle.

Natural resources included rich deposits of lead, zinc, and iron, and there were promising oil deposits. Also, asphalt, sand, gravel, and granite were abundant.

Today, 85 years later, Murray County does not look at all like its early days. Cattle are the main agricultural crop, and no dairies can be found. All rural schools have closed, and only two public schools remain in Sulphur and Davis. The county's largest employer is government with employees in public schools, the Chickasaw National Recreation Area, Oklahoma School for the Deaf, and the Oklahoma Veterans Center. An interstate runs along the west side of the county, state highways are paved, the state's smallest turnpike connects the interstate to Highway 7, and very few gravel country roads can be found.

Rural pioneers have moved the rocks, established and plowed the fields, built the roads, established schools and communities, and carved 271,360 acres of raw land into a thriving and beautiful place for over 13,000 people to call home.

This book is written to acknowledge our rural history and is prepared with respect for those before us—those who knew the meaning of being a neighbor, who experienced hard work, enjoyed play, and respected the gifts of nature from the Creator. It is also written to acknowledge the truly creative concept of the Cooperative Extension Service and the impact this network has had on the development of people, places, and the lands of Murray County.

One

Early Days to Statehood

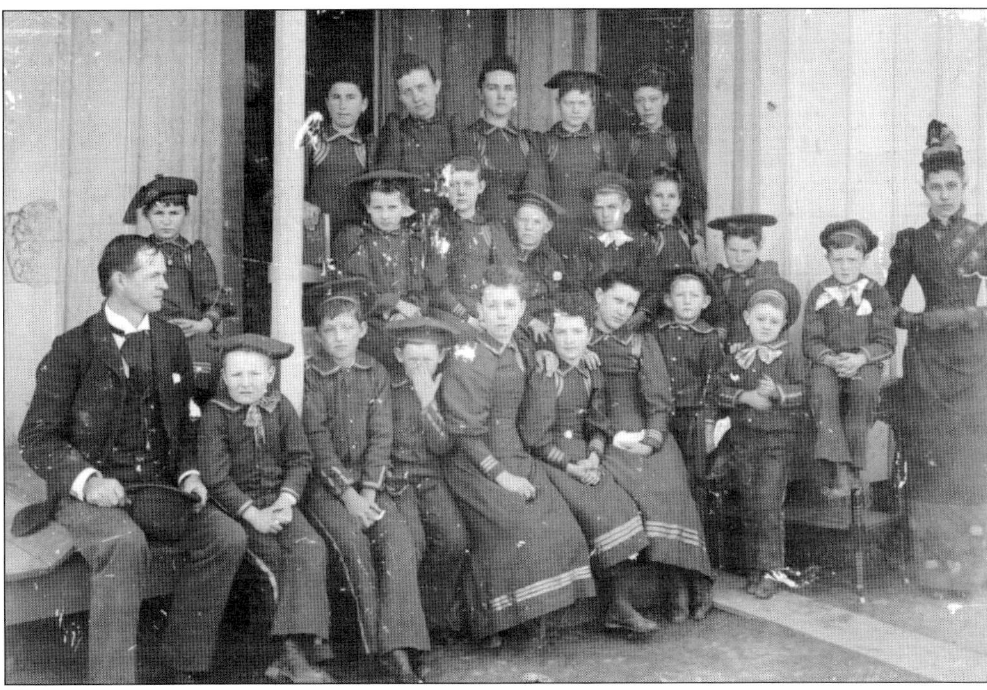

Schoolchildren and teachers are photographed in Indian Territory. The location of school in the county is unknown. There were three types of schools in early-day Indian Territories: subscription, mission, and tribal schools. A monthly tuition fee paid by the parents to the teachers funded subscription schools. Churches set up mission schools, and individual tribes funded tribal schools. (Davis Museum.)

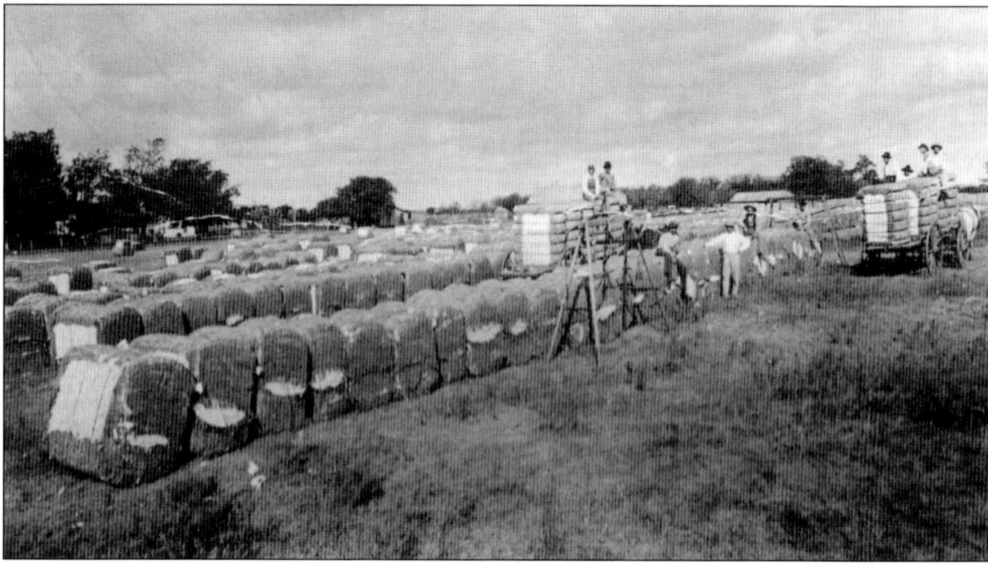

William "Bil" Findley owned this cotton yard located between Fifth and Sixth Streets in Davis, Indian Territory. Cotton was a major crop in the county, and the farming effects on the soils would play a role in the Dust Bowl that would occur in the 1930s. (Davis Museum.)

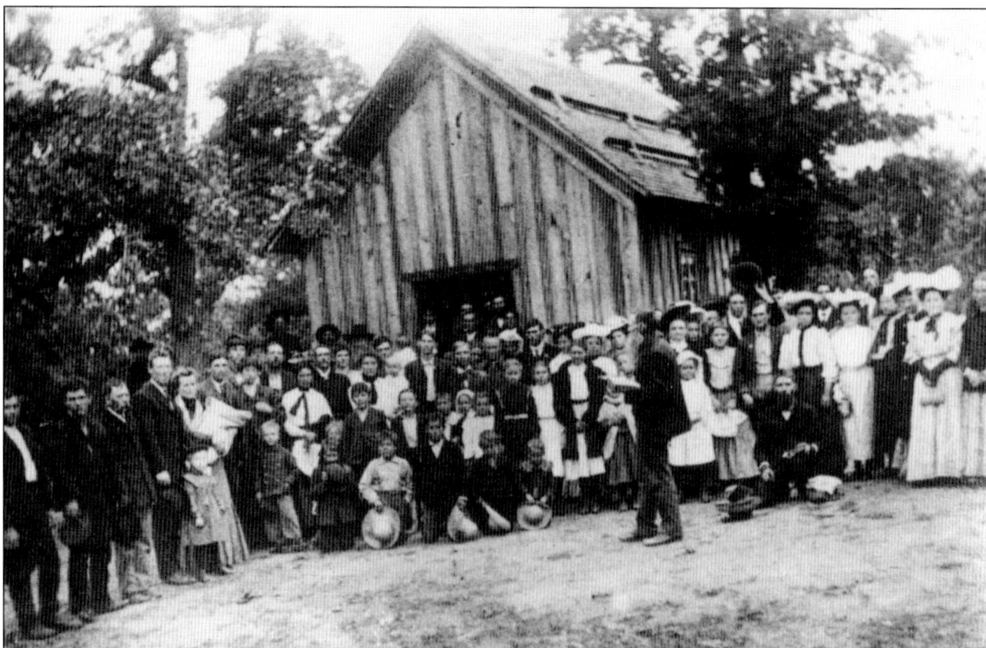

Missionary workers preach outside in the Chigley community. Prior to the Indian Removal Act, missionary workers from the seminaries and churches located in the east had begun work of "introducing Christianity" with tribes located in their original homelands in the south. Most of these missionaries were under the direction of the American Board of Commissioners for Foreign Missions, which was founded in 1810 by the Congregational and Presbyterian Churches. After removal, the mission work expanded to the Indian Territory where schools and churches were established. (Davis Museum.)

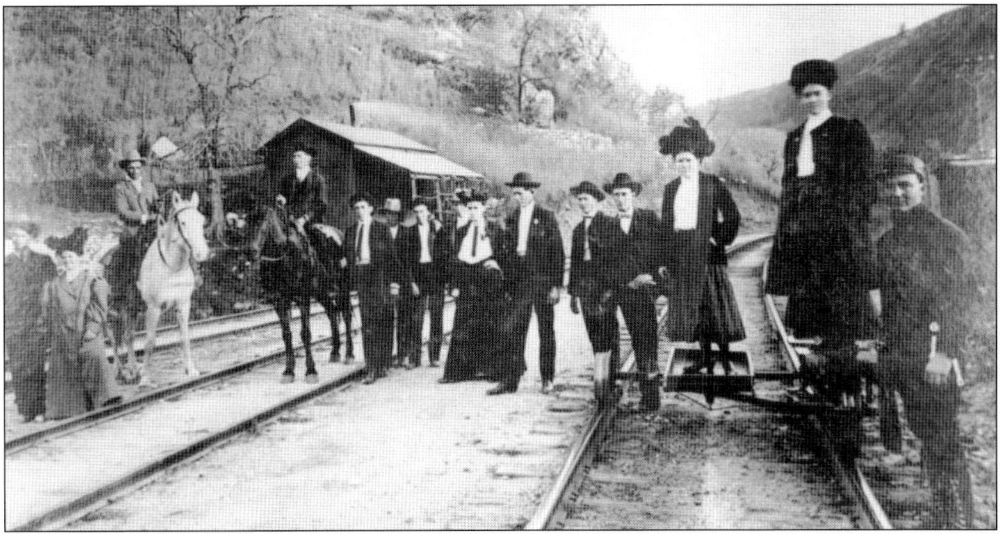

Here, workers are waiting for the Santa Fe train in the Arbuckle Mountains. The Atchison, Topeka and Santa Fe Railroad was one of the larger railroads in the United States and was established in 1859. The Santa Fe merged with the Burlington Northern on December 31, 1996, and later was renamed BNSF Railway. The train still runs through Davis, carrying freight north and south. (Davis Museum.)

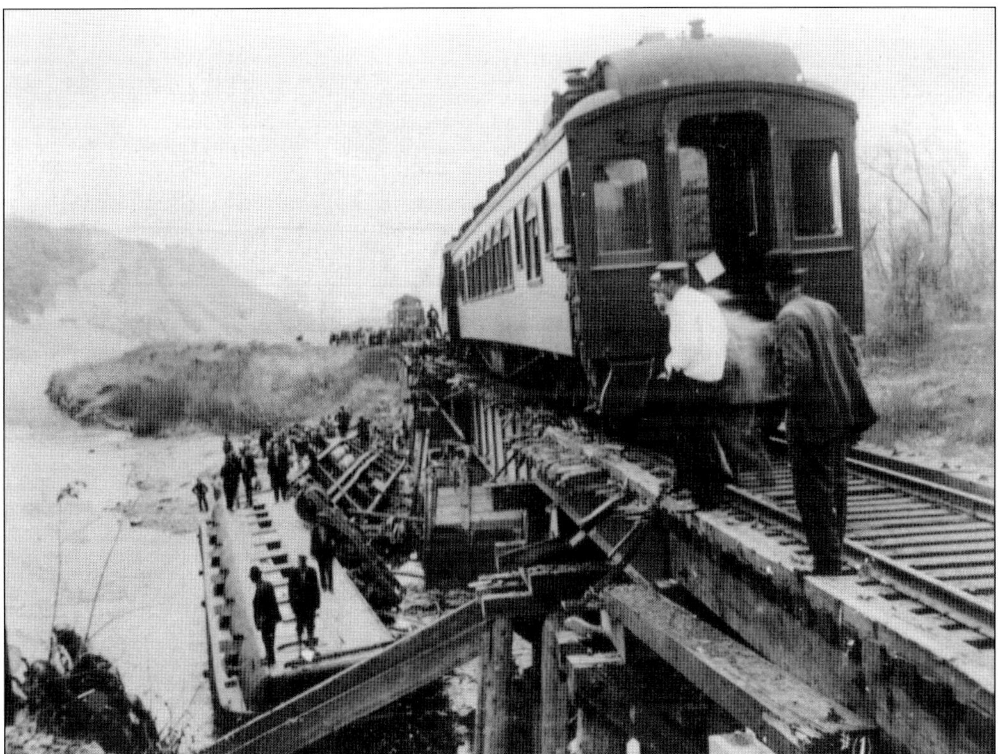

On Christmas Eve 1903, Santa Fe passenger train No. 5 derailed between Davis and Dougherty. Today, the Amtrak's *Heartland Flyer* travels the same cut through the mountains, carrying passengers from Oklahoma City to Fort Worth, Texas. (Davis Museum.)

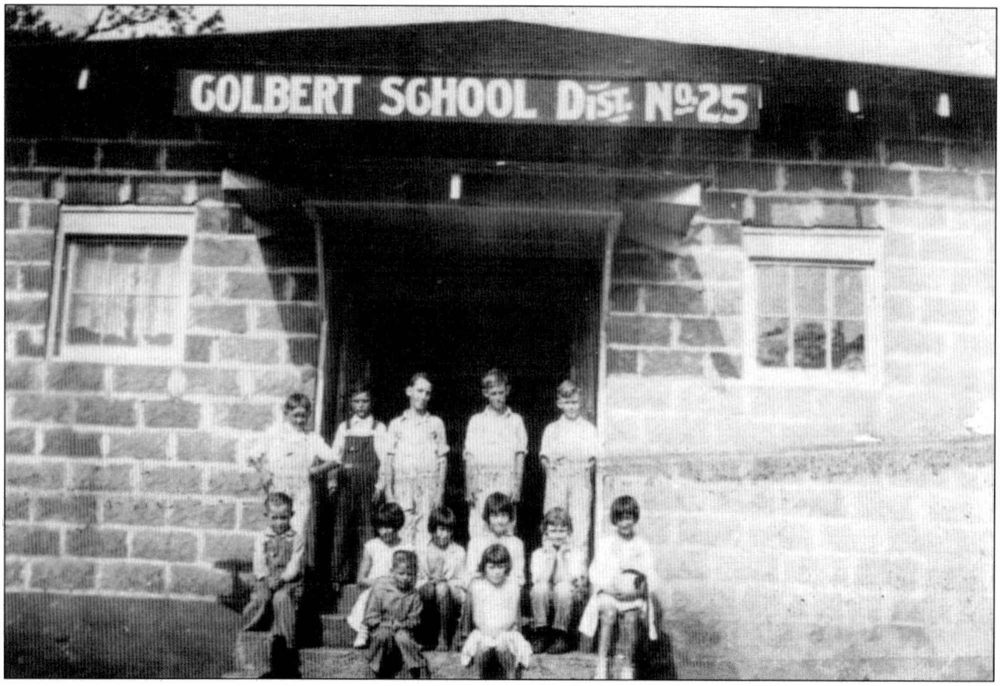

This photograph shows children at the Colbert School. The school closed in 1940 when it was annexed to Woodland School. The Colbert District No. 25 was located west of Davis. Woodland continued to operate until 1968, when it was forced to close due to low enrollment. Woodland was annexed into the Davis School District. (Davis Museum.)

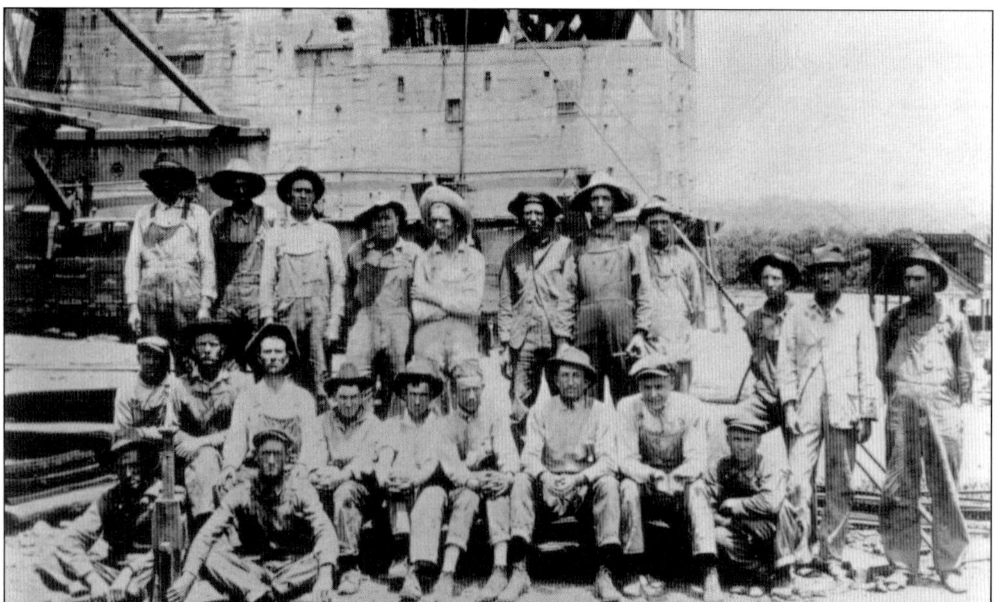

This is a 1918 photograph of the asphalt plant workers near Dougherty. Pyrite, quartz crystals, basalt, rhyolite, calcite, fluorite, porphyritic granite, Arbuckle limestone, anglesite, cerussite, dolomite, galena, hematite, smithsonite, elbaite, and Woodford Share are a few of the minerals mined today in Murray County. (Davis Museum.)

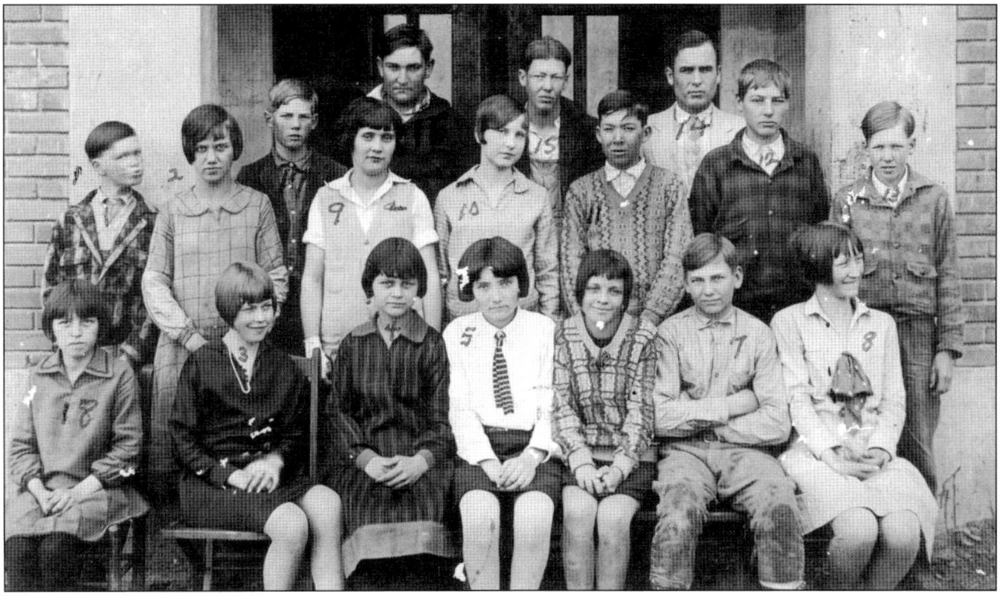

Pictured is a 1920s Hickory School class. Students are, from left to right, (first row) Fay Bradley, Imogene Welsh, Cora Bradley, Lahoma Gatlin, Vera Walters, James Smith, and Lillian Hicks; (second row) Halton Hyden, Thelma Hawkins, Liza Gond, Onilee Watson, N. Ozbirn, and Arthur Batson; (third row) J. Stidham, Gilbert Hewatt, Bill Whitsett, and teacher Lee Freeny. (Hickory Senior Citizens Center.)

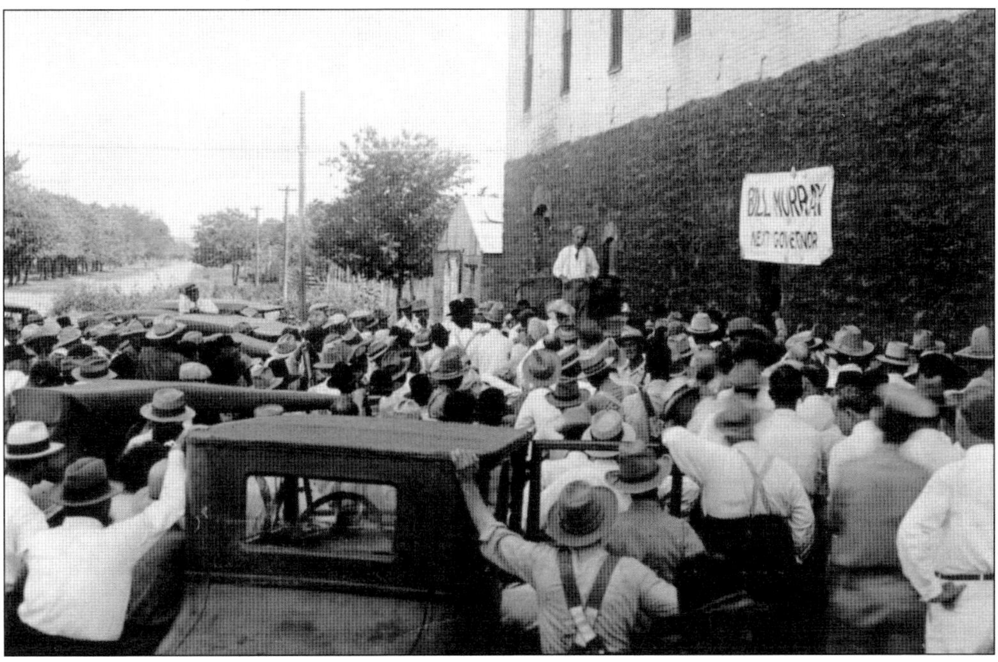

This photograph, taken in either 1910 or 1918, is of Bill Murray speaking to voters in Davis. Murray lost both the 1910 and 1918 elections for governor but was inaugurated as the ninth governor for the State of Oklahoma on January 12, 1930. Governor Murray and his family spent many summer days in Sulphur at the Artesian Hotel, enjoying the cool waters of the Platt National Park. (Davis Museum.)

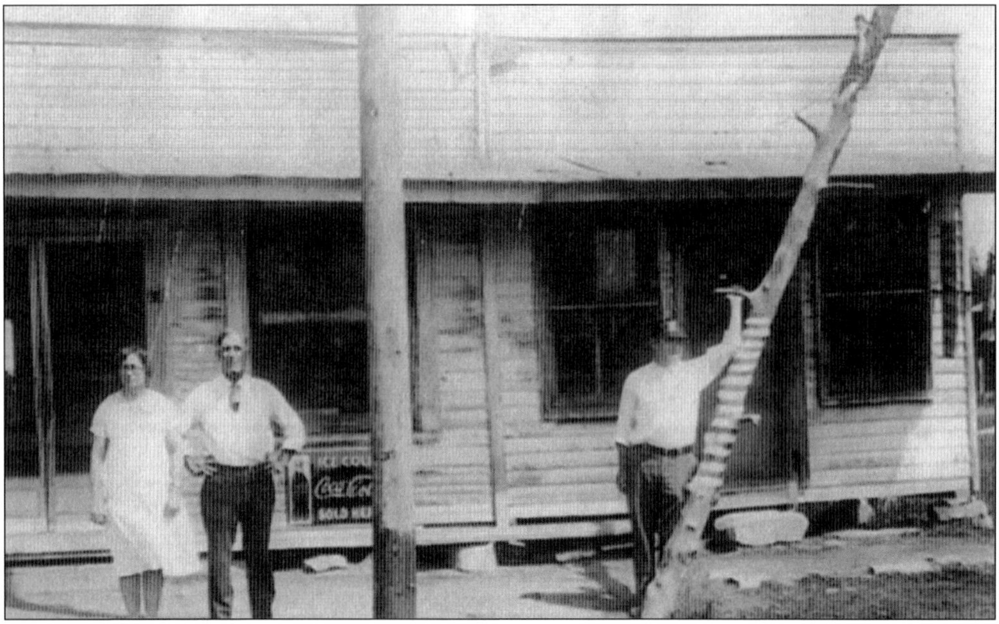

Taken in 1927, this photograph shows the Barvis Café and the Jess Payne Barbershop in Dougherty. Several Dougherty residents have tried to establish the location of these two businesses, but it remains a mystery.

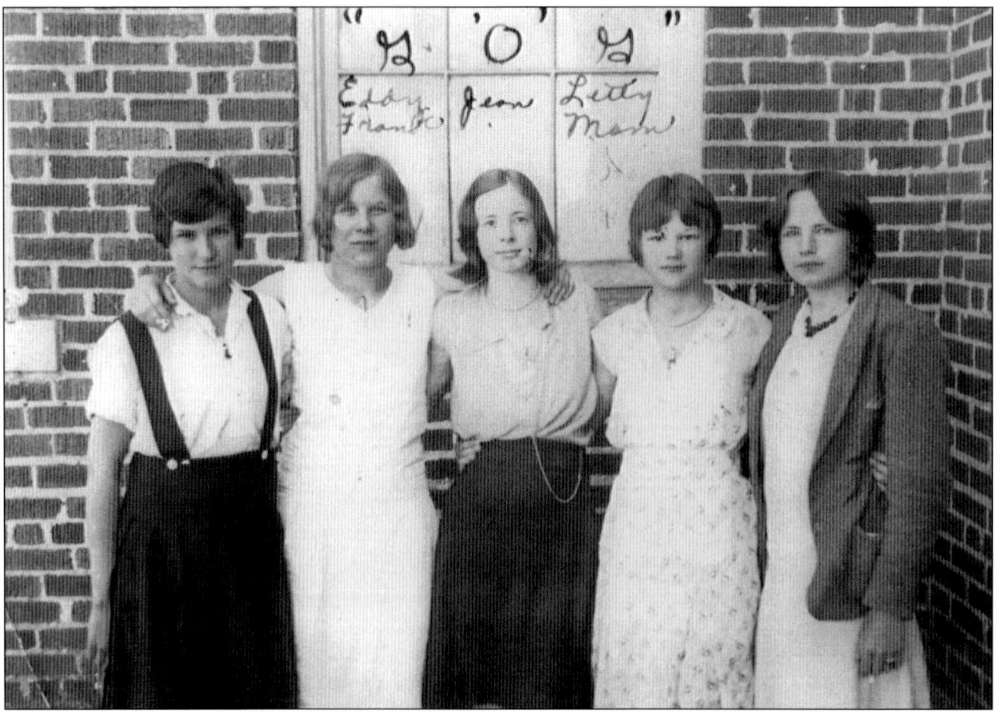

Pictured in 1929, friends from the Good O' Girls Club of Dougherty are, from left to right, Dollie (Hale) Deel, Frances Barrett, Bonnie King Pinkston, Oleta Stockton, and Oda (Easley) Richardson. Deel celebrated her 100th birthday on May 29, 2014. Pinkston was a teacher in Dougherty from 1931 to 1975, and Richardson was the postmistress for over 45 years in Dougherty.

Two

The Dirty Thirties

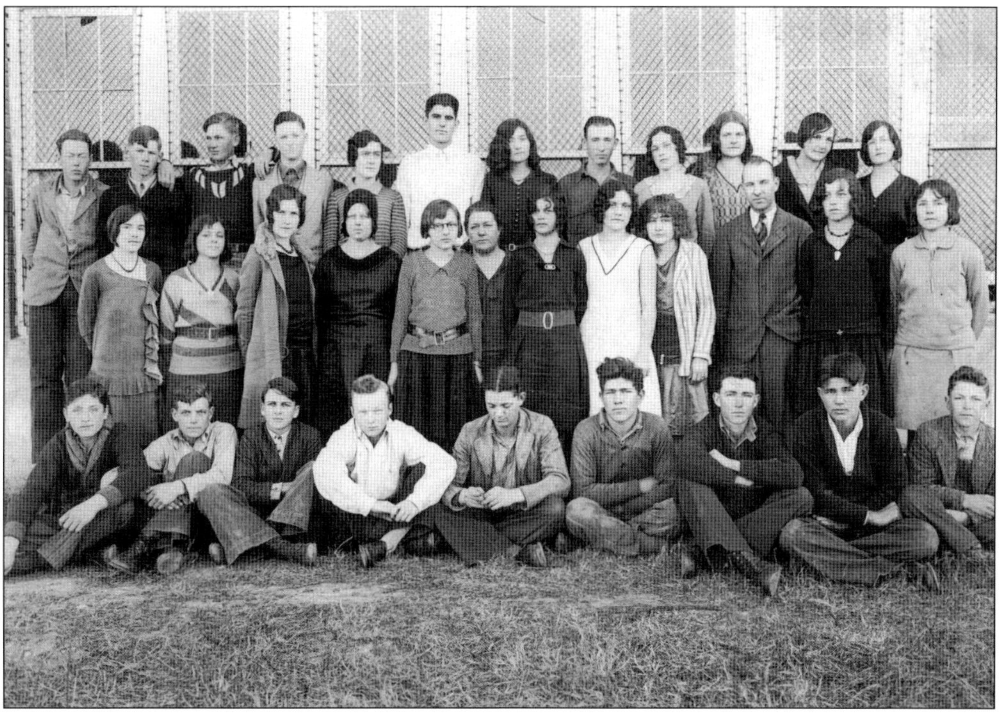

These Hickory High School students pose in a 1930 photograph. Pictured are, from left to right, (first row) O.L. Bynum Jr., Bill Jinks, Cecil Moore, A.P. Lewis, McGaha, Travis Crumb, Porter Craig, Lewis Crumb, and P.G. Waggoner; (second row) Juanita Roinson, Vera Walters, OnaLee Watson, Ruby Barrow, Maxine Bynum, Mrs. Smith, Cora Bradley, Liza Bond, Mary Goss, Ulysses Gaither, Fay Bradley, and Maybelle Craig; (third row) Bill Whitsett, Bill Lewis, Leonard Posey, Halton Hyden, Hughes, Paul Smith, Lahoma Gatlin, Wade Craig, Bessie Bond, Isabelle South, Batson, and Lucille Cockran. (Hickory Senior Citizens Center.)

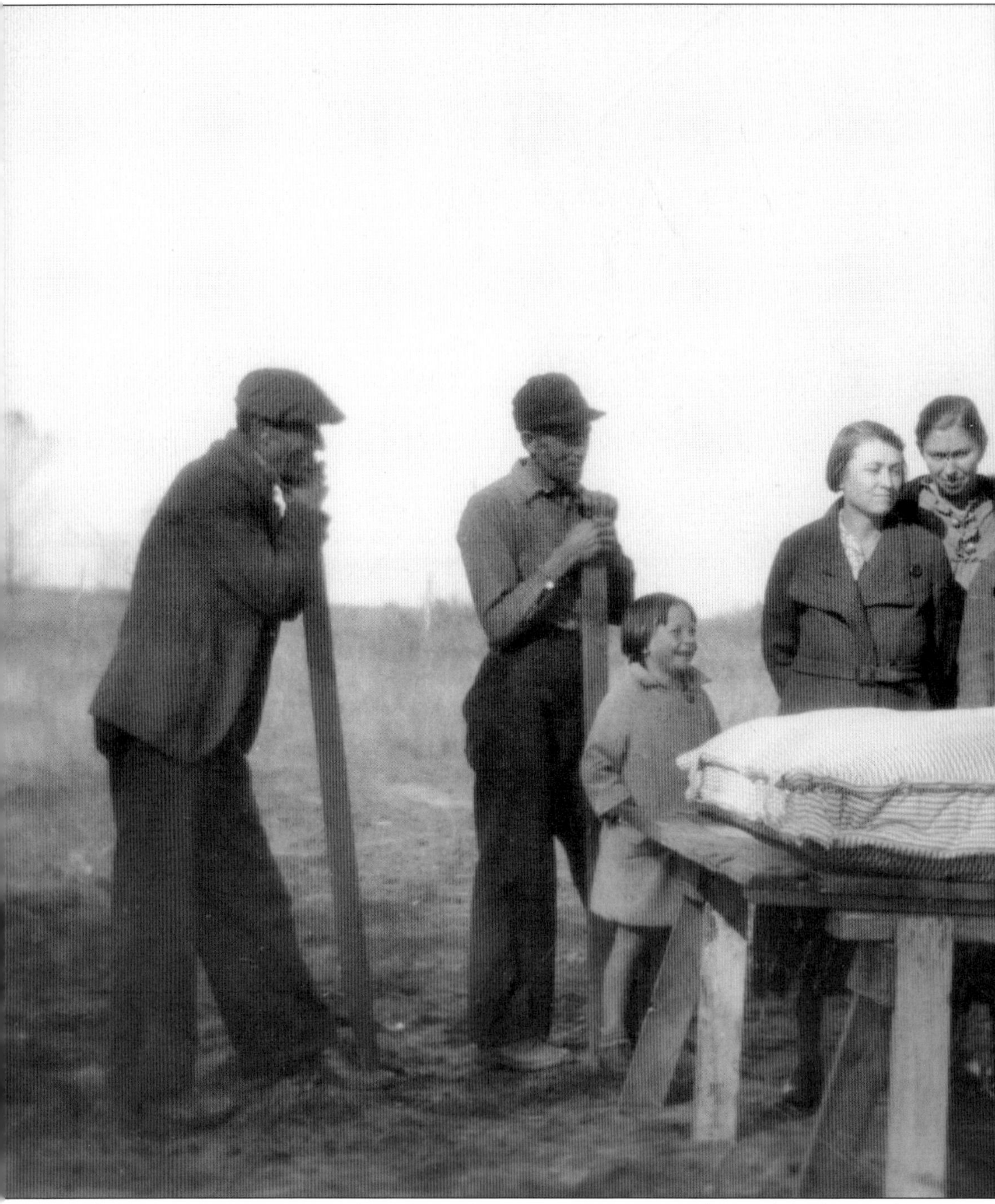

The extension program started in Murray County in 1929–1930, and one of the first goals was to make rural life more comfortable and healthier for rural families. In the first year of work, 512 families participated in educational meetings and programs. One of the first efforts included the home demonstration agent holding all-day mattress-making workshops, and home demonstration club women, often accompanied by their husbands, would gather to assist each other with mattress making. On a good day, they could produce two mattresses. This demonstration and workday

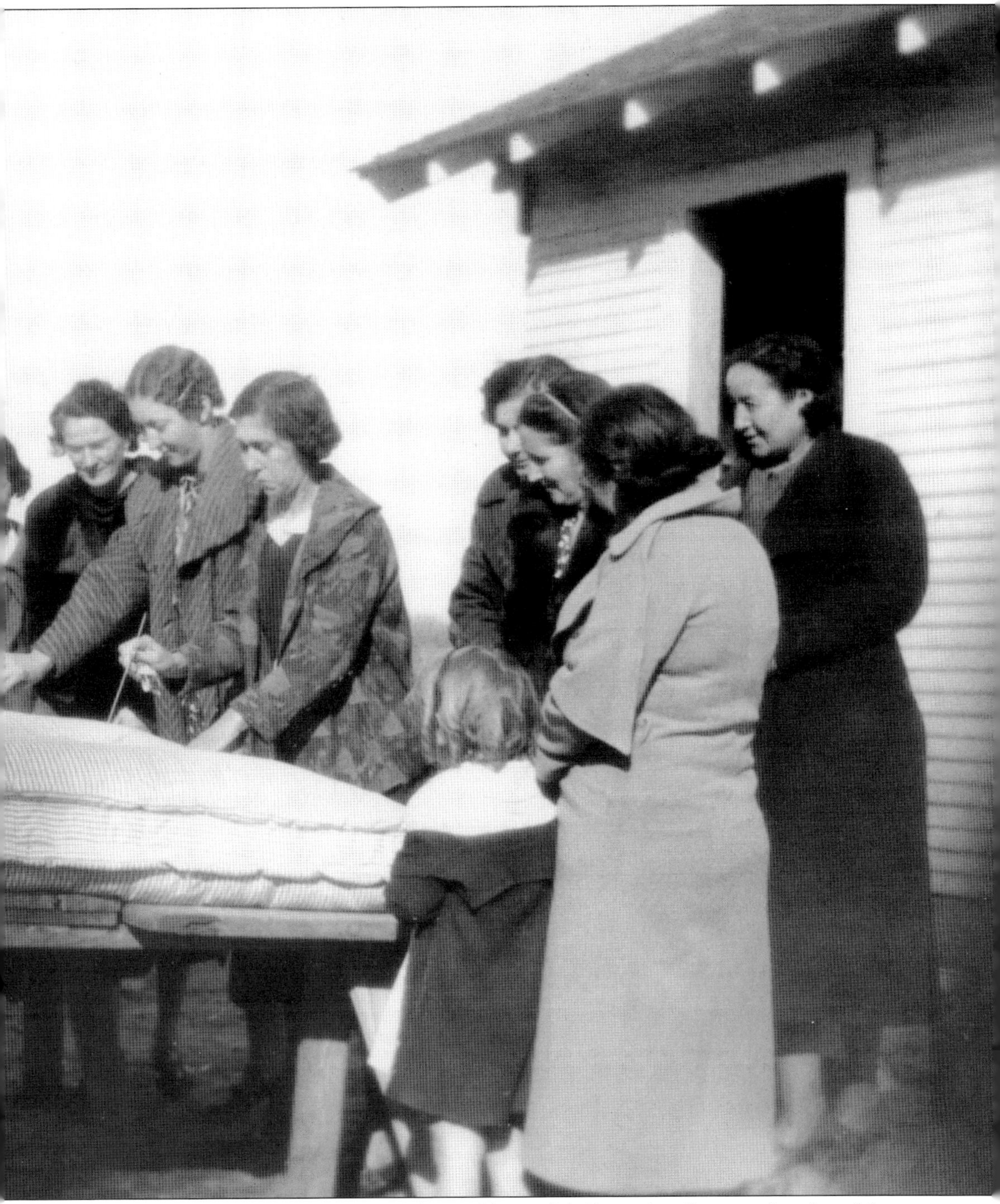

was at the home of Mrs. L.C. Spicer of the Buckhorn club. Records reflect sore hands and fingers and two very happy families. When extension work began, it focused on a program titled "Live at Home," which taught people how to provide for themselves by gardening, canning, improving the home with no or little cost, and making the family's clothing. The first extension office was in the Sulphur Creamery and moved to the courthouse in 1932, sharing office space with the county superintendent of schools.

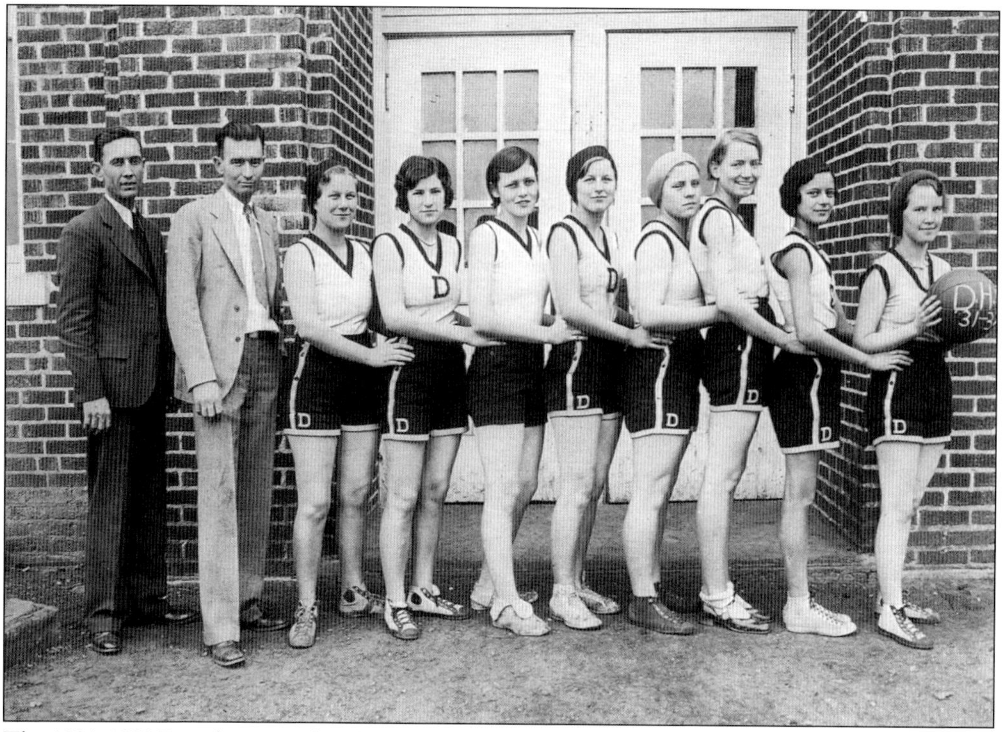

The 1931–1932 Dougherty High School basketball team poses for a team photogram. Pictured are, from left to right, Superintendent Hickman, Coach Newson, Frances Barrett, Dollie (Hale) Deel, Beatrice Neal, Essie Barrett, three unidentified players, and Bernice Loveless. (Judy Hale.)

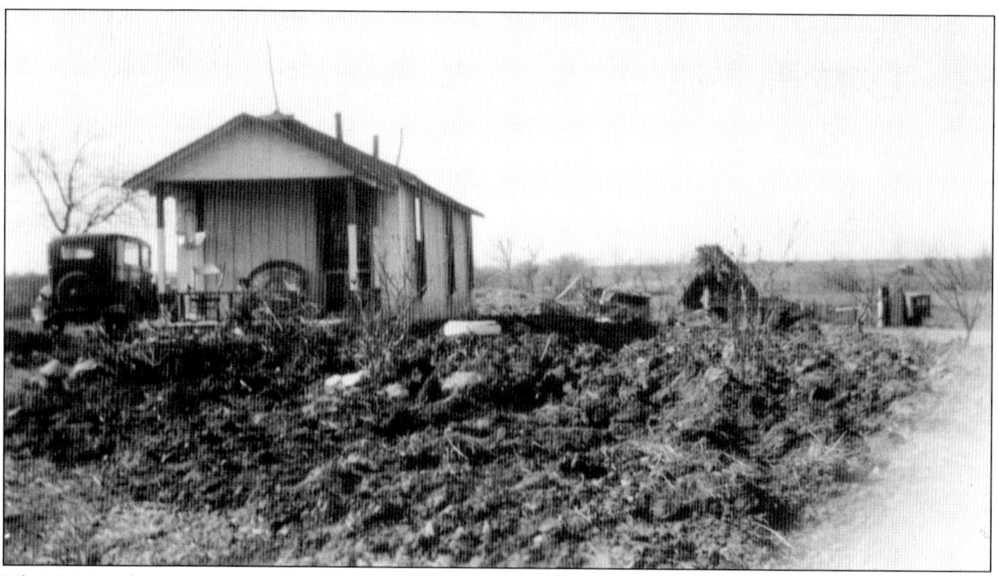

This image shows an example of a rural farmhouse in the late 1920s and 1930s in Murray County. Only a few homes had electricity, and even fewer had running water.

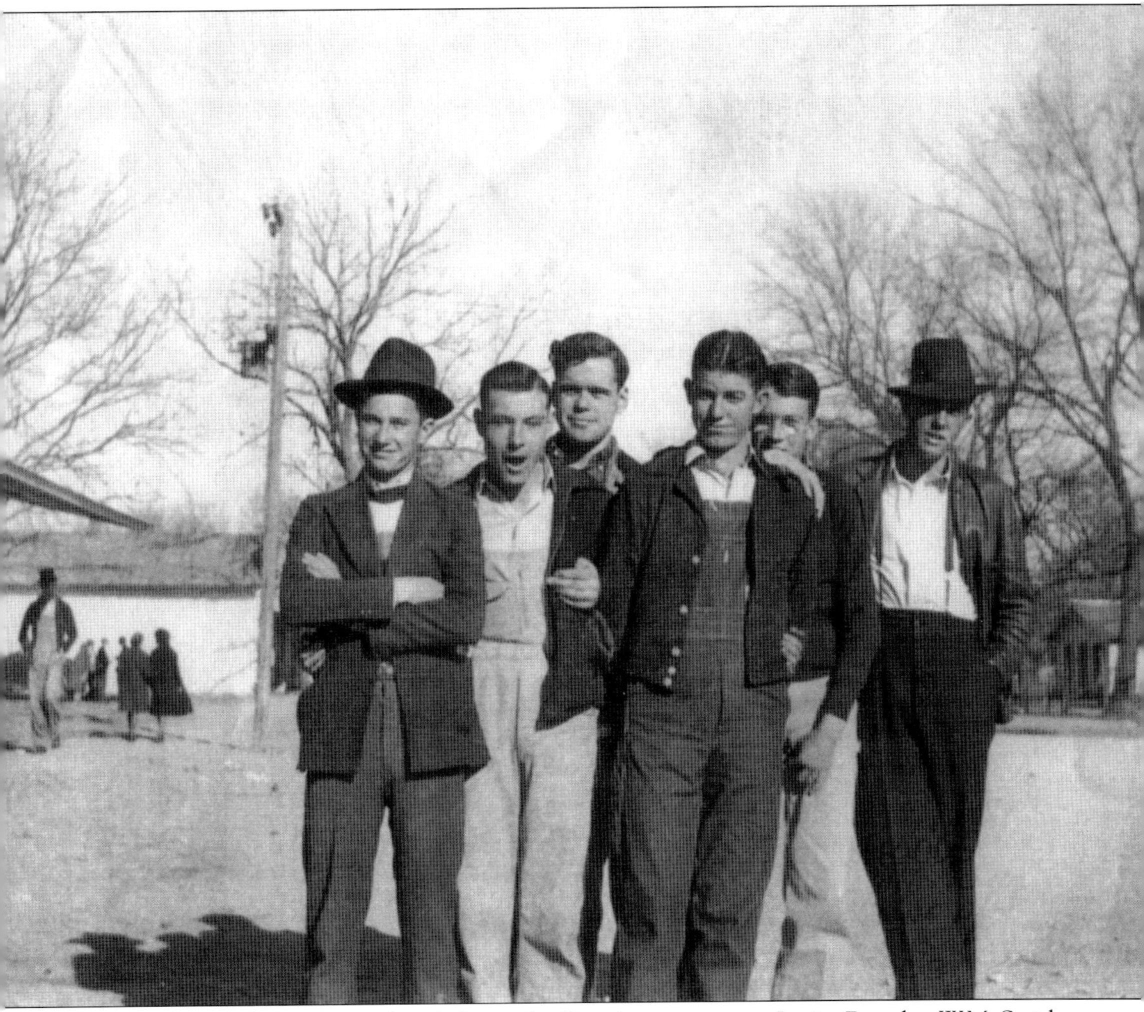

Pictured here in the 1930s are, from left to right, Dougherty teenagers Junior Donaho, W.M. Smith, J.C. Hunter, J.C. Pinkston, Don Loveless, and Paul West pose on Main Street. (Judy Hale.)

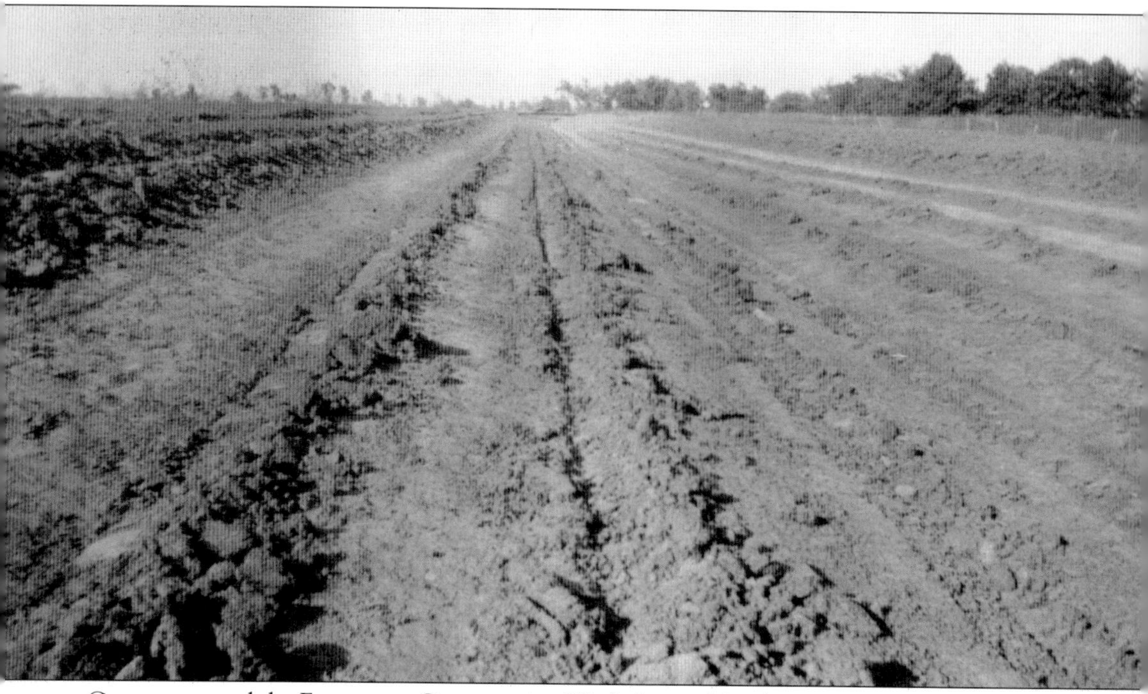

Congress passed the Emergency Conservation Work Act on March 31, 1933, under the direction of newly elected US president Franklin Roosevelt. In June of that year, Murray County began work on terracing. The county agent "ran lines" on 65 farms, and these terraces were built for an average cost of 95¢ per acre. It was estimated that the farmers land value was increased an average of $5 per acre with the terracing. With the exception of two farms, the work was done with the county road grader and county men. The average cost per day for the machine was $14. Records state, "The 12-foot machine did as much work in one day in building terraces as the average farm outfit could do in 10 days and did a much better job." Terraces were built on the farms belonging to the following men: H.G. Head, W.T. Hale, W.W. Jackson, R.L. Sandifer, S.A. DesMukes, Lee Martin, R.J. Horning, J.L. Jobe, J.B. Mosley, Fob Jones, J.H. Wilkins, and Collie Singletary. The 4-H Clubs also introduced terracing projects where boys were placed in teams. The Iona 4-H team represented the county at Oklahoma State 4-H Roundup competition in the same year, 1933.

Pictured is a traveling education car. On August 30, 1933, over 150 farm women attended the Farm Women's Camp held at Cold Springs in Platt National Park. A special visitor from the Kerr Jar Company, a Mrs. Bryant, spoke to the group on "Judging Fruits and Vegetables" and explained the different kinds of contests offered by the Kerr Jar Company. Bryant was traveling in one of the educational cars, carrying with her a large display of fruits and vegetables.

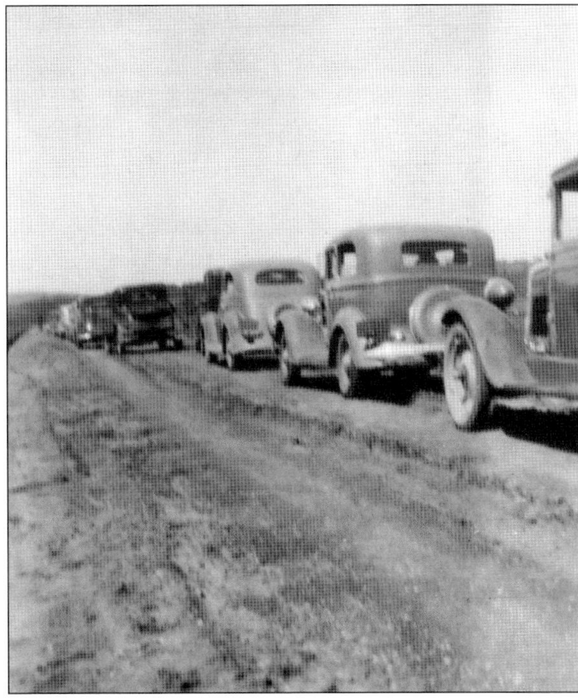

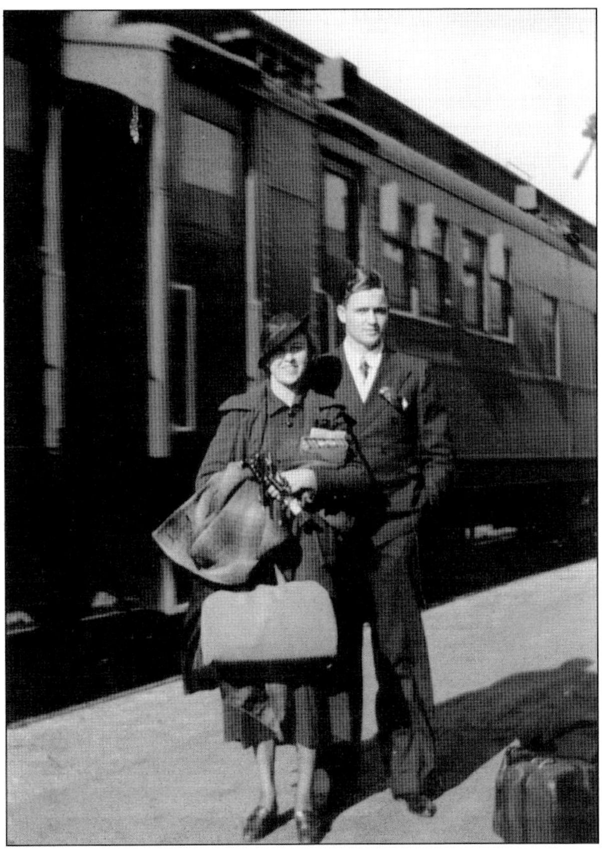

Wilma Moore of the Hickory 4-H Club and James Yingling of the Sulphur 4-H Club are shown returning from the International Livestock Show in Chicago. Moore was a "wash dress" contestant, and Yingling was the Oklahoma Health Champion. The 4-H delegates traveled by train, and this photograph dates from 1934.

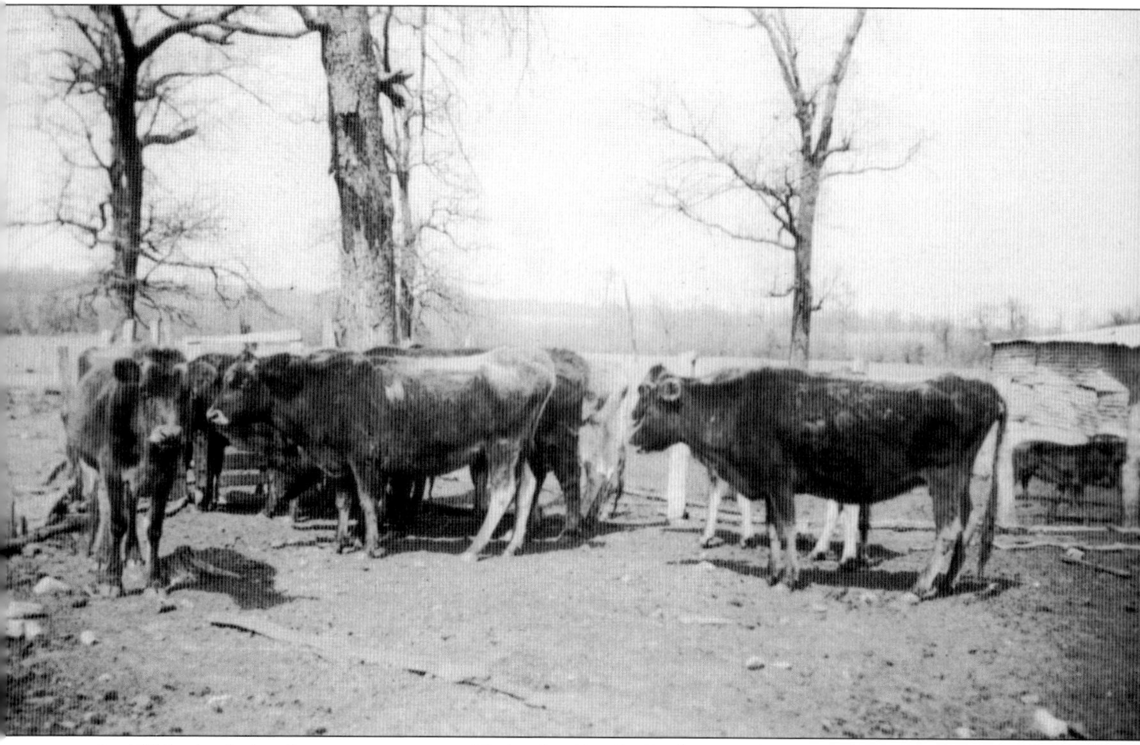

In 1934, the federal government established a Cattle Reduction Program because of the drought and the Great Depression. Over 4,400 cattle were slaughtered and removed from the county. Almost every "relief family" received part of a beef to can as food for their family. Many men lost jobs, and families were forced to grow and preserve their own food. Because of this emergency, the home demonstration agent set up canning schools in every community. The following is from a record about the emergency: "So many people were touched with the canning schools that the Davis community started a community cannery. Over 100 cans a day now, and as the work becomes more systemized we can do more and better work. On Monday, corn was canned for Jim Rowe, west of town. Tuesday more hot plates for using the pressure cooker were installed and 155 cans were canned for Walter Coffey." Also in 1934, two county banks were closed due to the Depression.

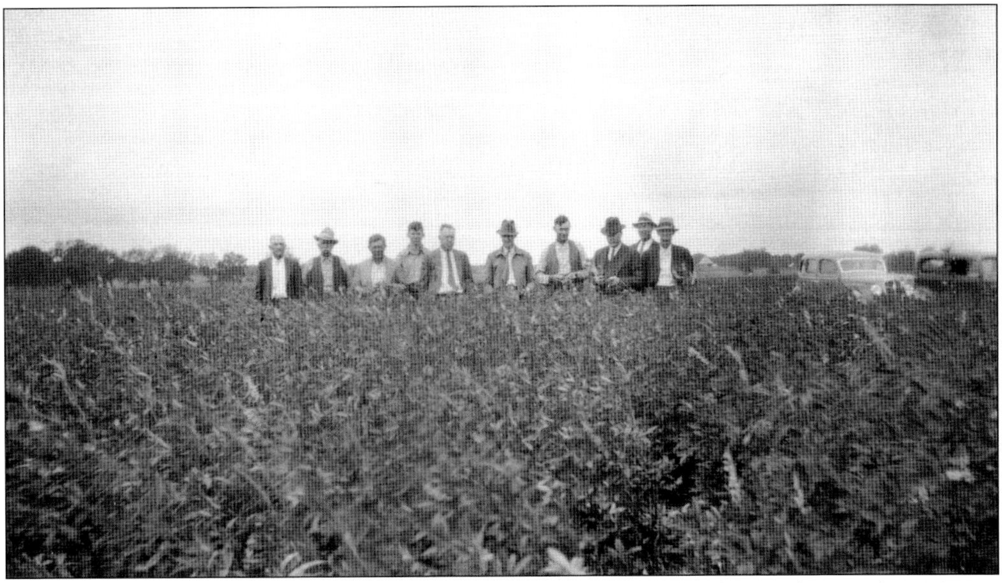

In December 1935, the federal relief program sent 30,000 pounds of Lespedeza seed to Murray County. Each of the 255 farms participating received 50 to 500 pounds of the free seed. This photograph was taken on the field of the Ross Smith farm west of Davis where Bermuda grass, lespedeza, and sweet clover were planted.

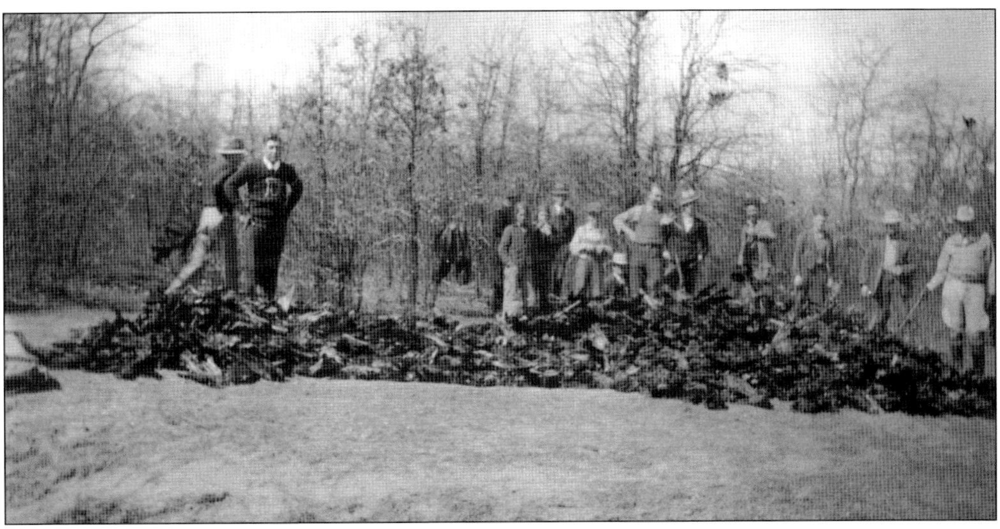

In 1935, rangers from the Oklahoma State Fish and Game Department set off 50 "bombs" in a crow roost near Hickory. Bombs were made of dynamite sticks placed in paper cylinders with shot taped around them. At 9:00 p.m., the bombs were set off, killing 4,346 crows and crippling around 2,000. The reason for this action was to reduce the damage the crows were inflicting on the area. Crows are omnivorous and will eat insects, spiders, fish, and snakes, as well as dead animals, fruits, nesting birds, vegetables, and nuts.

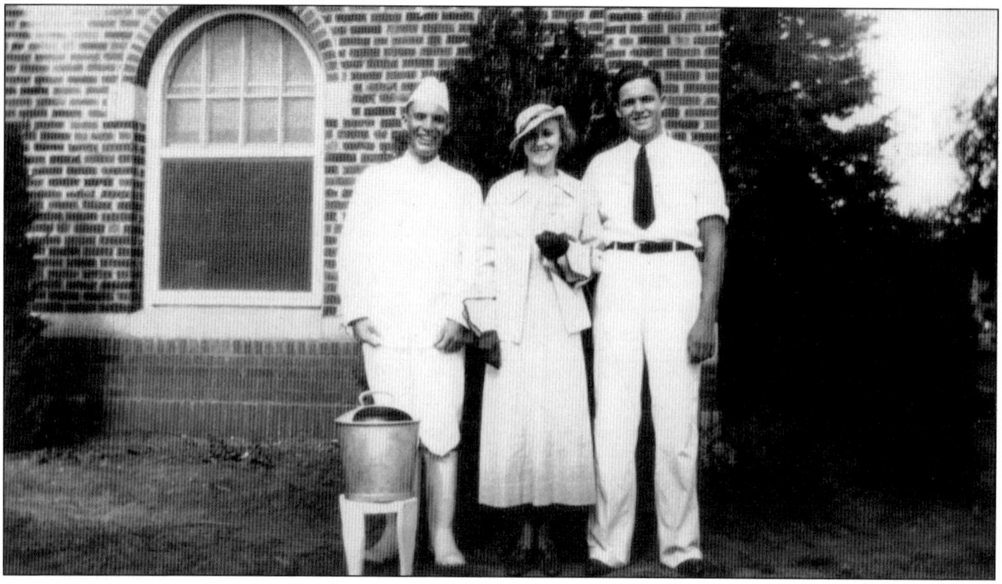

Pictured are three first-place winners at 4-H Roundup held on the Oklahoma A&M campus in 1935. From left to right are Carl Herring (winner of the dairy outfit contest), Wilma Moore (winner of the cotton wash dress contest), and James Yingling (winner of the health contest). The 4-H's work in the county was growing stronger, and 4-H youth chosen to lead the county that year were Fred Huffines of Joy as president, Essie Edgmon of Davis as vice president, Wilma Moore of Hickory as secretary, Bonnie Howard of Sulphur as song leader, Jimmie Frazier of Oak Grove as game leader, Herbert Clinton of Dougherty as stunt leader, Lucille Girod of Sulphur as reporter for the *Sulphur Daily News*, and Ora Mae Pullen of Davis as reporter for the *Davis News*.

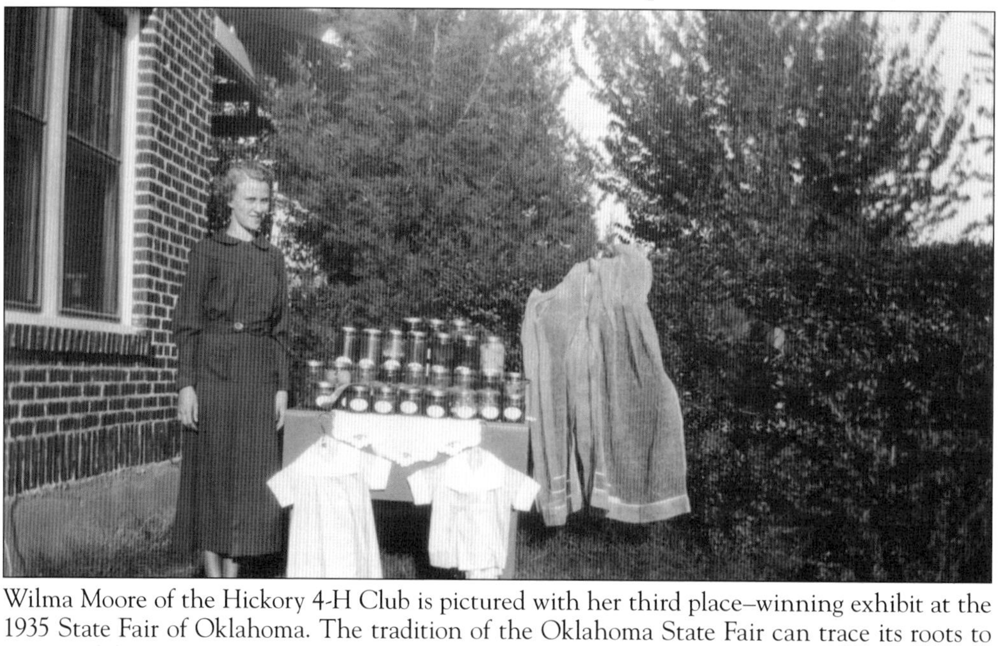

Wilma Moore of the Hickory 4-H Club is pictured with her third place–winning exhibit at the 1935 State Fair of Oklahoma. The tradition of the Oklahoma State Fair can trace its roots to territorial days. The first fairs were held in the eastern portion, or Indian Territory, and like most fairs, it centered on agriculture. This served as an opportunity to educate American Indians on "modern" farming practices and to also provide a social occasion for rural residents.

Here is the "brother and sister" outfits sewn by Wilma Moore of the Hickory 4-H Club. These outfits placed third at the 1935 State Fair of Oklahoma. Other ribbons were awarded to Virginia Yingling of the Nebo 4-H Club, who won third place in clothing judging and fourth place in canning and baking. John Bounds of Davis placed eleventh in dairy, and Thomas Smith of the Woodland 4-H Club placed eighth and tenth place for his wheat exhibits.

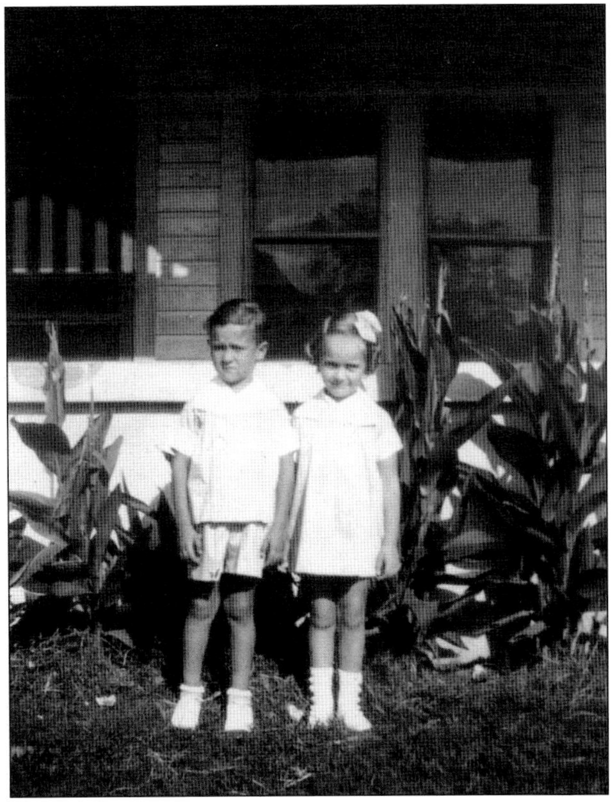

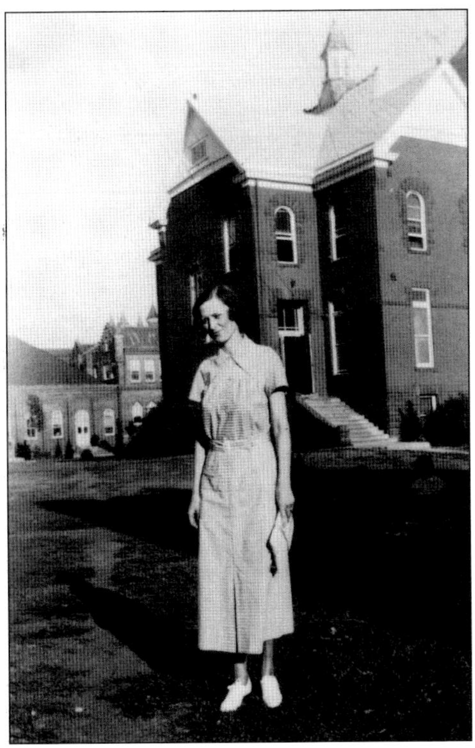

Mrs. Dick Grant of the Woodland Home Demonstration Club placed second for her housedress at the Stillwater Roundup in 1935. A housedress is a relatively simple and inexpensive dress that is suitable for housework.

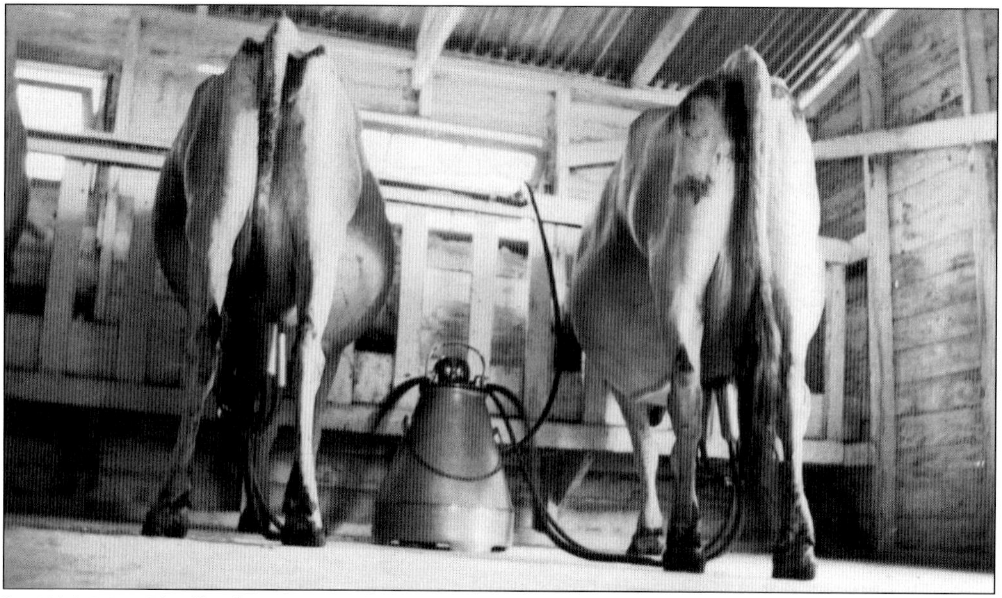

In 1936, Mac Chaffin demonstrated a new milking machine for a group of farmers on a farm tour. During this decade, there were many large dairies located in the Murray County, and J.B. Mosley had the largest dairy, milking 50 cattle a day. In cooperation with the Murray County Cheese Company, the county agent handed out 300 bulletins on homemade barrel milk coolers. Records show the quality of the milk improved for those who installed the coolers.

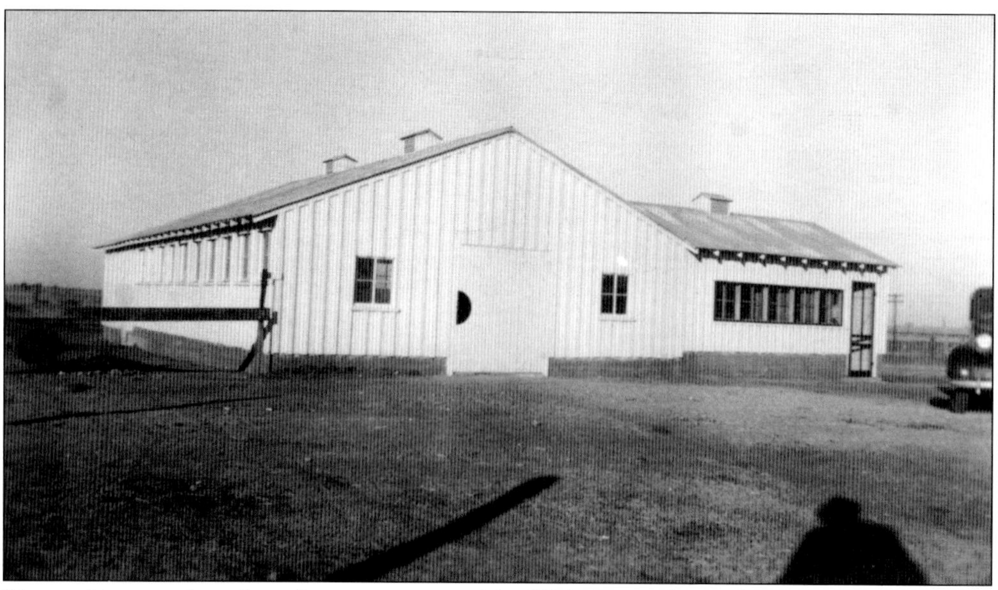

Pictured is a modern dairy barn constructed by W.A. Donaghe on his farm in the Scullin Community in 1936. The county agent assisted with the design of the barn.

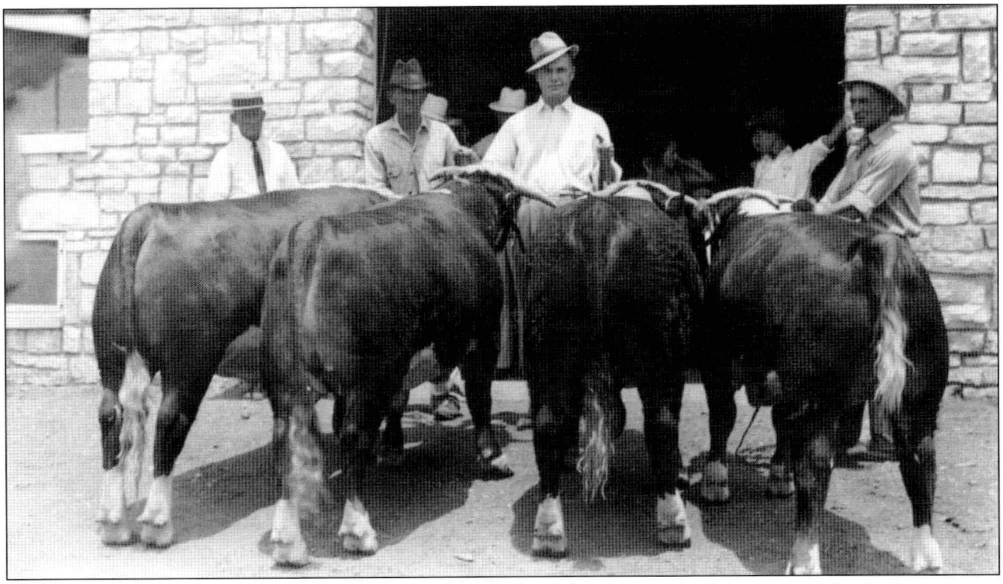

The Harper-Turner Ranch, located six miles east of Sulphur, presented four young bulls for viewing by area ranchers in 1936. The historic barns are still being used on the ranch, which is known today as the Jacobs Ranch. Jason Jacobs, the son of the late Bill Jacobs, operates and manages the ranch today.

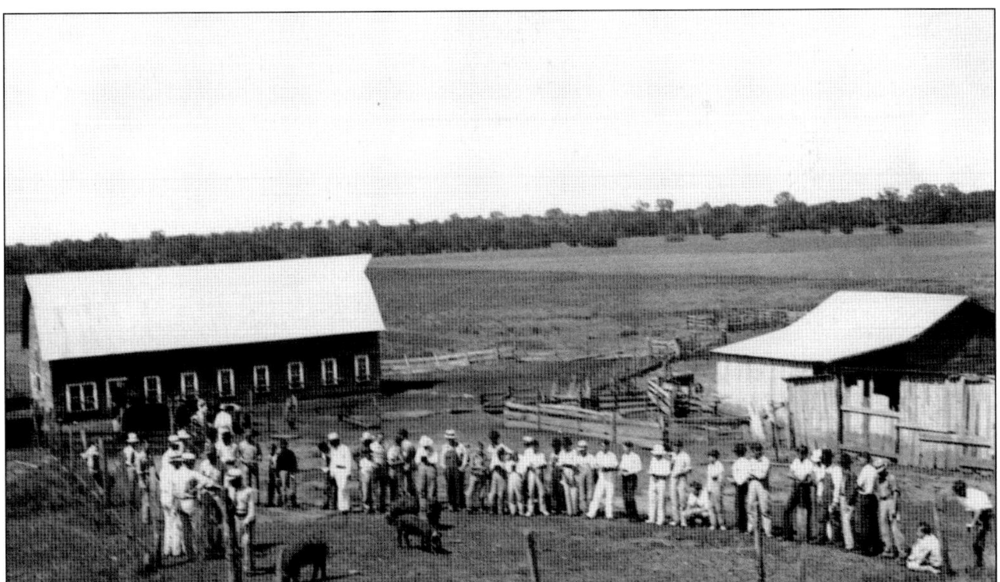

The 1936 district livestock judging school for 4-H youth held on the campus of Cameron College near Lawton, Oklahoma, is seen here. Boys would attend these schools to learn the characteristics of a quality animal, focusing on hogs, beef, dairy cattle, sheep, and chickens.

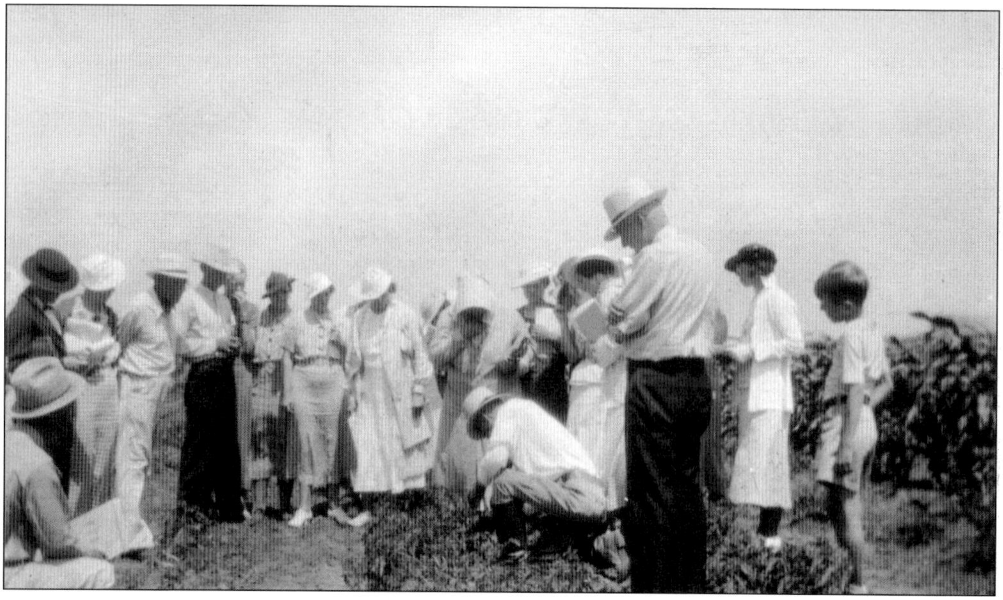

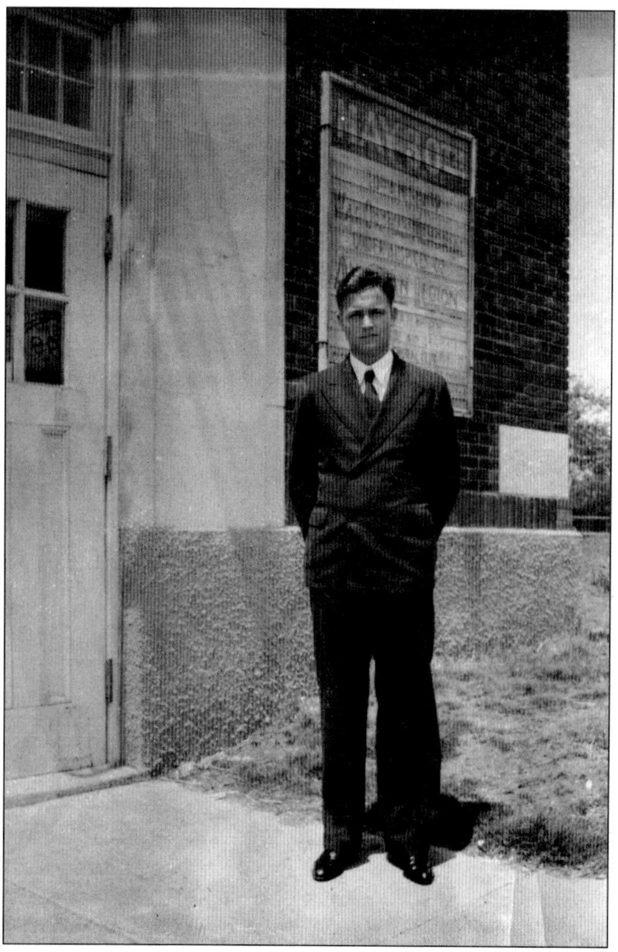

On June 1, 1936, nine counties were represented at the garden judging school held in Murray County. County agents would share the newest ideas on gardening, and during the growing season, a county-wide competition was held annually to select the best garden in the county.

James Yingling, the Sulphur 4-H Club appropriate dress champion, is pictured in 1936. The appropriate dress contest was designed to teach 4-H members how to select and care for garments and what was considered "appropriate" for the occasion.

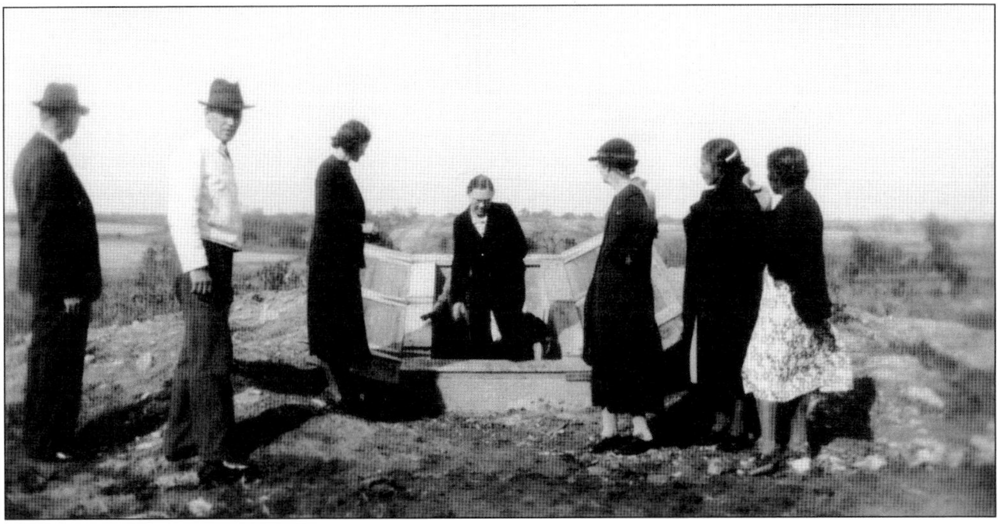

Farm men and women held an annual kitchen and cellar tour. This tour shared ideas of improvements that could be made to the home and farm. This cellar belonged to Alpha Kahler. Cellars provided not only safety from the tornadoes and storms, but also storage space for the jars of canning that took place every summer. The cool, dark environment helped the food keep its natural colors longer and provided a constant temperature for storage.

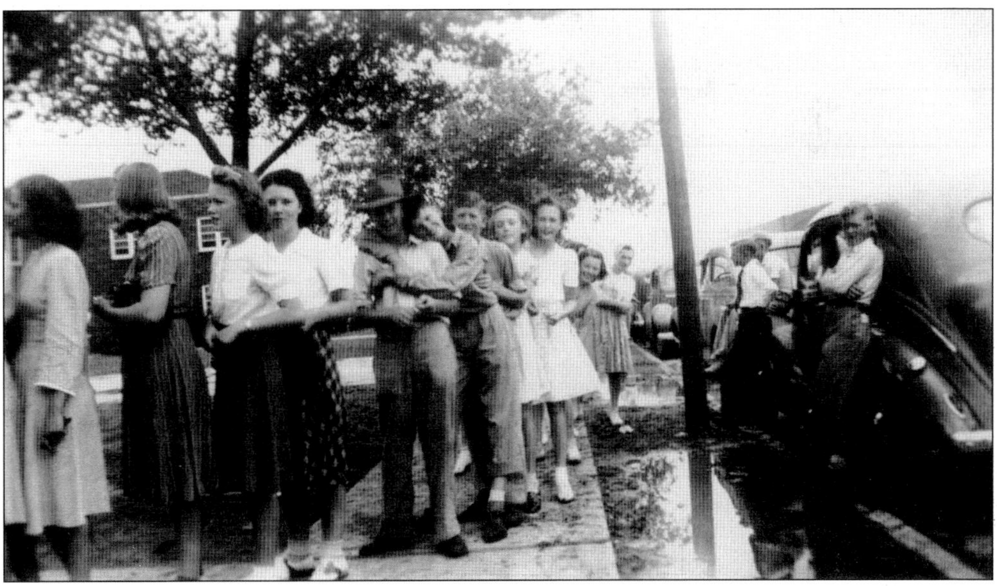

Murray County delegates are shown attending district judging school in Lawton. They would learn how to judge everything from clothing to baking and from garden produce to sheep. These schools usually were three to four days in length and were attended by agents and extension specialists as well as adults and 4-H club members.

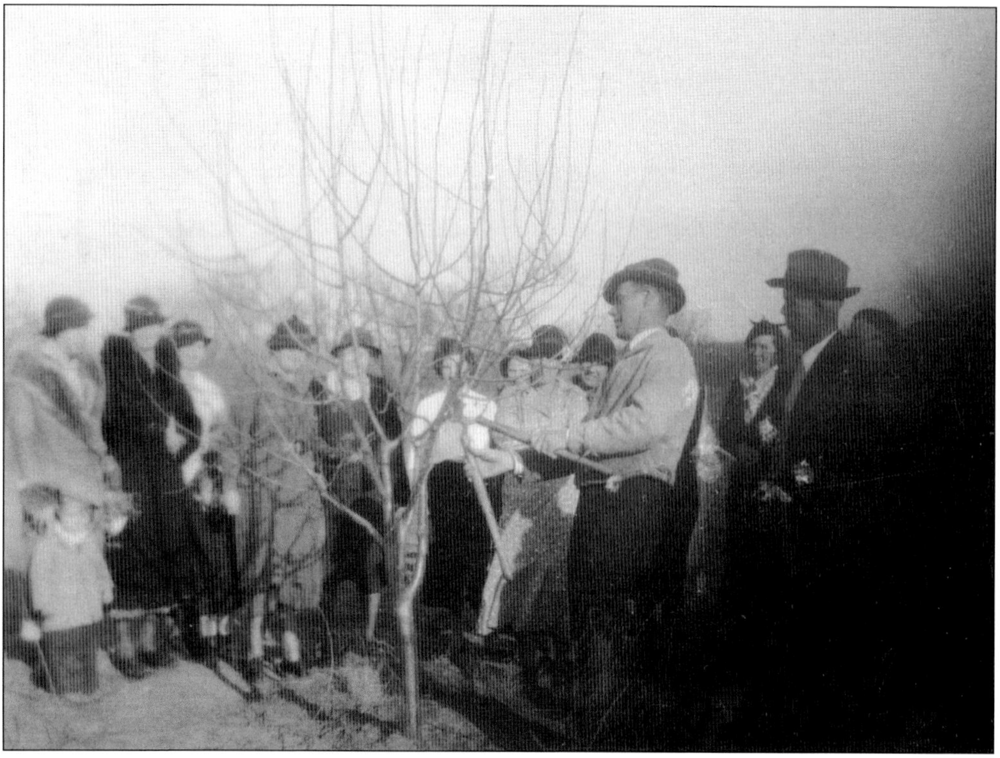

A specialist from the A&M campus would travel from county to county to demonstrate new techniques for ways to prune trees and shrubs. A horticultural specialist is shown here presenting a demonstration to the members of the Palmer Home Demonstration Club. The demonstration method of teaching is still used by the Cooperative Extension Service today.

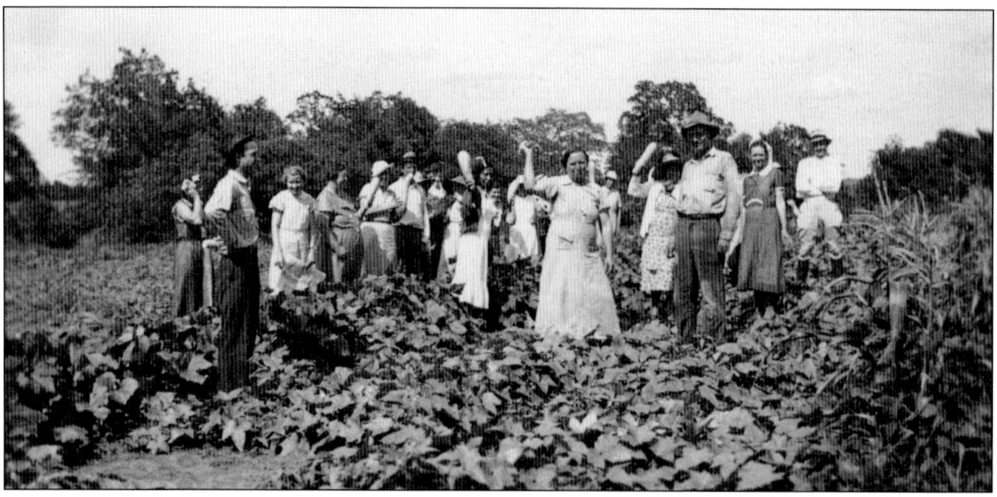

Annual garden tour participants inspect the garden of Mrs. W.M. Skelton of the Koller community. The Koller community was located on the eastern side of the county near Hickory. The tour visited Carr Chapel where they viewed the yard of Mrs. L. Tolliver and then the gardens and yards of Mrs. M.K. Stoddard, Mrs. Leon Jobe, Mrs. J.L. Jobe, Mrs. Jim Arms, and Mrs. Nova Ferguson. After lunch, the tour continued by visiting Merel Kahler, Mrs. W.M. Wright, Mrs. W.B. Chilcoat, Mrs. Andrew Hudson, Mrs. Otis Warren, Mrs. D.G. Daniels, and Mrs. Sam Harrison.

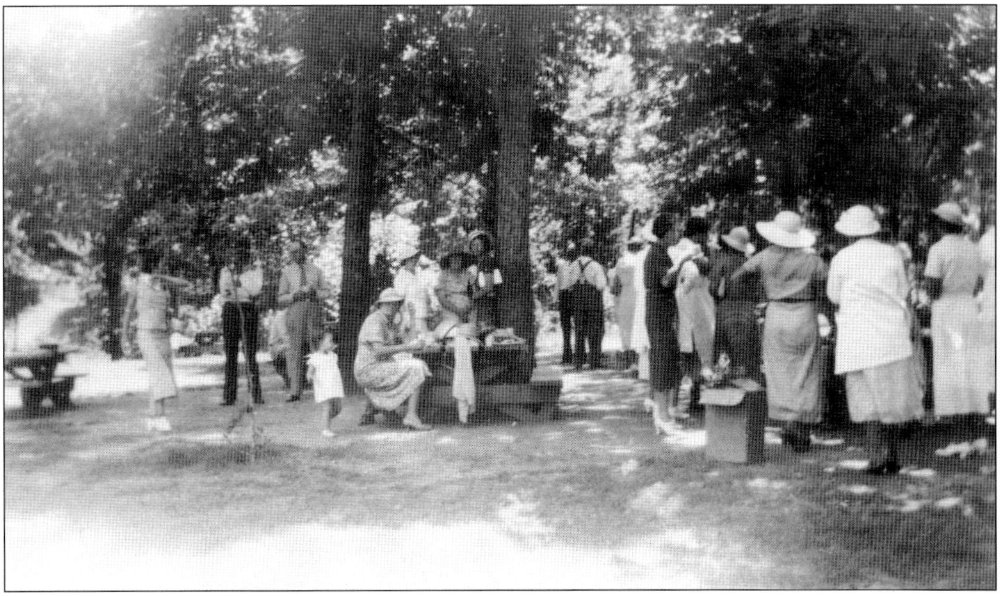

The 1936 garden tour participants enjoy a picnic at Buffalo Spring in Platt National Park. A total of 65 people attended the tour. In order to transport the 65 tour participants, cars were furnished by the Sulphur Chamber of Commerce, Mrs. R.D. Ross, Millard Lowrance, R.S. Goffe, B.F. Keith, J.L. Bostick, W.H. Leeper (of the Mays Lumber Company), Dora Pease (a home demonstration agent), and Oran Stipe (assistant agent).

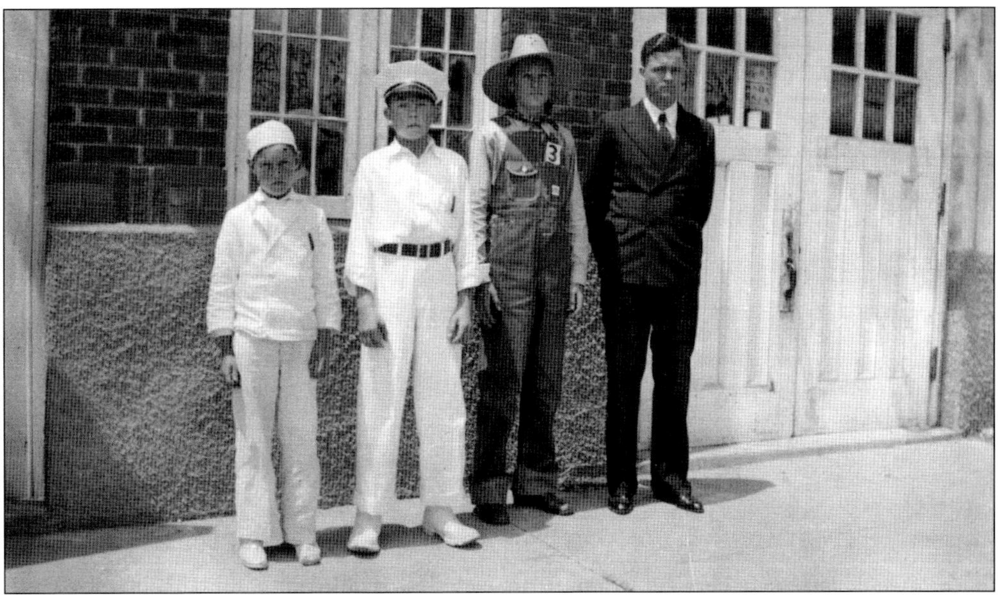

From left to right, Louie Gene Richard of Buckhorn 4-H, Johnnie Lee Currie of Davis 4-H, Delmar Salers of Sulphur 4-H, and James Yingling of Sulphur 4-H model their farm and street dress attire in the county appropriate dress contest held April 29, 1936. The contest was held in the Convention Hall in Sulphur with 47 girls and 31 boys competing.

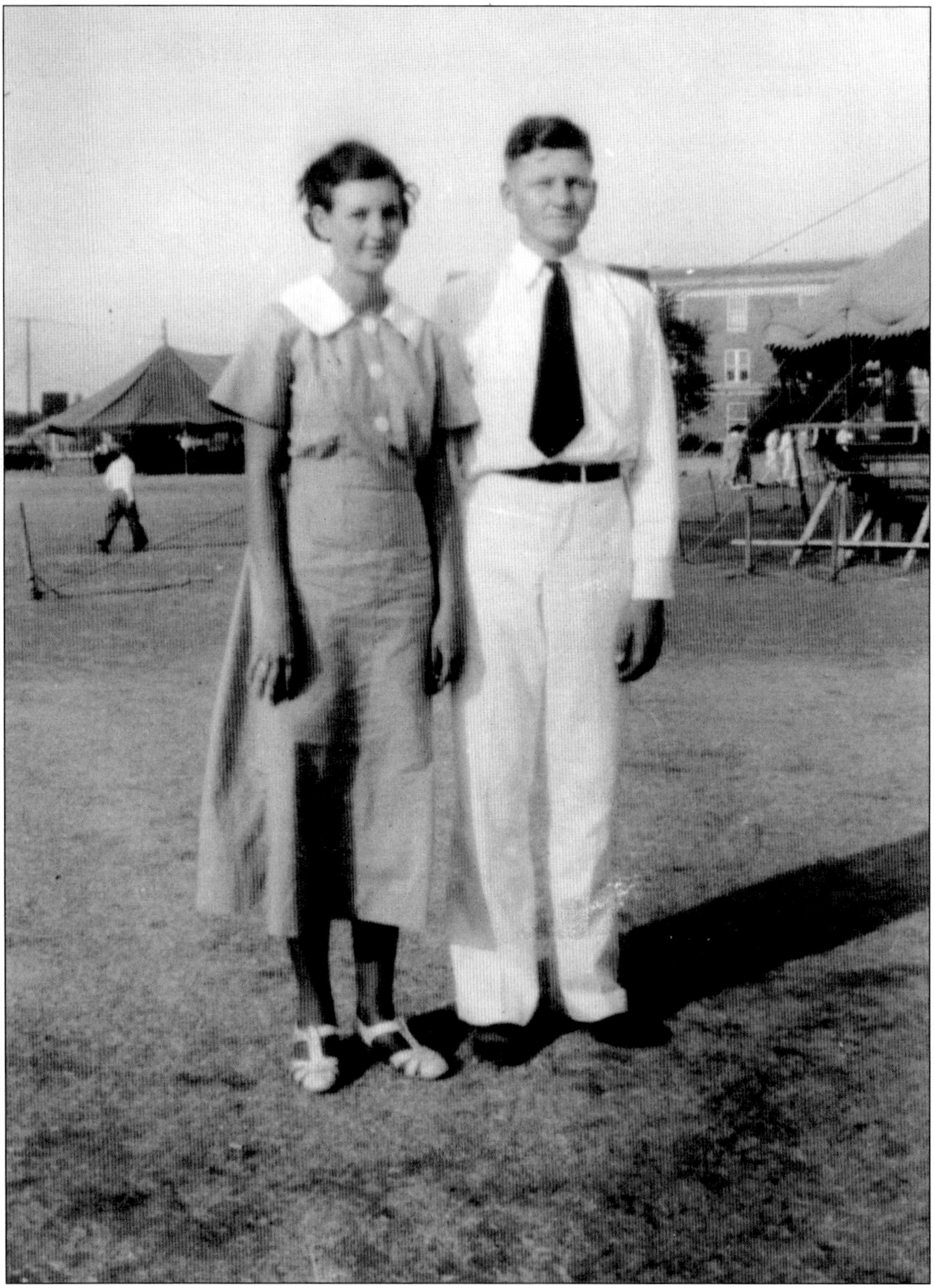

Jennie Wren Thompson of Joy 4-H and Alfred Ashton of Sulphur 4-H represent Murray County in the health contest held at 4-H Roundup in 1936. To compete in this contest, 4-H members studied food and health habits using a health chart that suggested foods to build strong bones and teeth, give good color to skin, and make hair gloss and the eyes clear. They also focused on correct posture and the proper care of teeth. Record keeping was an important part of the health project.

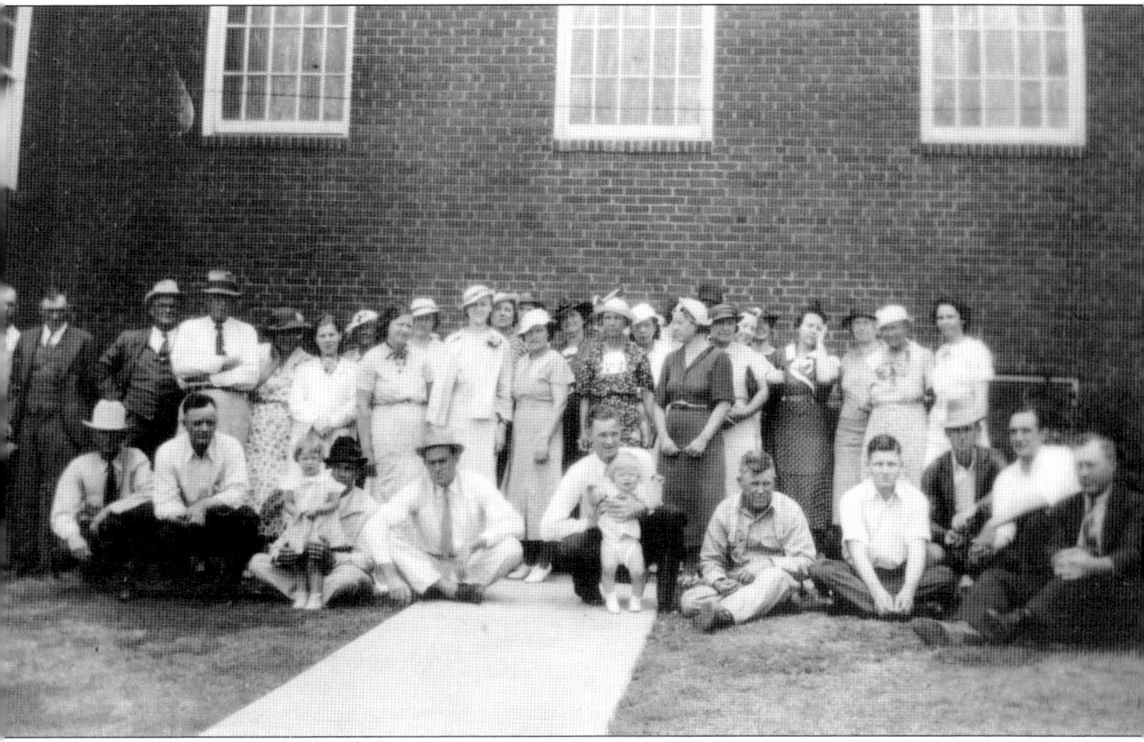

The Murray County Extension Advisory Committee met in joint session with the farm ladies. Officers elected for 1937 agriculture program were C.C. Clinton, chairman; Joe L. Bostick, vice chairman; and B.F. Keith, secretary. The agriculture advisory committee and the farm women committees met with agents to select major and minor projects that needed addressing by extension. Major projects selected this year were soil erosion control, 4-H Club work, dairy improvement, pasture and legume improvement, horticulture, and agriculture conservation programs. Minor projects were crop improvement, insects, marketing, and livestock.

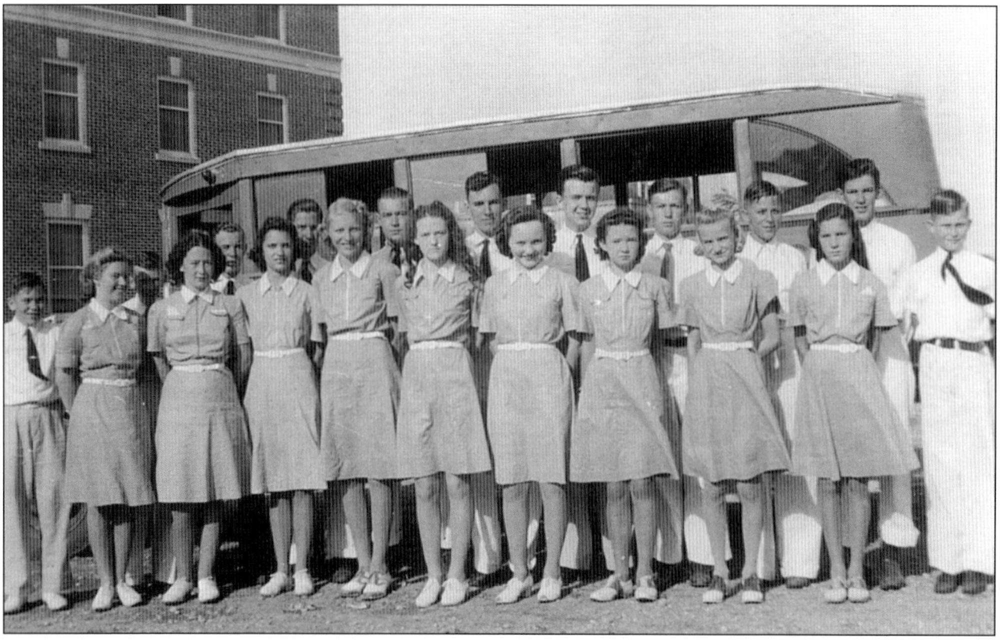

Murray County 4-H delegates are shown attending the 1937 4-H Roundup in Stillwater. Delegates attending this event were housed in homes across Stillwater or in tents pitched on campus grounds. There were twenty 4-H members and three coaches, Ethel Bounds, and Mr. and Mrs. A.D. Davis, along with the two agents. At 8:00 p.m. that evening, delegates from all over the state gathered under a big tent to kick off the weeklong 4-H conference. Roundup continues today as a major event for 4-H members and is still held on the campus of Oklahoma State University in Stillwater.

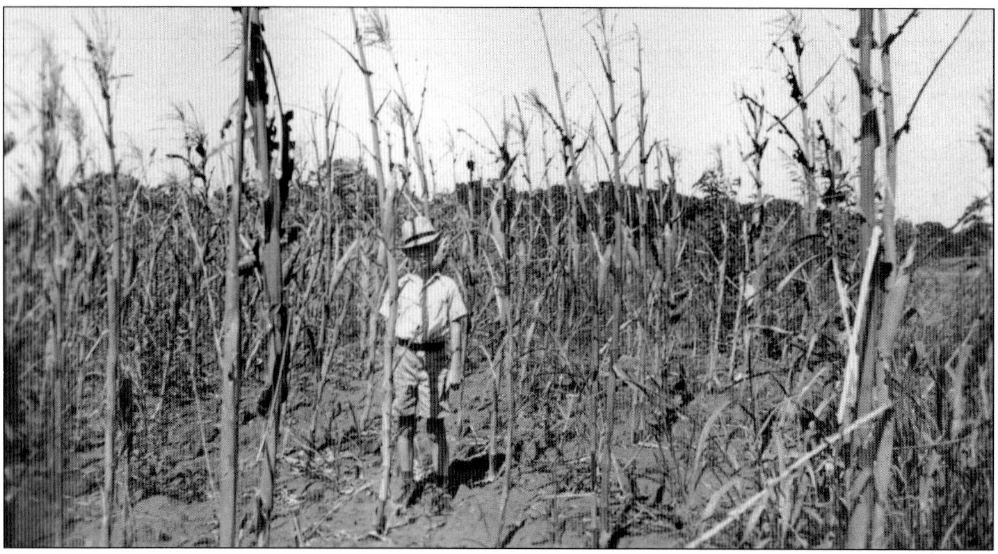

This photograph depicts 1937 grasshopper damage on the John Hassen farm north of Sulphur. The extremely dry weather during 1937 caused the grasshopper damage to be widespread and devastating. The dry period was not just a season; in fact, the 1936 records state, "no rain fell the first four months of the year. A killing frost and freeze hit April 2 and 3. A plague of grasshoppers arrived in May; the drought began to hurt in June. Burning heat scorched gardens and crops the summer thru. Such was the garden season of 1936. Worst in the memory of man."

Shown here is a sample of vetch from the C.C. Clinton farm near Dougherty. Growing vetch, which is a member of the pea family, added nitrogen to the soil, something county farmers were trying to improve after the mistreatment of the soil by growing cotton. Pasture development became important during this time, and both new and existing grasses were closely watched. Grasses included lespedeza, sweet clover, burr clover, yellow hop and black medic clovers, Bermuda grass, Dallas grass, and ryegrass.

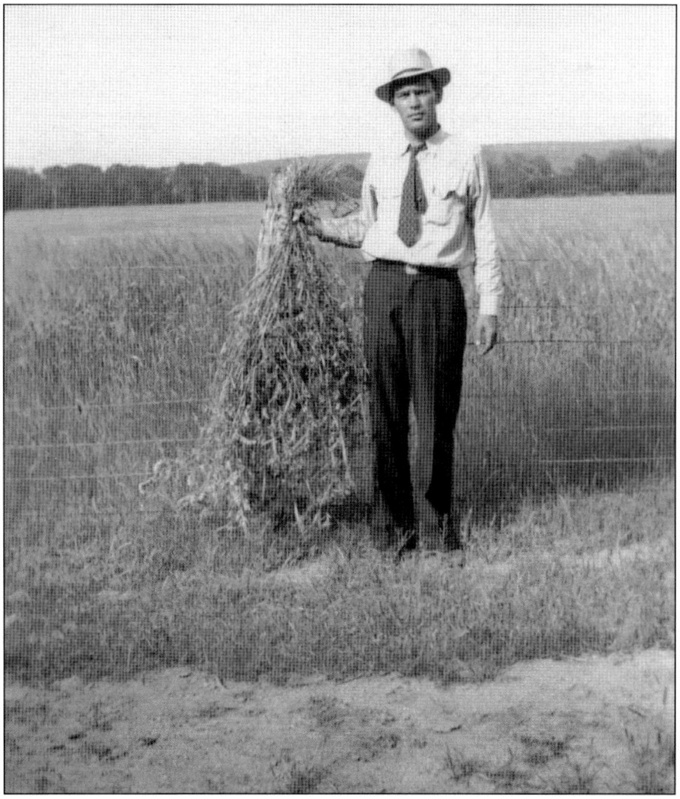

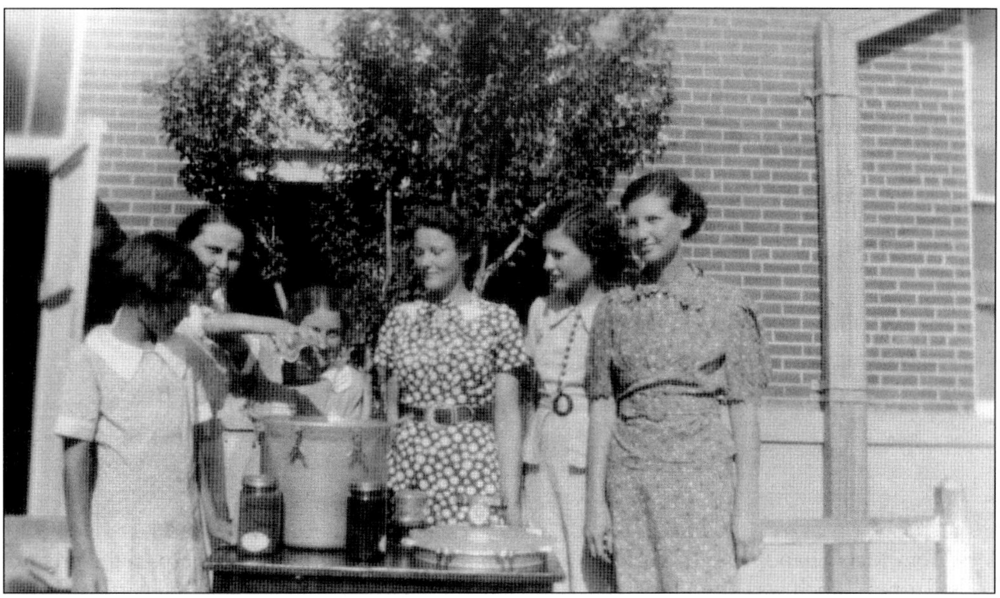

4-H girls assist home demonstration agent Dora Pease in giving a canning demonstration to the girls of the Joy 4-H Club in 1937. Food preservation was a major program of work in Murray County. There were 260 adult home demonstration members enrolled in food preservation. In 1937, the 260 members preserved 19,942 quarts of vegetables, 16,618 quarts of fruit, 12,227 quarts of meat, 24,138 pounds of meat preserved by salting or drying, and 4,365 gallons of lard.

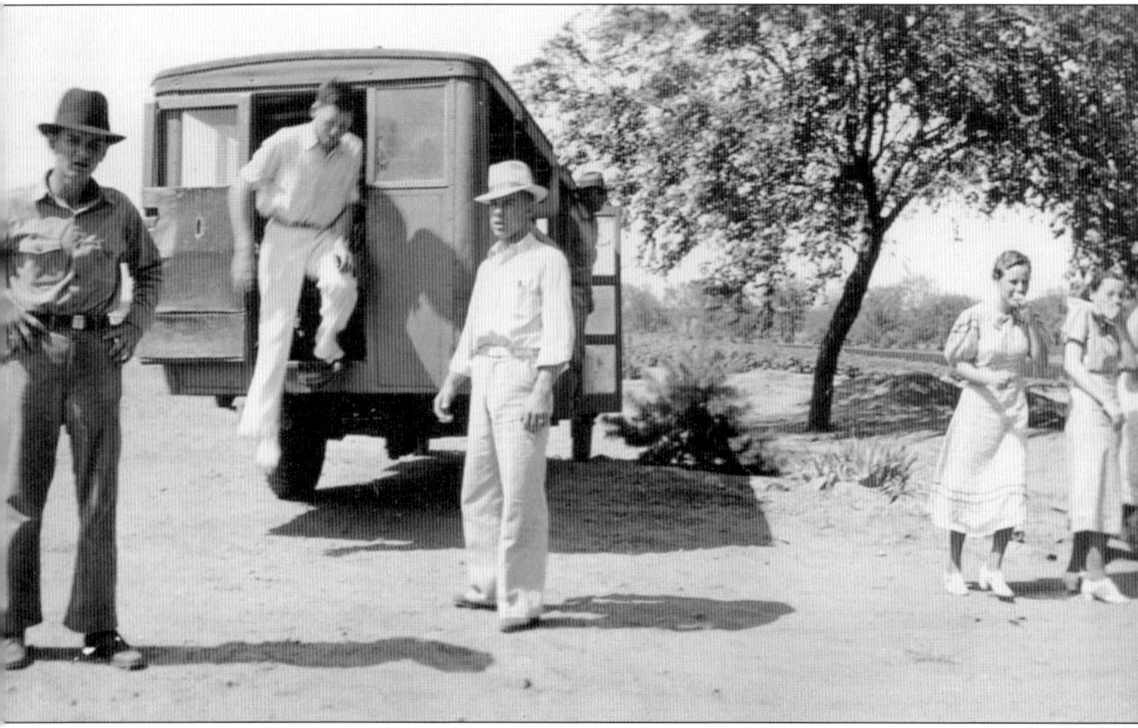

Murray County 4-H delegates are seen on a picnic while traveling to the 1937 Stillwater Roundup. The trip took several hours of travel because of rough roads. Oklahoma A&M president Dr. Henry G. Bennett gave the welcome address to 4-H members from across the state gathered under the large tent. He told the delegation that 4-H Roundup was a "rare experience in cooperative living in a larger group where you have no special privileges." Members spent the week living together, meeting new people, experiencing educational workshops, and experiencing life on a college campus.

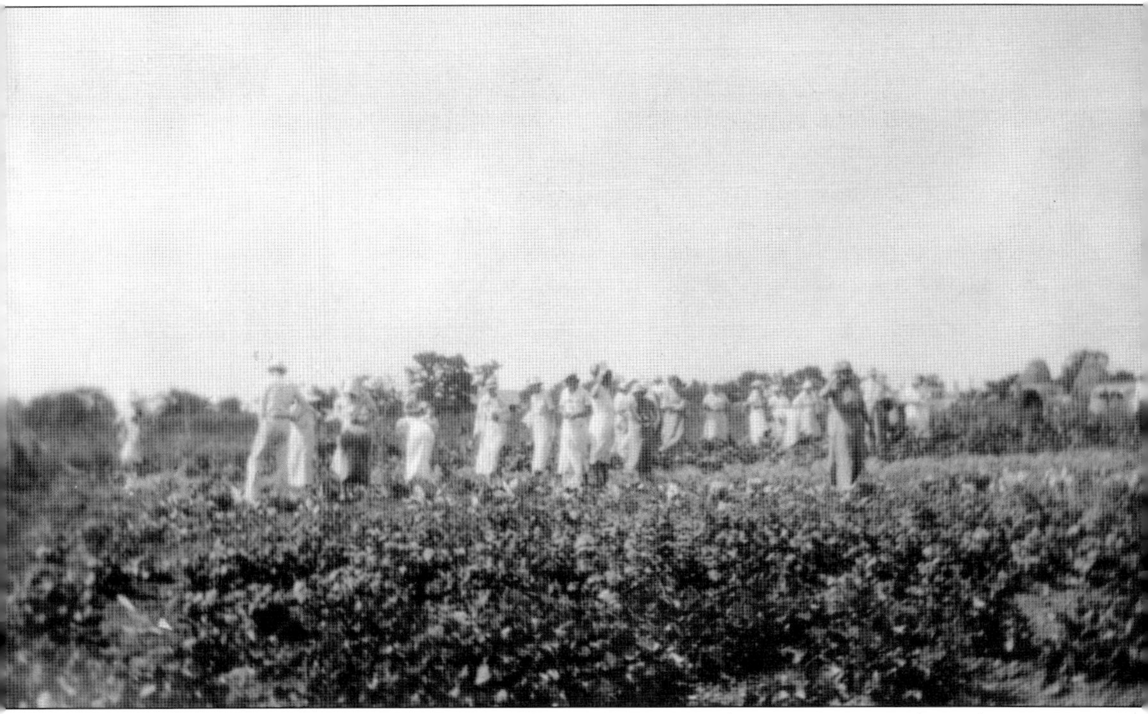

Farm men and women take a day off farm work to participate in the 1937 county-wide garden tour. Here, they are inspecting the garden of Mrs. Walter Teel of the Joy community. The emphasis of yard improvement was implemented to teach people pride in their homes and to show them that the native materials available in the county made improvements possible at a minimum cost. In 1937, there were 122 participants in the yard improvement project, and these demonstrators planted 676 trees, 1180 shrubs, and 330 vines. The number of flower beds built numbered 223; a total of 136 members planted Zennia flowers, 54 pruned their plants and trees, and 89 sprayed yard plants. Sanitary conditions were improved with around 78 new wells, 57 sidewalks were made, and 37 new buildings were constructed, not including 9 new homes.

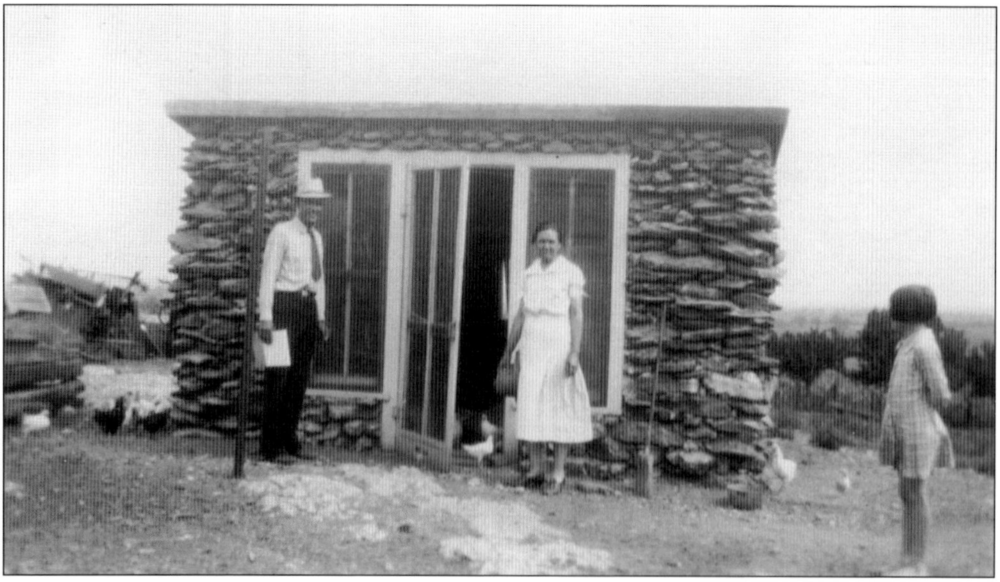

Mr. and Mrs. W.L. Skelton constructed a rock brooder house on their farm. The cost was $9 for cement, $1.30 for asphalt roofing, 85¢ for glass panes, 20¢ for catches for the windows, and $1.10 for the stovepipe. The total spent on the project was $12.45, which was a big investment for this family. County agent R.E. Chiles is photographed with Mrs. Skelton. Extension building and material recommendations were used for this design.

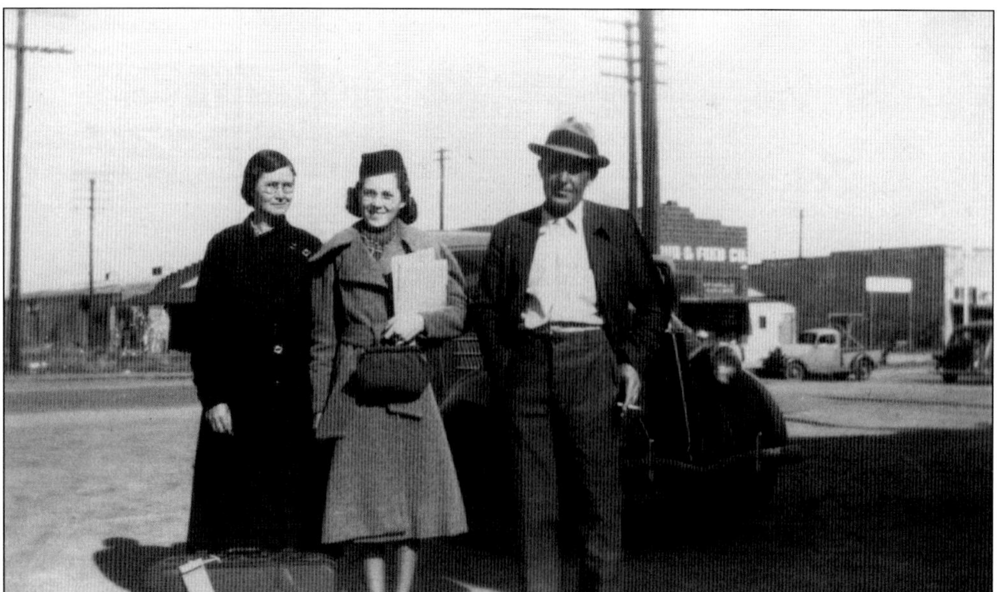

Mr. and Mrs. C.B. Pullen and daughter Ora Mae pose before Ora Mae travels to the 1937 Chicago International Livestock Show where she competed as a member of the Oklahoma State 4-H baking judging team. The Oklahoma team placed fourth.

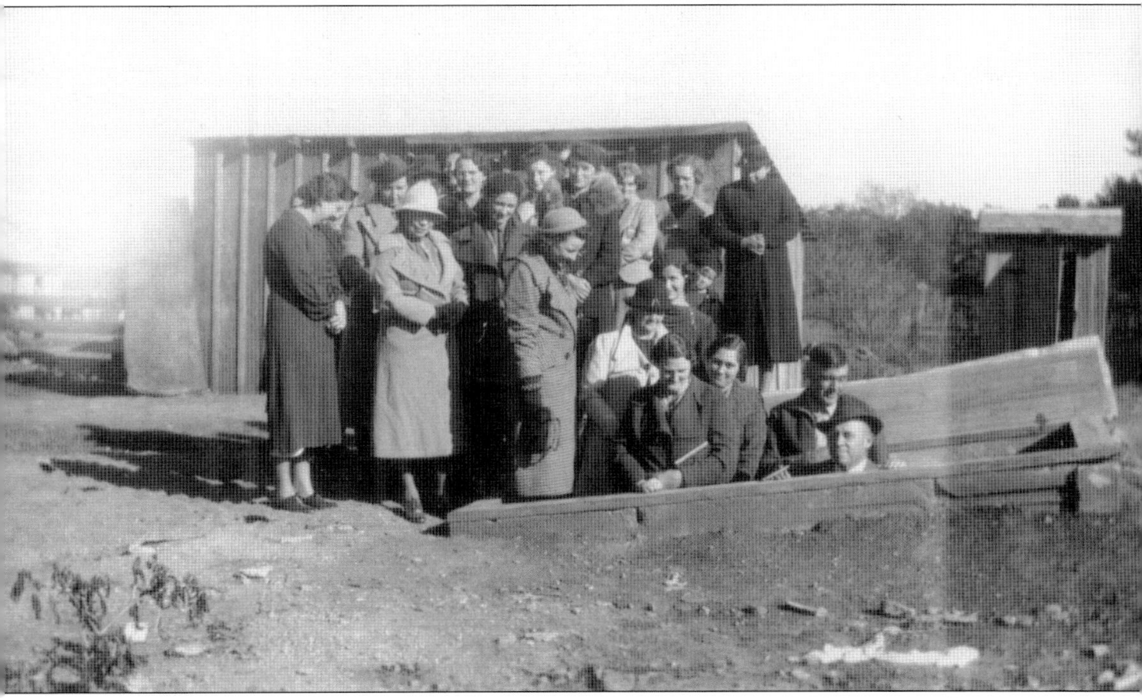

Home demonstration club members are inspecting the canned goods and the new cellar of Prue Morton of the Woodland Home Demonstration Club. Members attending the tour would bring their sack lunch and gather in the Platt National Park for a picnic lunch.

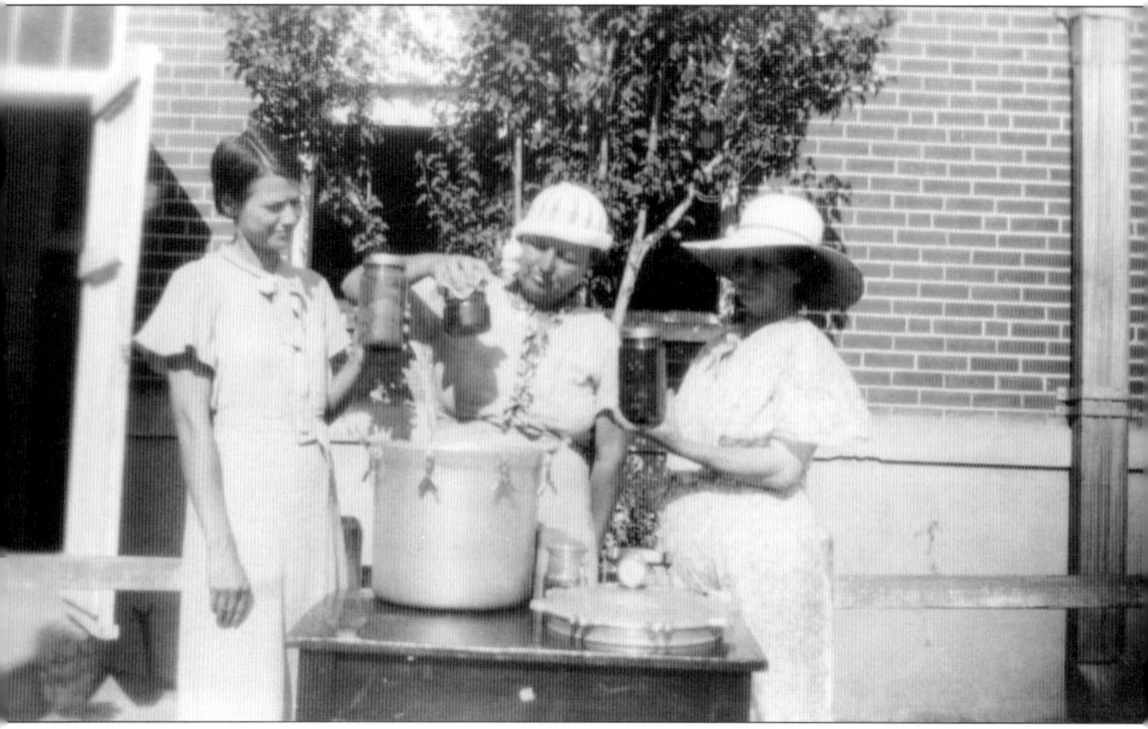

From left to right, Mrs. Paul Nowlin, Mrs. Walter Teel, and Mrs. D.G. Daniels present a fruit-canning demonstration. Home demonstration work not only taught a particular skill, it also offered opportunities for developing leaders in the various rural communities.

Mrs. W.M. Wright poses by a pecan graft placed on the tree by Mr. W.D. Armstrong, assistant horticulturalist. Pecans are native to Murray County, and the art of grafting introduced new varieties to the area.

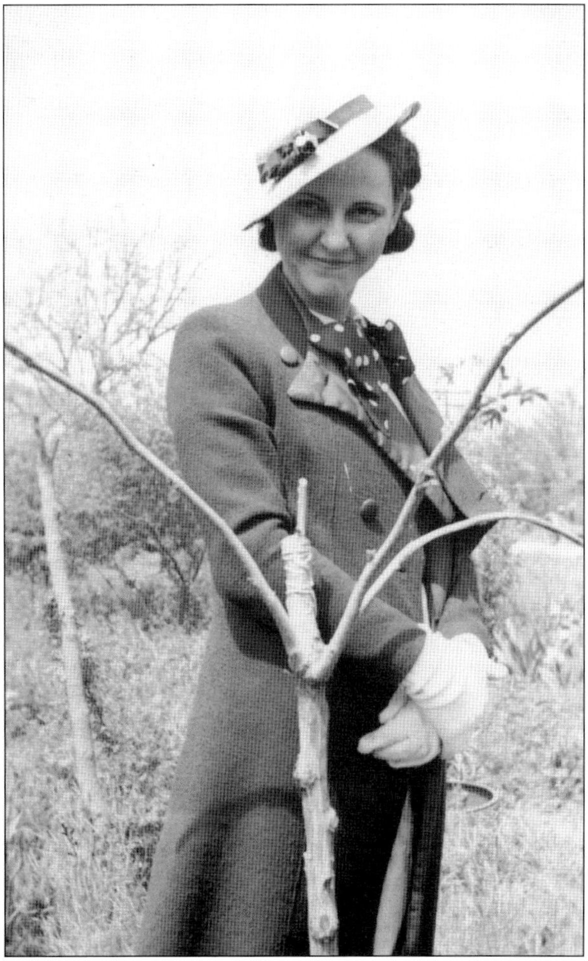

The 1937 Farm Congress, held in August on the A&M campus had 31 Murray County delegates in attendance. This was a five-day event filled with short courses on foods, clothing, yard improvement, gardening, child development, health, house furnishings, and sanitation. Many women considered this trip their vacation and saved money all year in order to attend.

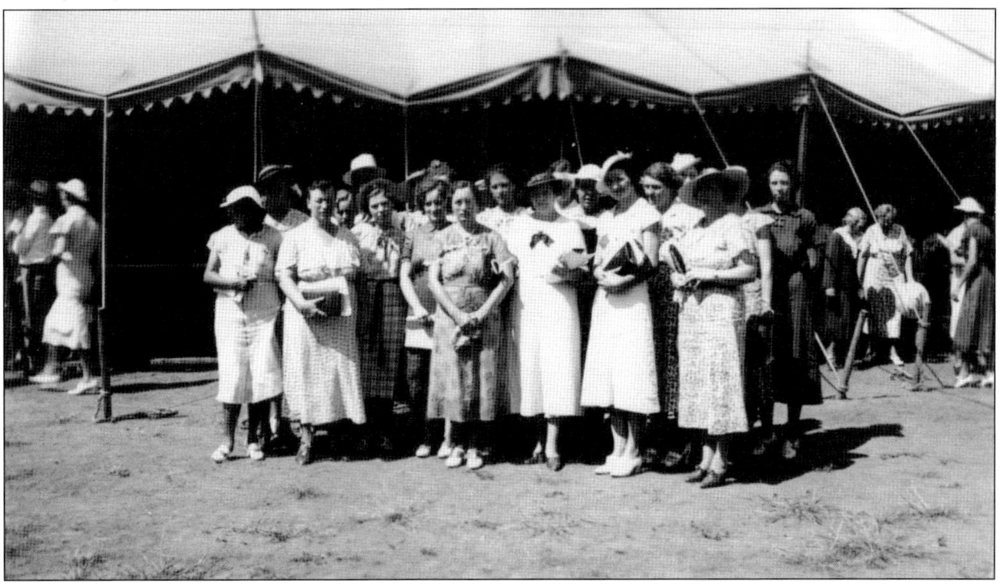

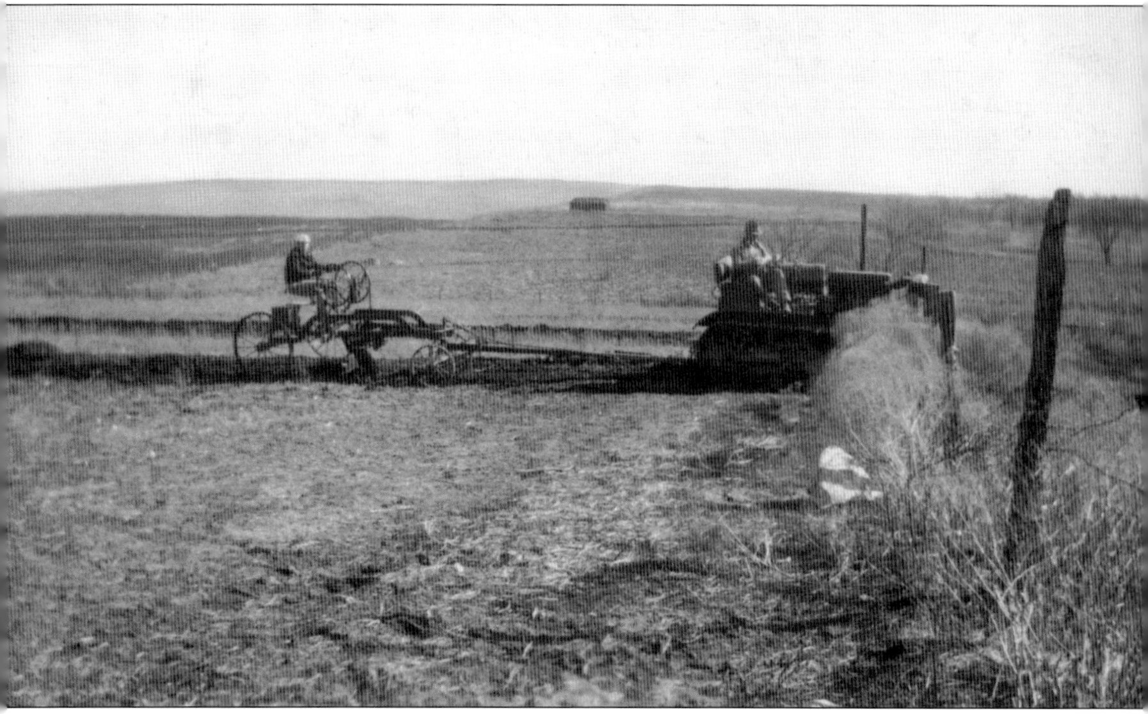

On December 28, 1937, county agents received instructions on how to work with their county in establishing a soil conservation district. Their job assignment consisted of the following three steps: educate, assist with the legal process of creating the district, and finally, help setup the office. The county farmers voted on the establishment of the conservation district on March 4, 1938. Conducting the election was E.F. Wiggins, J.E. Ballenger, and L.H. Greer. Voting would take place in the following locations and under the direction of J.L. Bostick, W.D. Biggerstaff, and Charles B. Thompson of Sulphur; Ross Smith, A.L. Pitchford, and Richard Morton of Davis; B.E. Turbyfill, Jess Lee, and J.L. Neil of Hickory; W.L. Hale, C.C. Clinton, and W.T. Motsenbocker of Dougherty; B.L. Bulen, George Little, and T.B. of Vickery and Fletcher; Tom McGiboney, J.W. Watson, Reece Hale of Drake; and L.J. Atterberry, J.P. Brownlee, and O.J. Arms of Oak Grove. The votes were cast, and 97 voted for the creation, and 20 voted against. In this photograph, J.H. Brassfield is using a tractor and grader to build terraces on his farm west of Sulphur as a step in soil conservation.

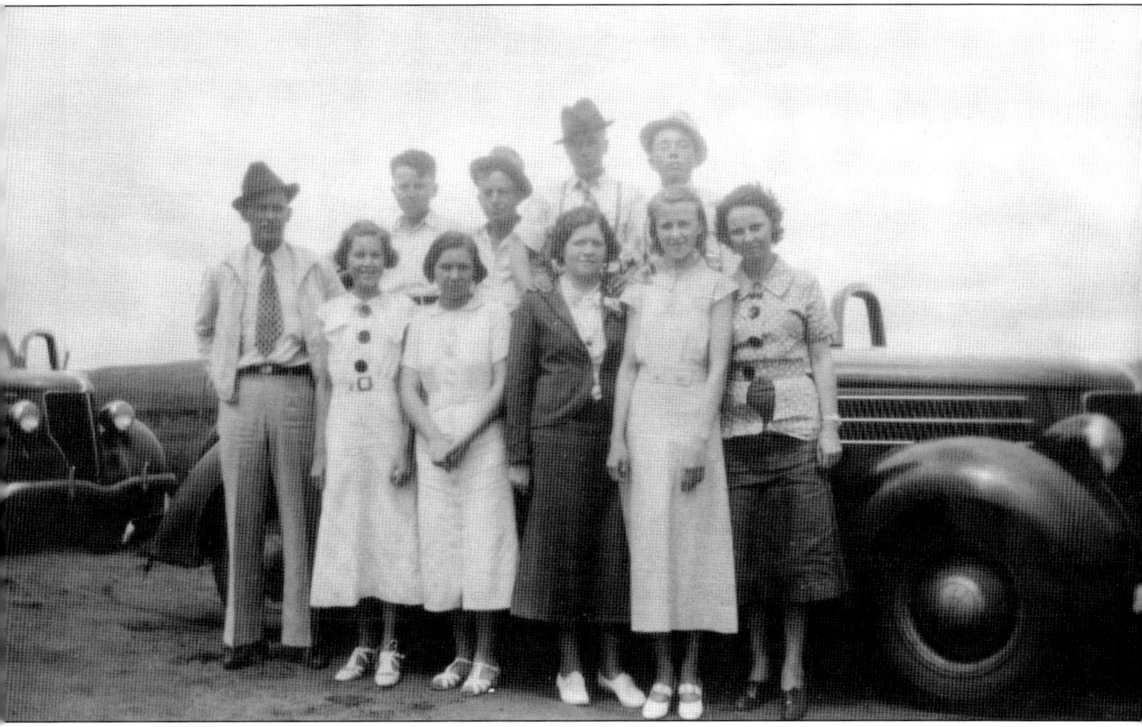

These Murray County delegates are shown attending the 1936 district judging school in Lawton. Judging schools were usually two to three days in length, and delegates were housed on the Cameron College campus.

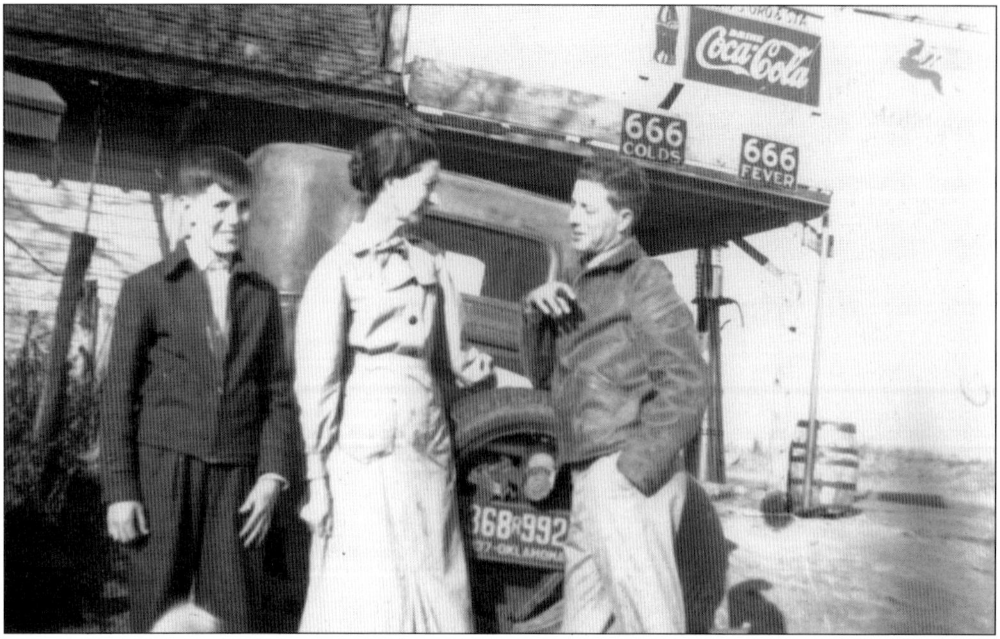

From left to right, Albert Jr. poses with his mom, Maggie Clary, and brother Aubra in front of the Hickory Grocery and Station in 1937. Albert Jr., known as "Junior," and his wife, Margaret, raised their family in the Sulphur area, where Margaret taught the first grade in Nebo and Sulphur. The couple still makes their home in Sulphur, and Margaret continues as an active member of the Oaklawn Home and Community Education Club, today's name for extension club work. (Loyce Gerth.)

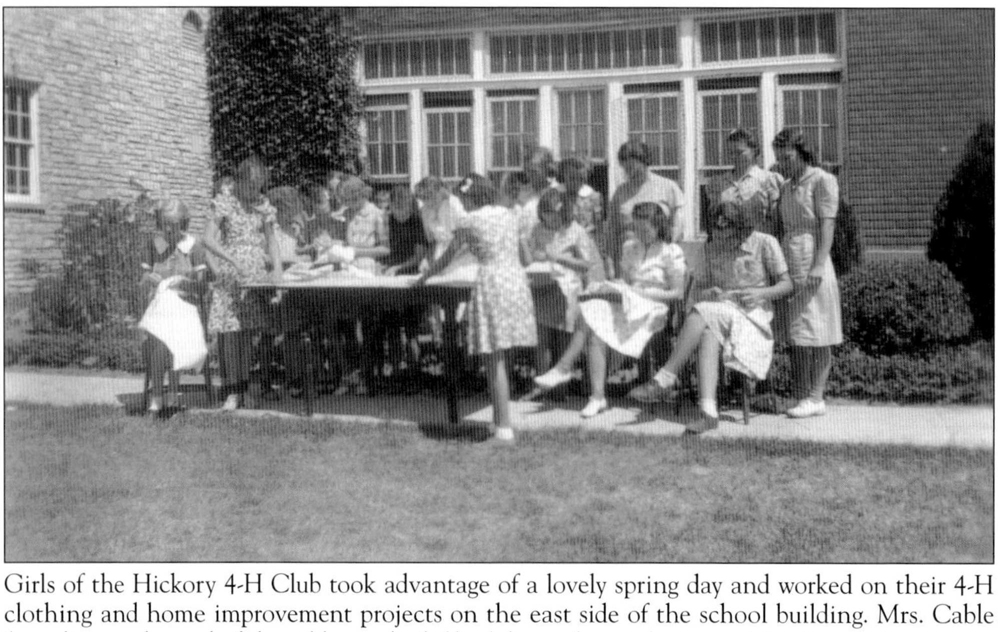

Girls of the Hickory 4-H Club took advantage of a lovely spring day and worked on their 4-H clothing and home improvement projects on the east side of the school building. Mrs. Cable (standing at the end of the table on the left), club coach, can be seen giving instruction to one of the younger members.

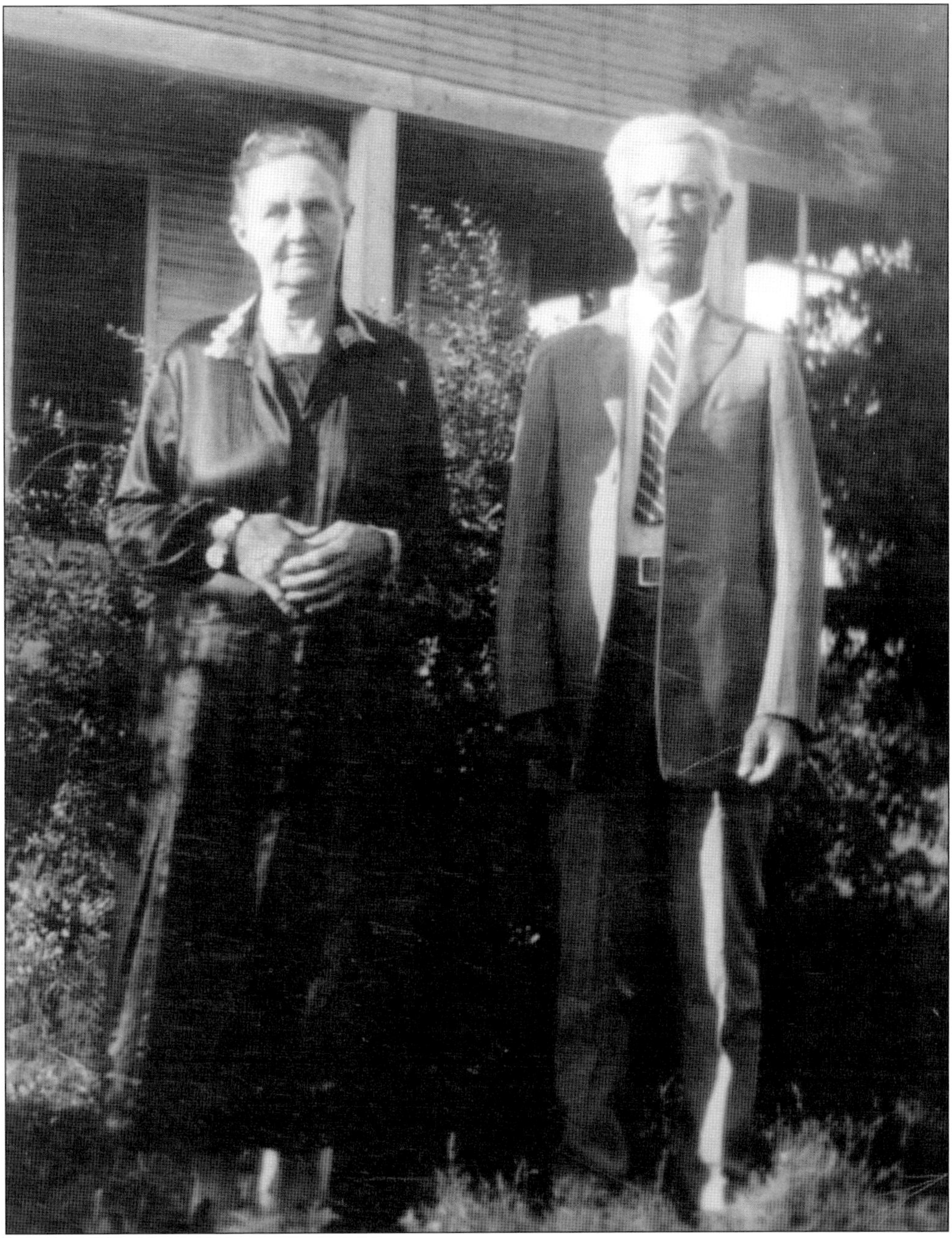

E.H. and Alice Jayne are shown in this photograph. The Jayne family farmed the area that was located one mile north of the currently located Murray County Exposition Center, on the left side of the road. The Jaynes' daughter Bessie married Tom Albright, and they farmed cotton on the land where the Sulphur Methodist Church stands today.

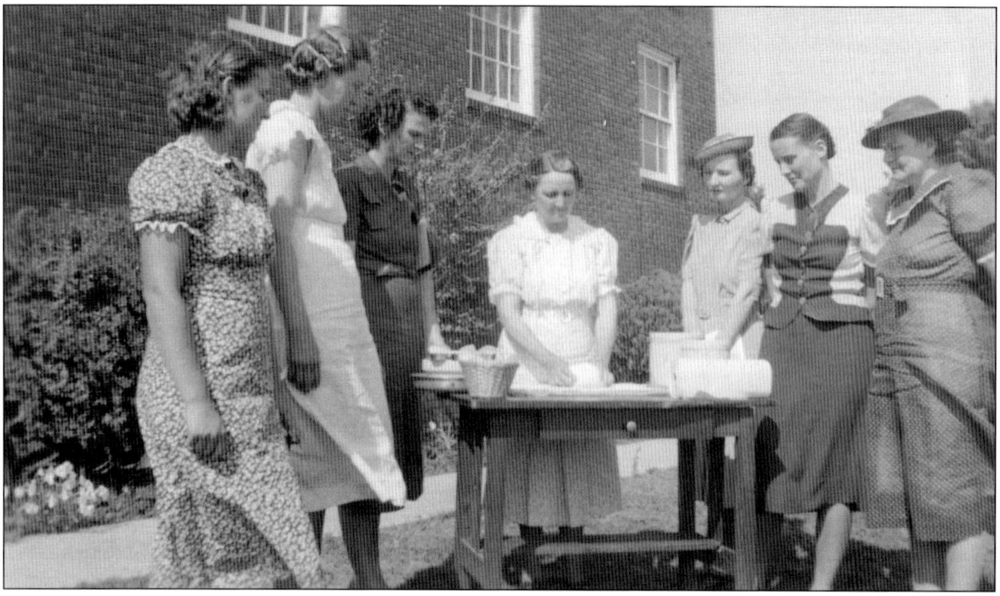

On Friday, May 5, 1939, Mrs. Ross Smith of the Woodland club gave a bread making demonstration for members attending the Murray County Home Demonstration Council meeting. She demonstrated how to make cloverleaf Parker House rolls. Mrs. Smith learned how to present this demonstration by attending the 1938 Farm Congress held on the campus of Oklahoma A&M College.

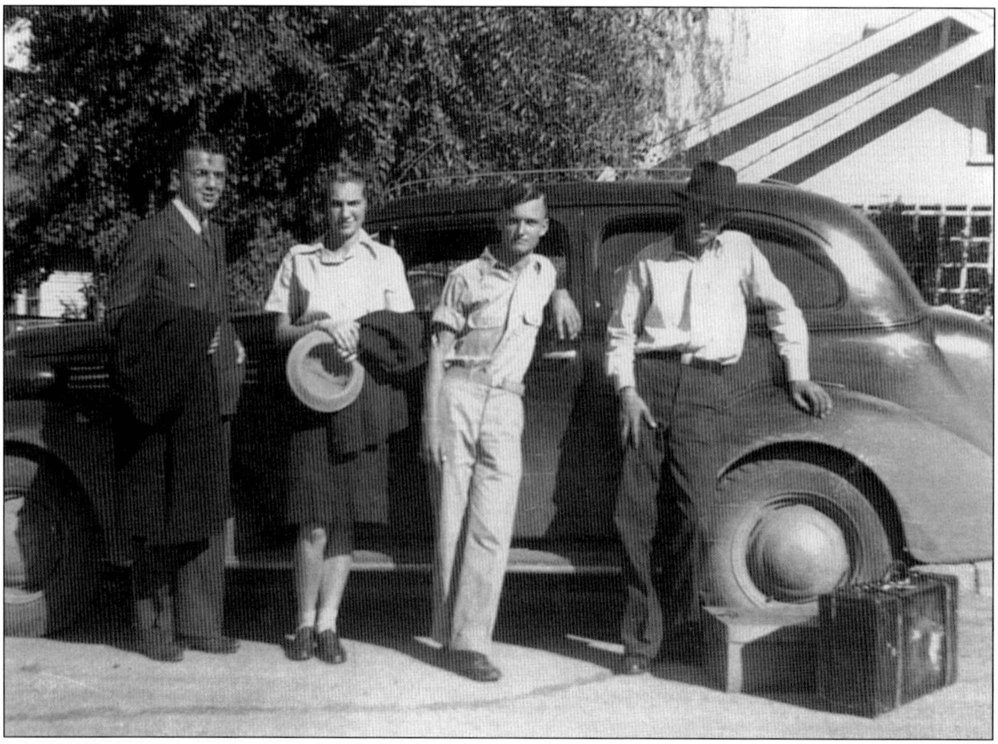

These 4-H members are packed for Kansas City to attend the 1939 American Royal Livestock Show. Traveling are, from left to right, George Ashton and Ethyle Steward of the Sulphur club, Billy Vickery of Hickory, and Harold Watson of Sulphur.

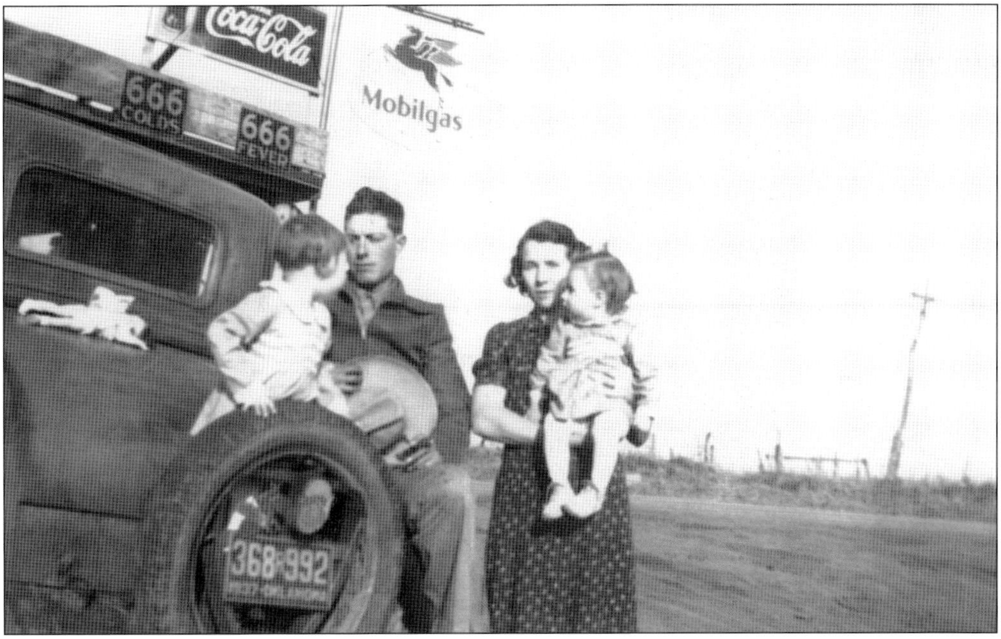

Hickory residents Aubra and Maybelle Clary are shown with daughters Wilma and Loyce. At one time, Hickory was a busy town with several businesses, a school, a post office located in the grocery store, and churches. (Loyce Gerth.)

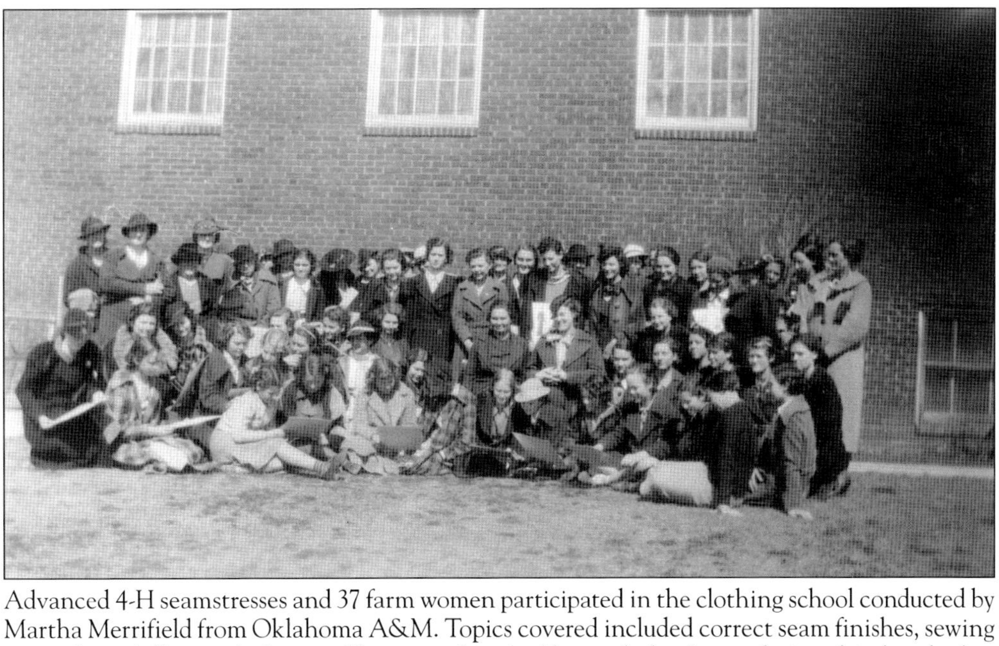
Advanced 4-H seamstresses and 37 farm women participated in the clothing school conducted by Martha Merrifield from Oklahoma A&M. Topics covered included correct seam finishes, sewing on pockets, different plackets and hems, and worked buttonholes. It was during this decade that the US government used the slogan "Use it up, wear it out, make it do or do without," so making everything the family needed was part of life and part of being a good American.

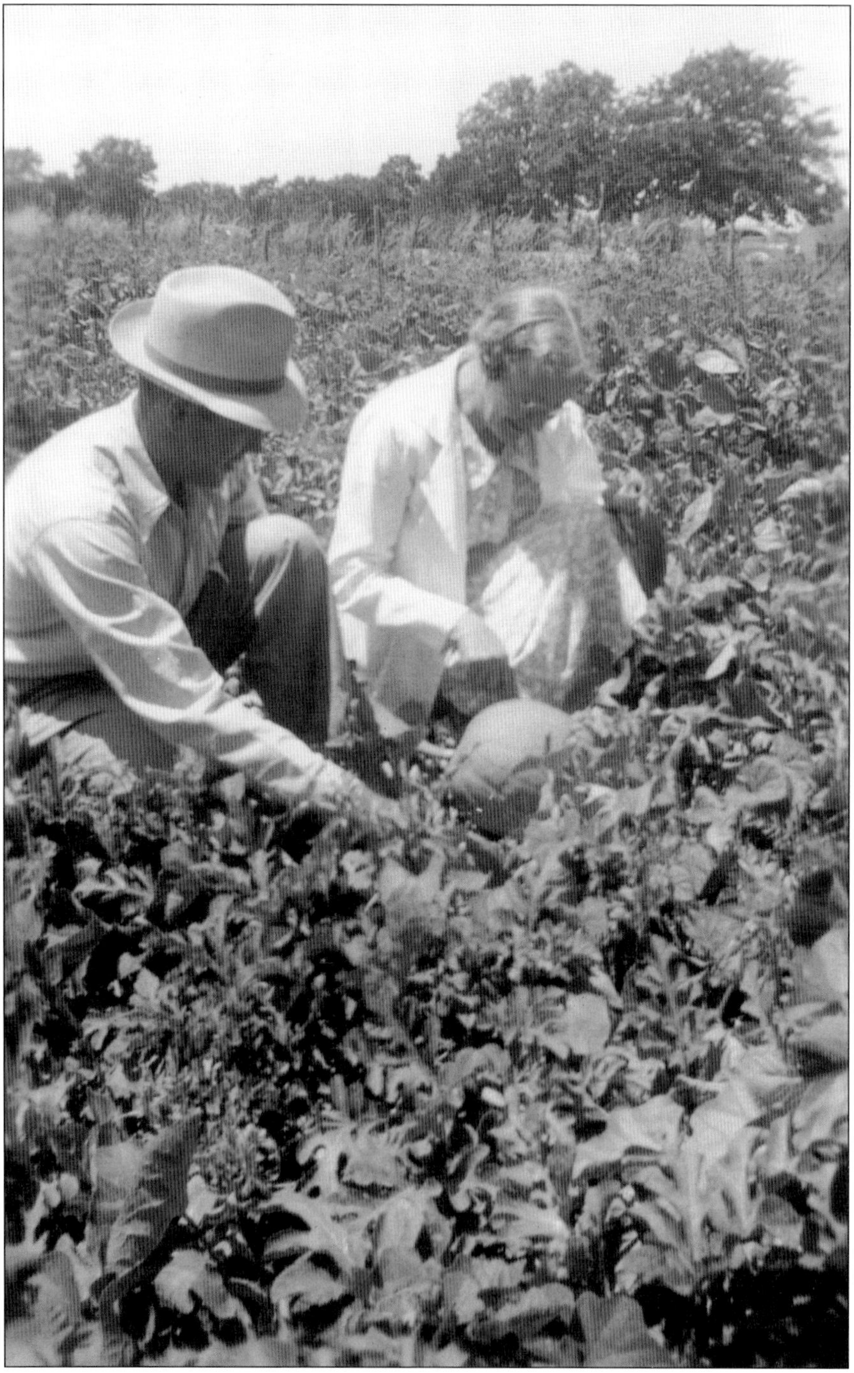

Mr. R.E. Chiles, county agent, and Mrs. G.H. Head are shown inspecting the watermelons grown by Mr. and Mrs. Head. Mrs. Head was a member of the Oak Grove Home Demonstration Club and was known for her outstanding gardens. The Heads also participated in the 1937 kitchen and cellar tour. Those attending recorded, "Mrs. Head has made a serving a table from a trunk tray which came from Germany. Another interesting convenience she made was a garbage pail made from an old cream separator."

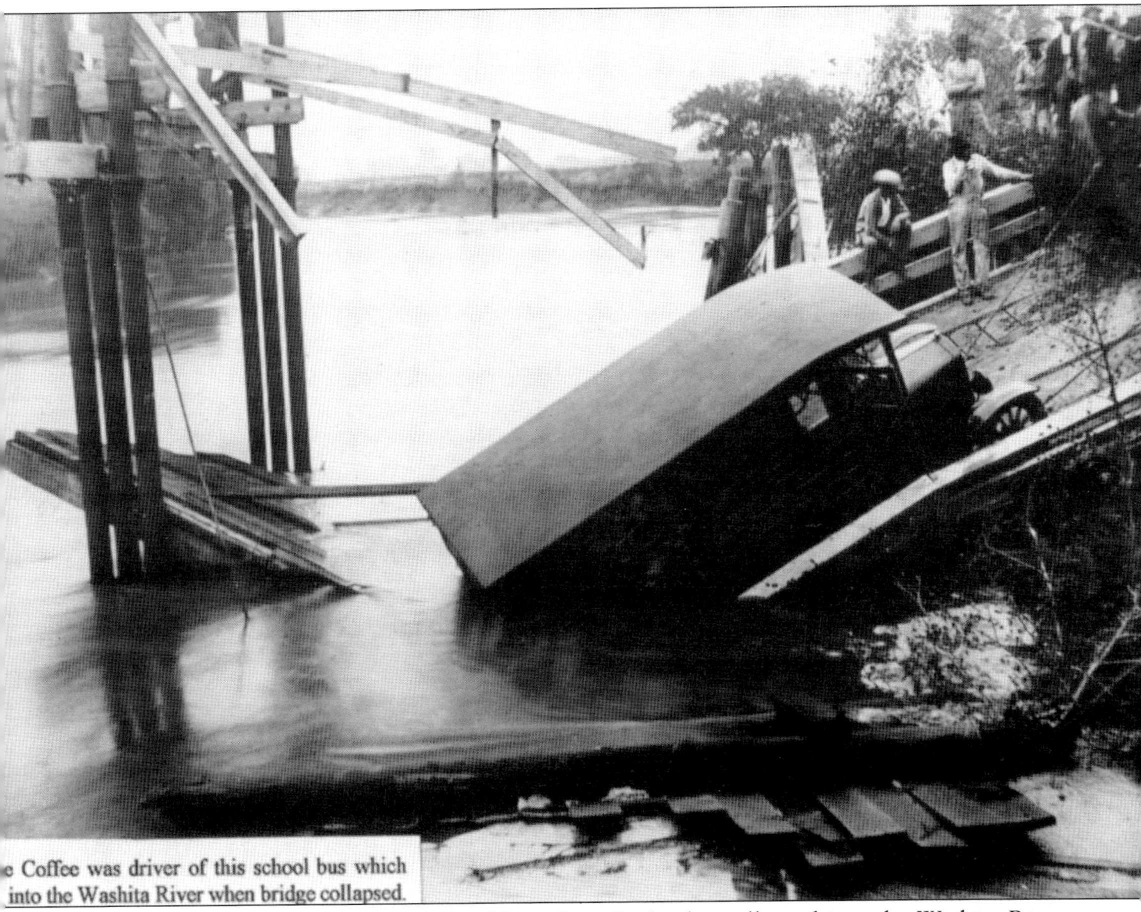

Lige Coffee was the driver of this school bus when the bridge collapsed into the Washita River in 1939. Coffee was able to get all the schoolchildren on board to safety.

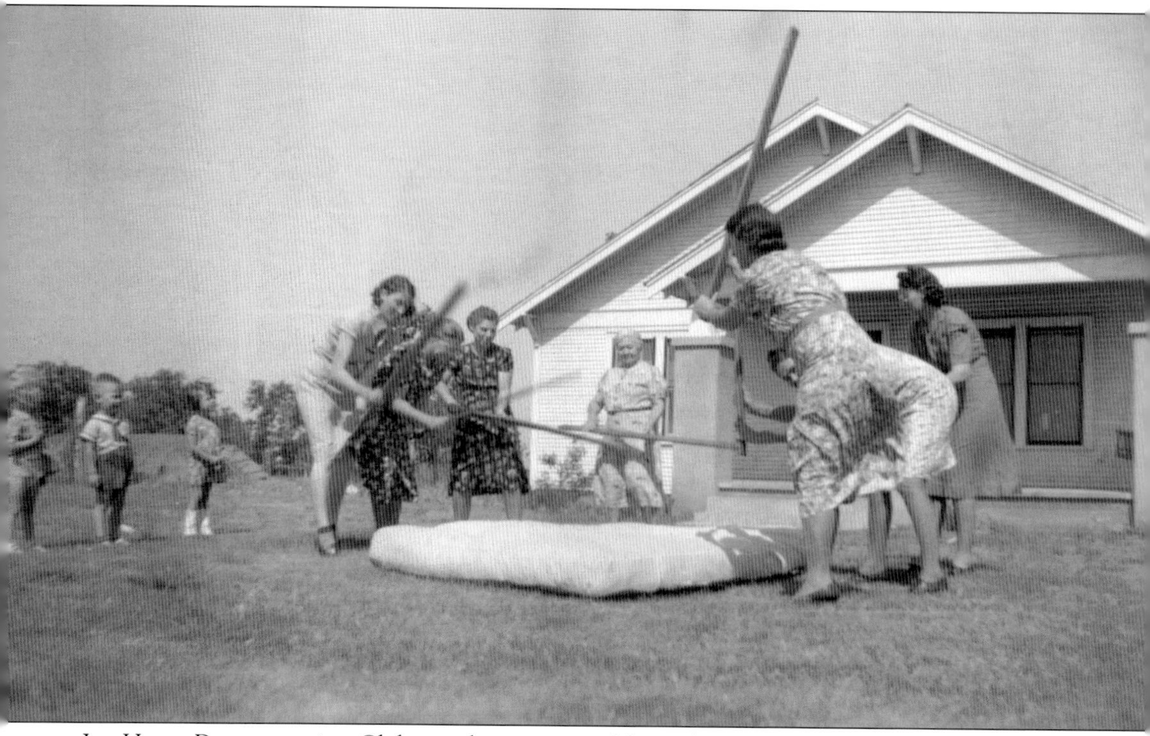

Joy Home Demonstration Club members meet on November 7, 1939, to make two mattresses. The photograph shows members beating one of the mattresses before starting to put in the roll. At this time, there were 19 clubs in this county, and each club sponsored at least one community project as well as regular club projects.

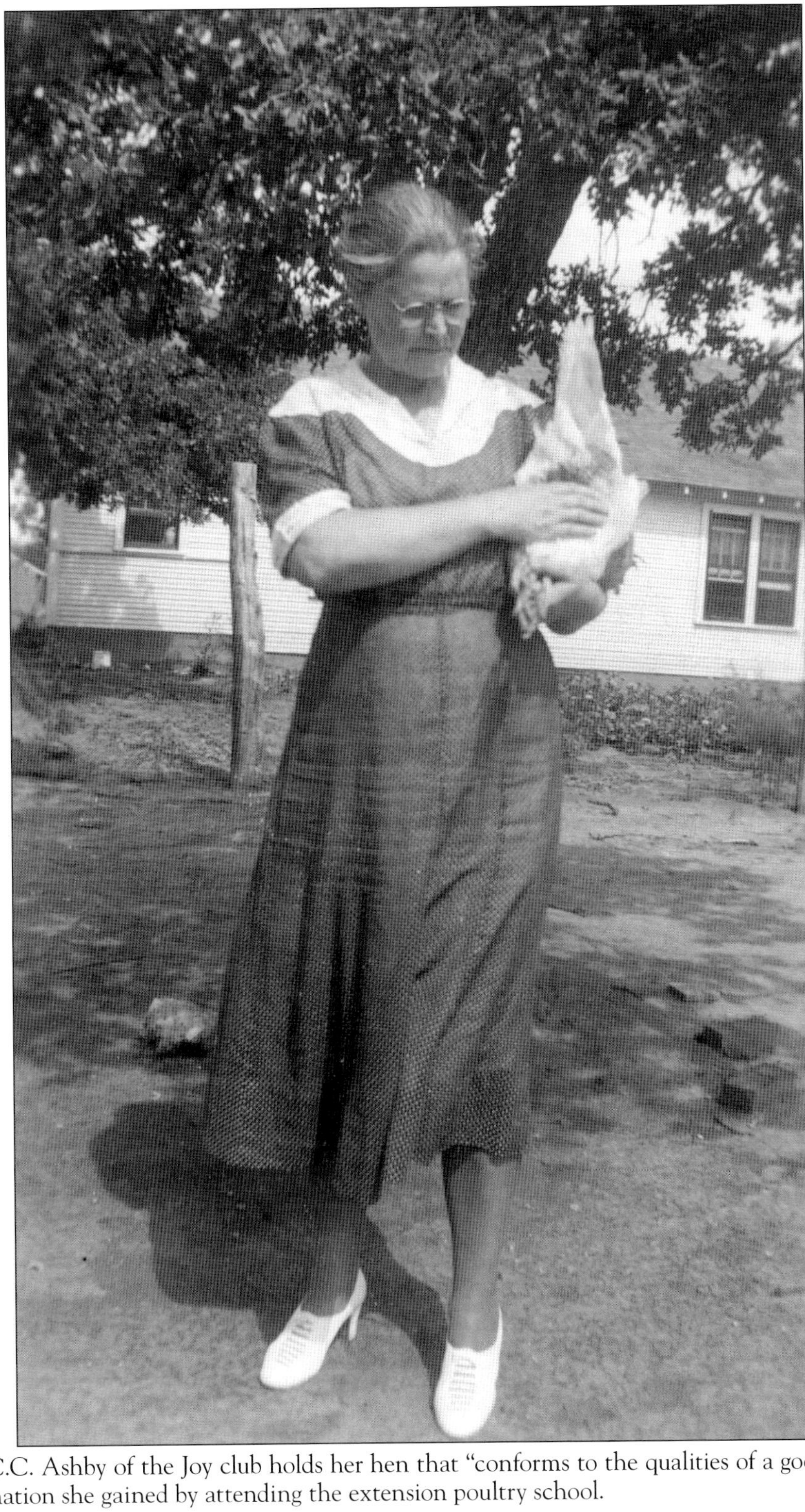

Mrs. C.C. Ashby of the Joy club holds her hen that "conforms to the qualities of a good layer," information she gained by attending the extension poultry school.

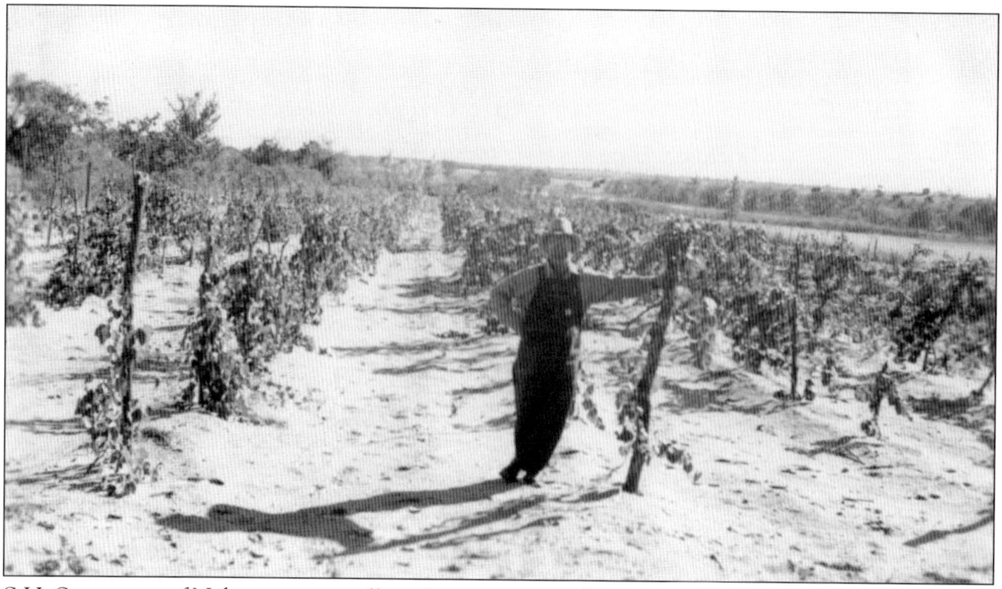

S.H. Stevenson of Nebo poses proudly in his two-year-old grape vineyard. The Nebo community is located south of Sulphur, close to the Carter County line.

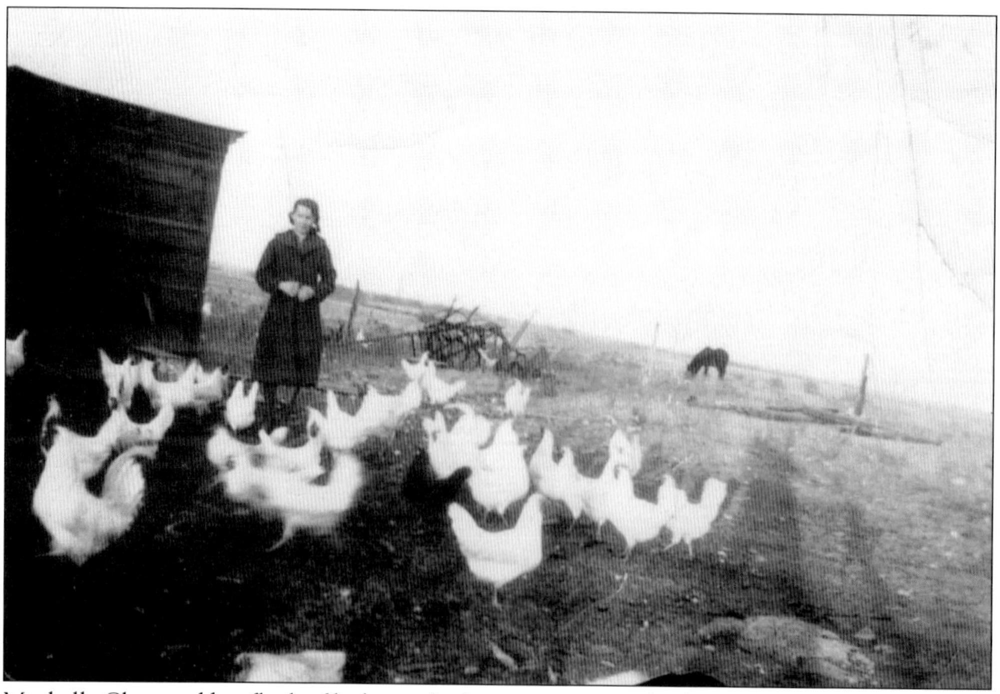

Maybelle Clary and her flock of leghorn chickens are seen on the farm in Hickory in 1939. Most county farms raised chickens for use by the family, and often, the eggs were sold to folks in town to earn extra money.

Three

FROM THE DEPRESSION TO WORLD WAR II

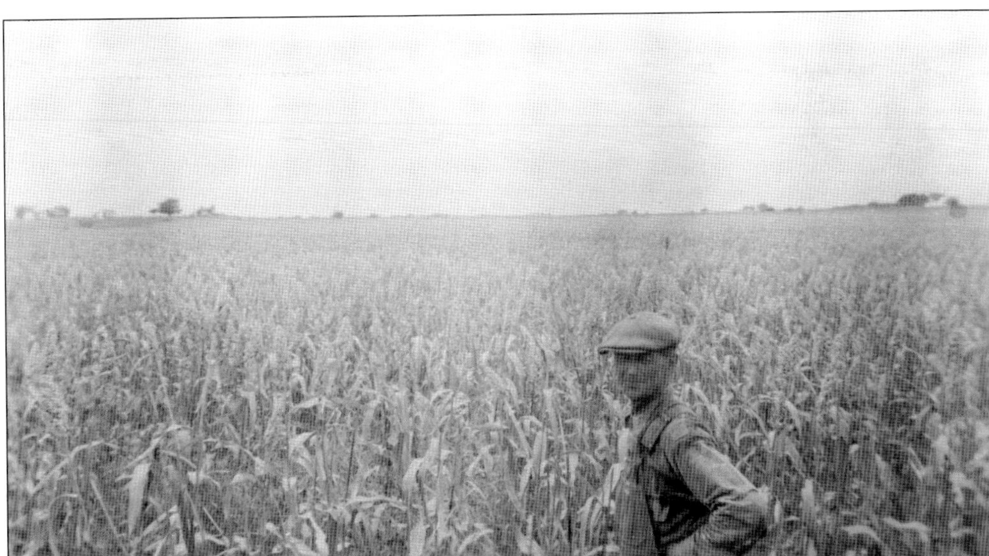

T.B. Vickory stands in the field of hegari sorghum, a new crop introduced by the county agent. It was grown for forage and grain. This field was equal in value to a cotton crop grown on the same acreage. The 1940s decade saw the introduction of several new varieties of grasses and grains into the county.

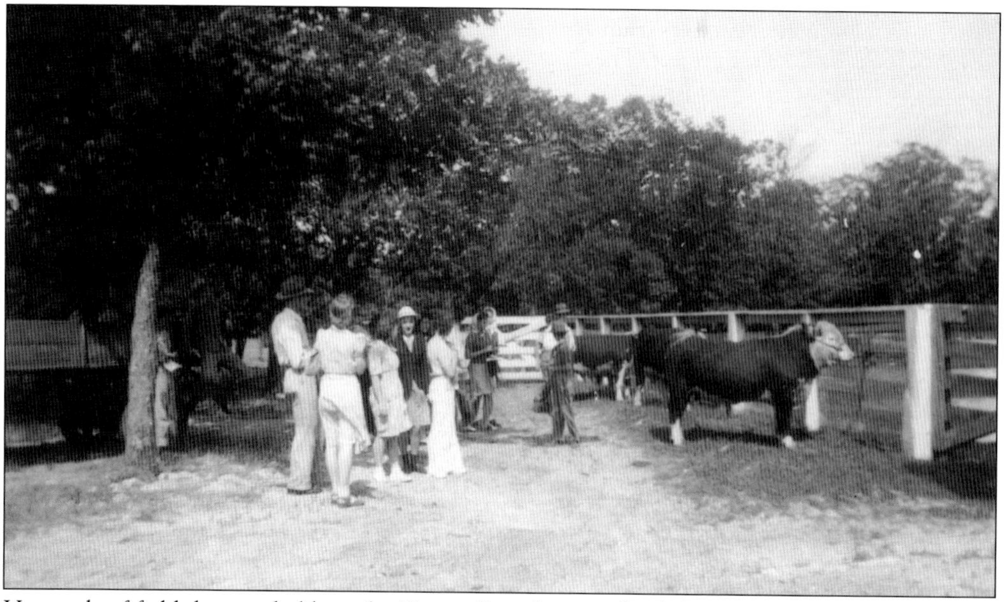

Here, a beef field day was held on the Turner Ranch east of Sulphur. Polled Herefords were the prized cattle on the ranch and were cared for by Tom McClelland, ranch manager; Hubert Little, farm manager; and Dr. "Doc" Easley, ranch veterinarian. It took a large number of people to manage the ranch operations with several of these people being known as specialists in their fields.

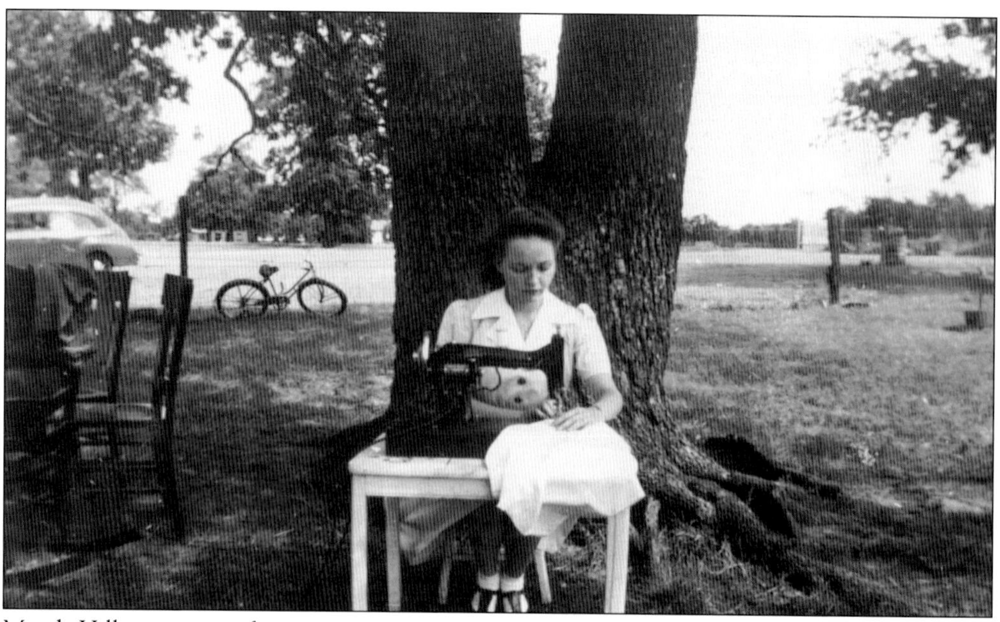

Maude Hill sews a pair of new pajamas on one of her friend's new electric sewing machine. Sewing projects are still part of today's 4-H program.

Carrie Grant, a Woodland 4-H member, used her 4-H baking manual for this cake recipe. Extension and the US Department of Agriculture produced many project manuals on a variety of topics for distribution to 4-H members. The manuals were used to teach new information and to give project requirements to the members.

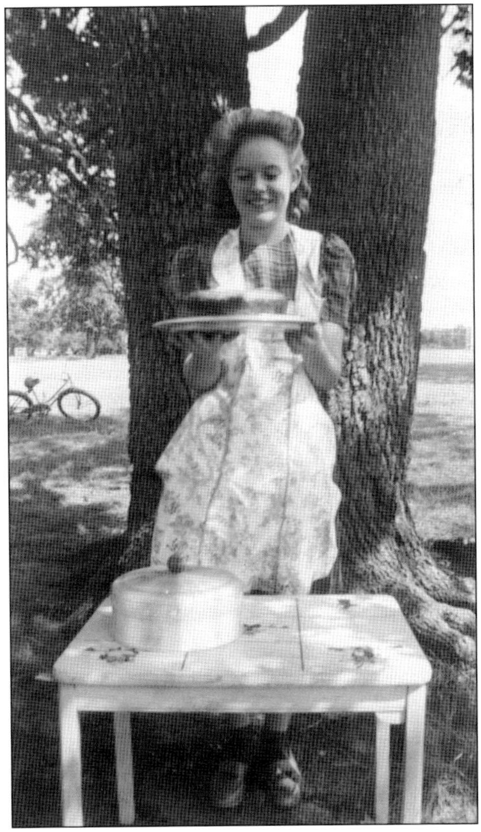

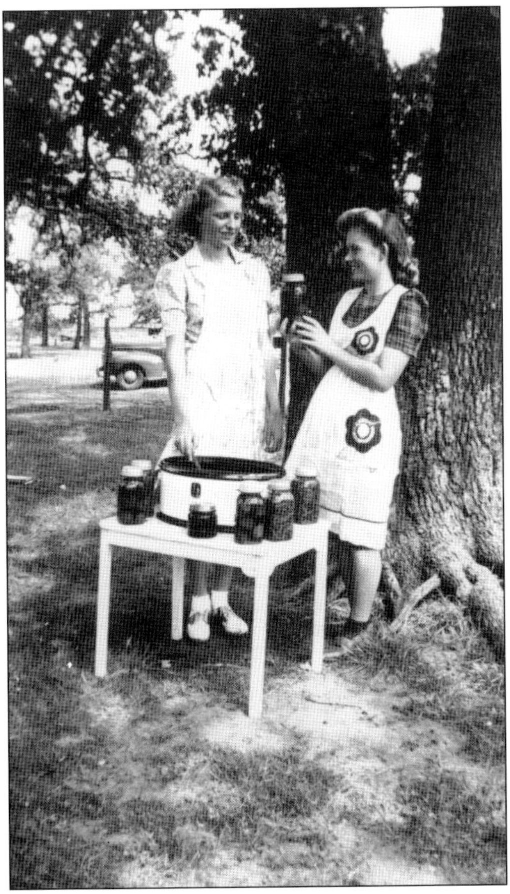

Carrie Grant (right) explains her canning methods for a jar of beets to fellow 4-H member Mary West. Both girls were active members of the Woodland 4-H Club.

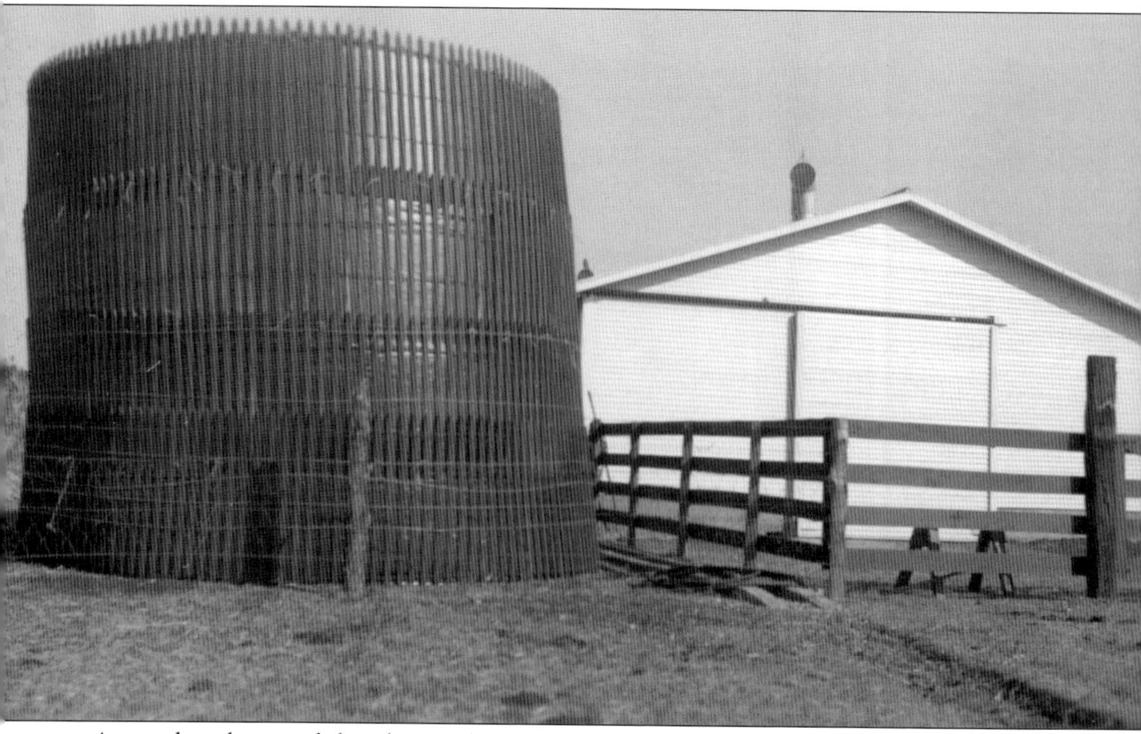

A new dairy barn and slat silo were built on the Arvin Eidson farm east of Sulphur in 1940. A silo is a structure for storing bulk materials such as grain.

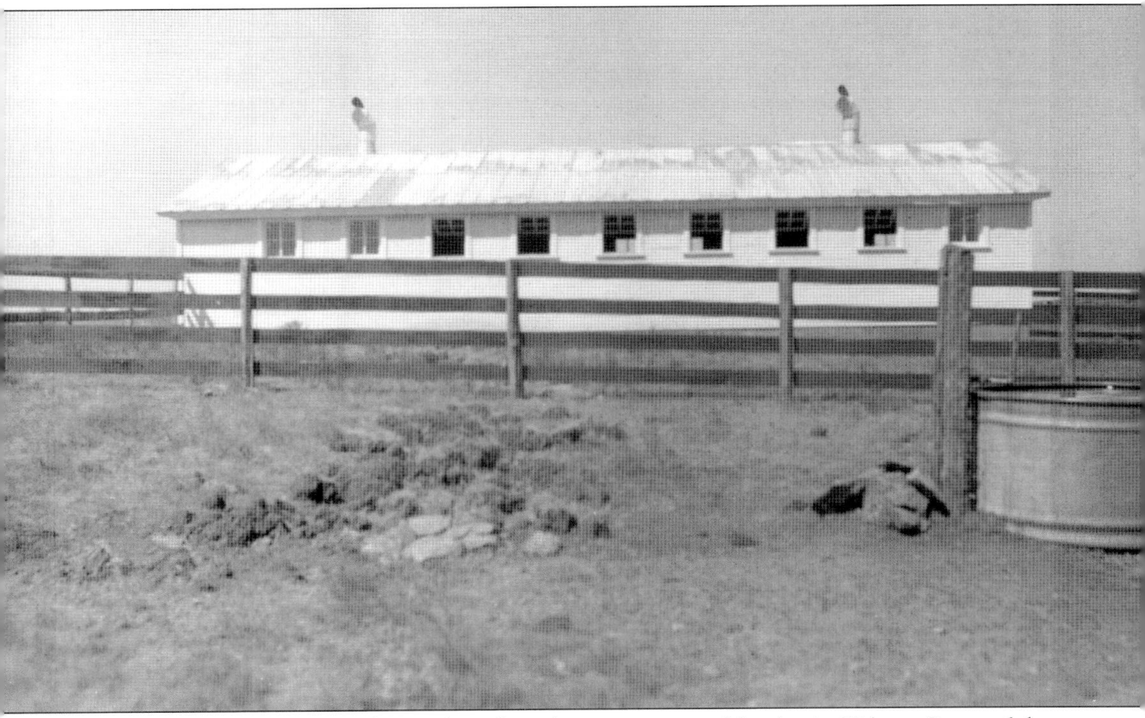

Shown here is a side view of the modern dairy barn constructed by Arvin Eidson. Some of the Eidson family still make their home in Murray County, including Wayne Eidson, who owns and operates a large Chevrolet and Buick dealership in Sulphur.

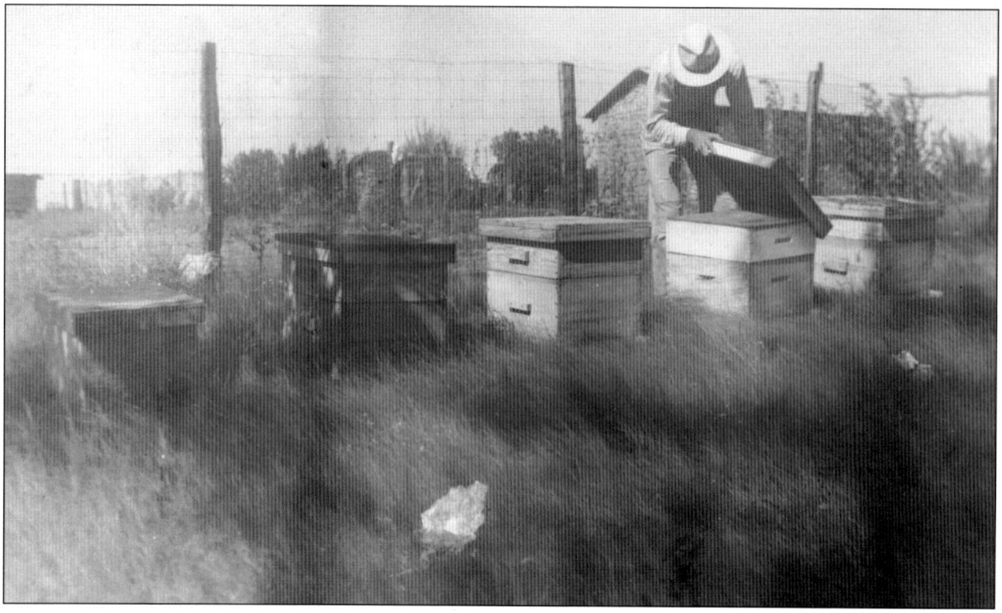

G.R. Scott of Hickory harvested 140 pounds of honey in one season. He earned $15 in sales and saved the rest for home use.

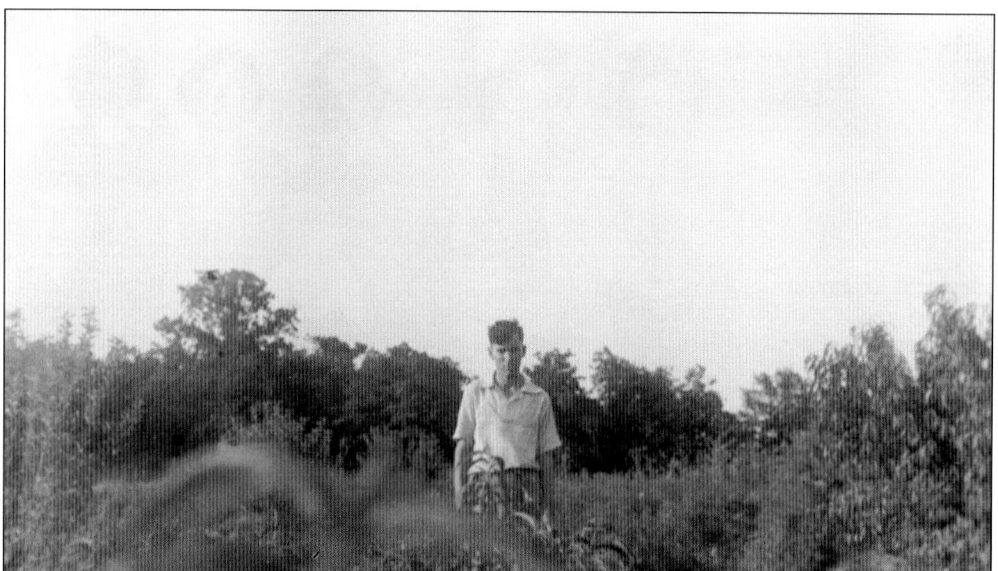

G.R. Scott, a Hickory 4-H member, is shown in his peach tree nursery. G.R. used these trees for his budding work. His orchard was 1/3 acre in size. In 1940, 21 orchards were planted county wide by 4-H boys and girls.

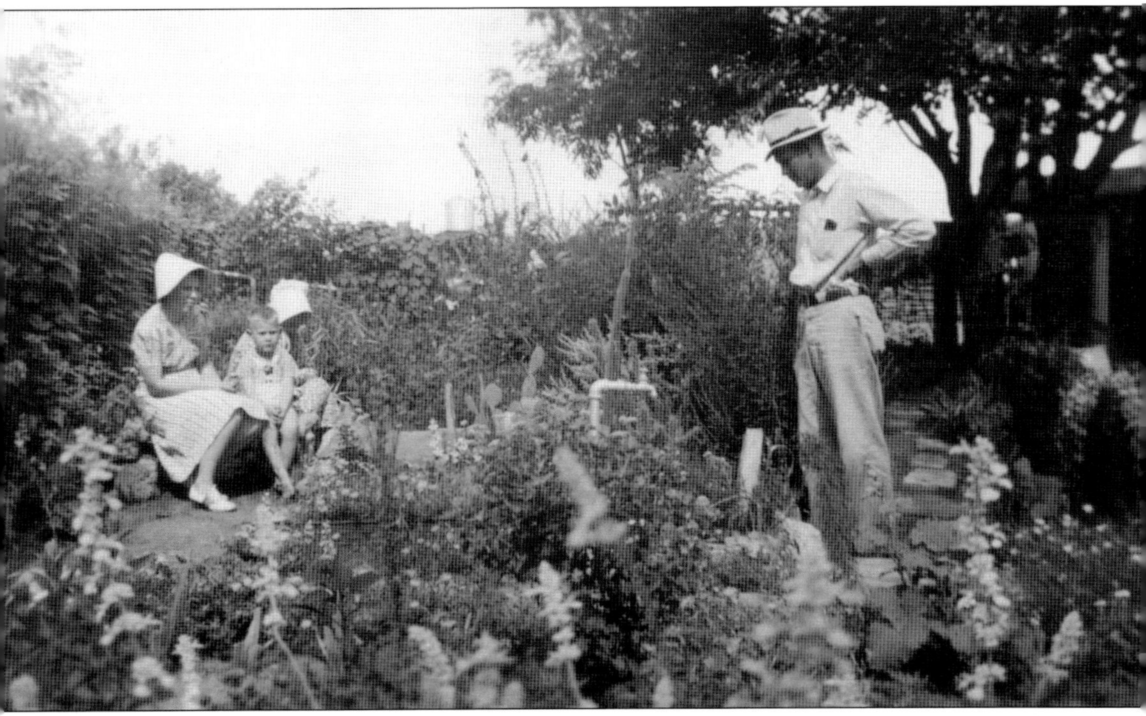

Pictured here is the flower garden of Mr. and Mrs. Matt Wolf Sr. Two years before this photograph was taken, the area was a chicken yard. Mrs. Wolf's garden was quite large and included an outdoor living room, complete with a gold fishpond. This information, titled "Planting Friendship," was found in old extension records, and it goes on to state the following: "Mrs. Matt Wolf of the Joy Home Demonstration Club has a unique way of cultivating neighborhood friendship with a hoe. In her backyard, Mrs. Wolf has a large flower bed which she prizes very highly because it is here that she has planted flower plants given her by her different friends. Mrs. Wolf can look out her kitchen window on to this friendship flower bed and name the person giving her each plant. By this method, Mrs. Wolf can associate her many friends with the flowers, which she loves so much."

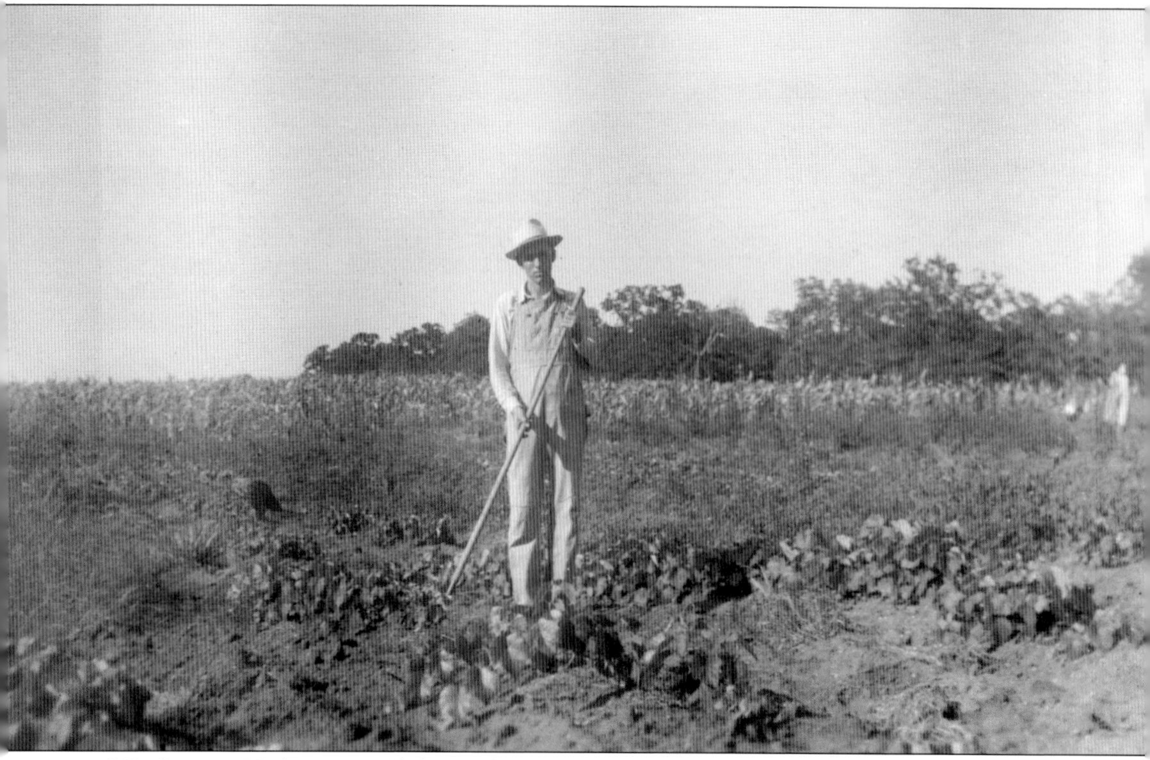

G.R. Scott, a Hickory 4-H Club member, set out 250 grape cuttings in the field to grow for one year before transplanting to the vineyard. In 1940, thirteen 4-H boys completed the work in the home vineyard project. Horticulture specialists from Oklahoma A&M would come to Murray County each fall and spring to present demonstrations across the county on budding and grafting pecans, pruning grape vines and fruit trees, and pruning shrubs and roses.

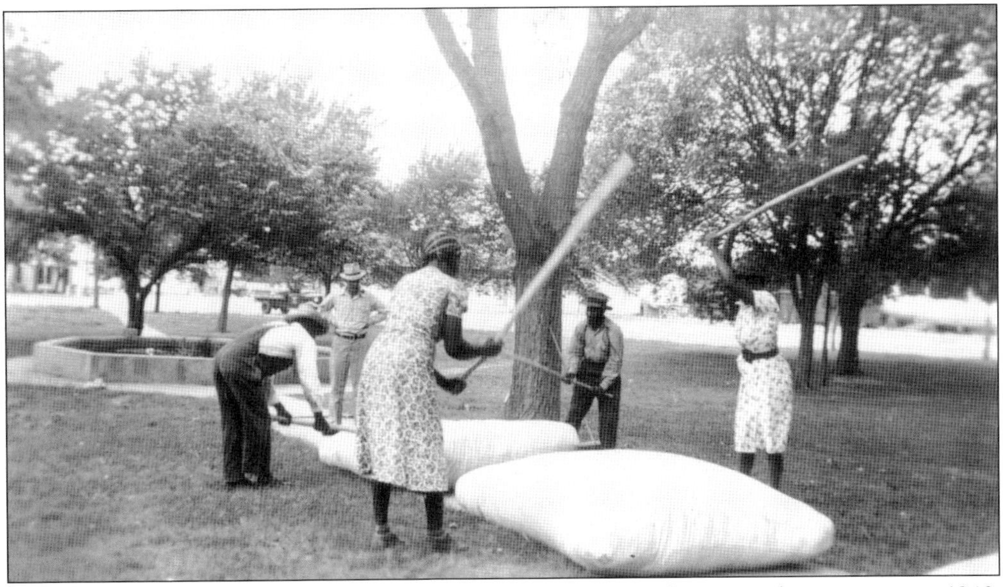

This image shows African American men and women learning how to make a mattress in 1940. Extension records kept numbers and ethnicity of people they served, and the terms used during this period were "Negro," "White," and "Indian."

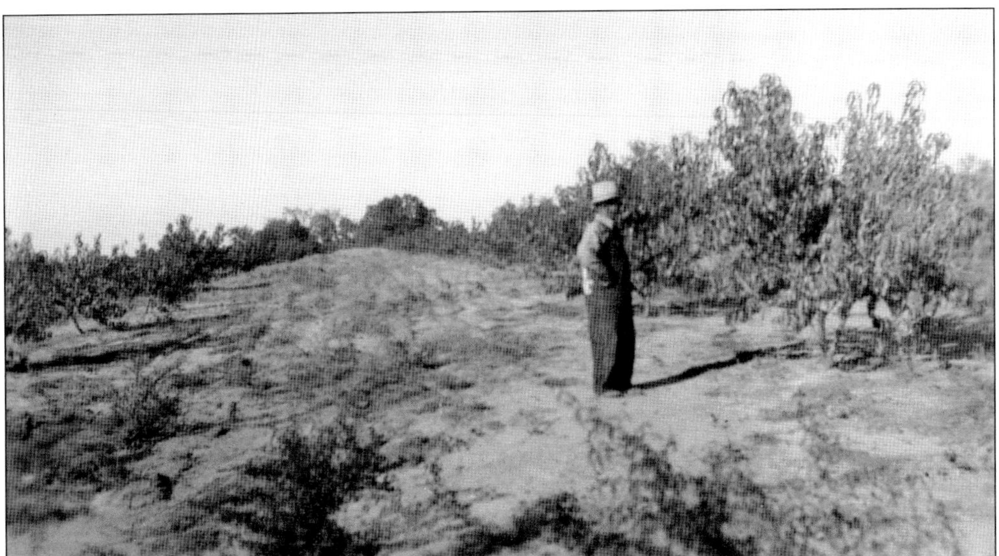

Two-year-old peach trees are shown on the Stevenson farm in Nebo. In the spring, the native peach tree would flower in pink, and the fruit these trees produced was small with a tough skin. Today, very few fruit trees can be found in the county compared to the early 1900s.

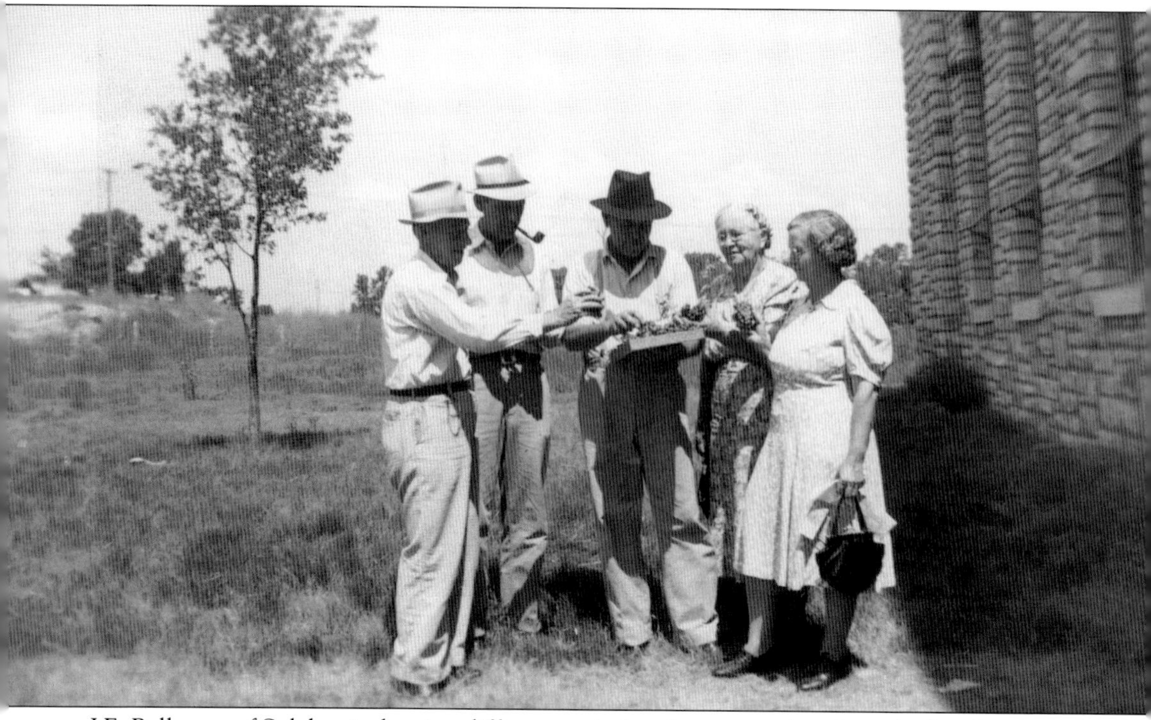

J.E. Ballenger of Sulphur is showing different varieties of grape cuttings furnished to the county by the Oklahoma A&M Department of Horticulture. The varieties were being tested on his farm in 1940.

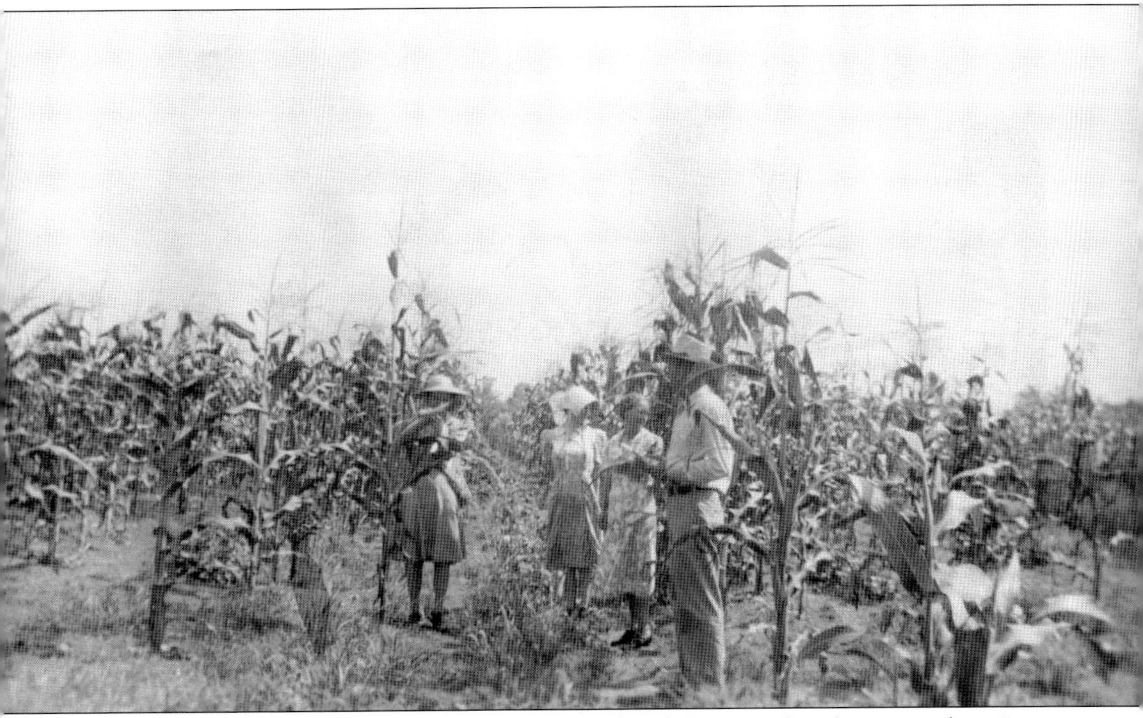

A field of Reid's yellow dent corn grown from registered seed. Registered seed was something "new and improved," and the extension agent used planting demonstrations in order to show farmers what could be produced. Farmers would make annual tours of farms growing the registered seed to inspect the demonstration field's final harvest.

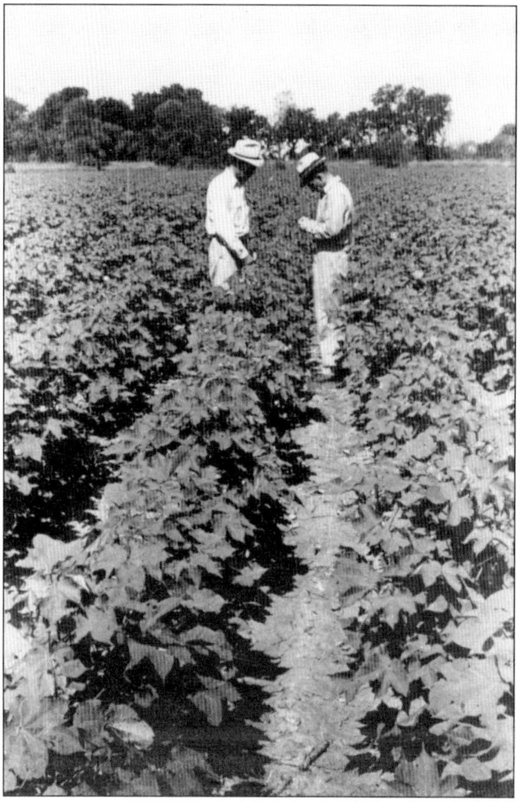

Here, Dick Grant and county agent R.E. Chiles inspect foundation planting of Acala 8 cotton on the Grant farm. Dick Grant was a member of the Davis Cotton Improvement Association.

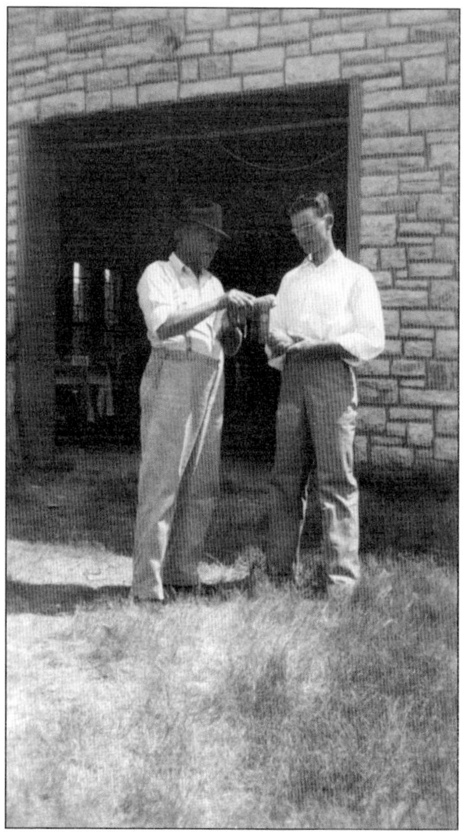

J.E. Ballenger and 4-H member Ross Badget take a look at the first-place corn from the 1940 county fair.

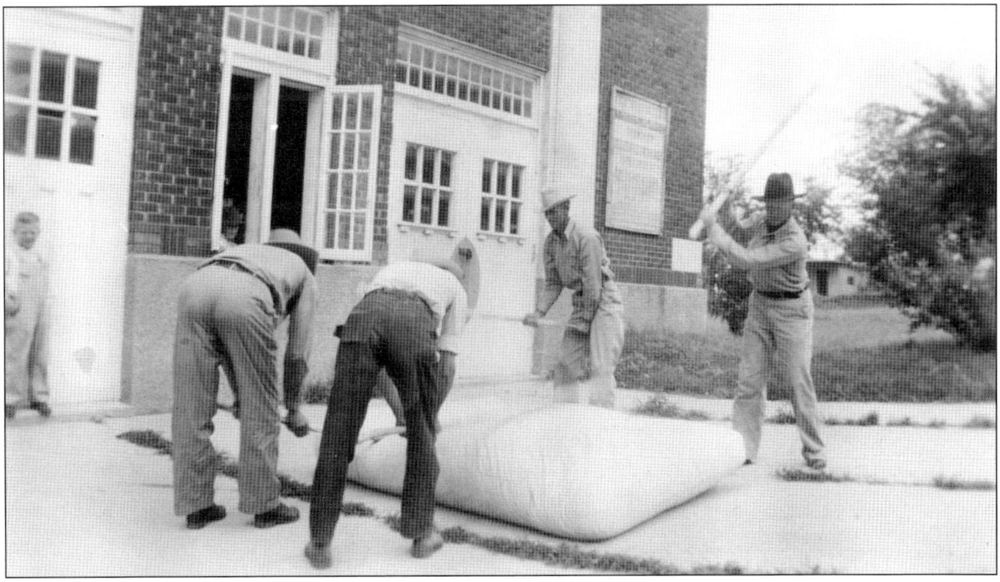

Pictured are men assisting with mattress making. Because one of the steps in mattress making was beating the mattress, men would often perform this labor-intensive task. In 1940, the count was 112 mattresses made county wide.

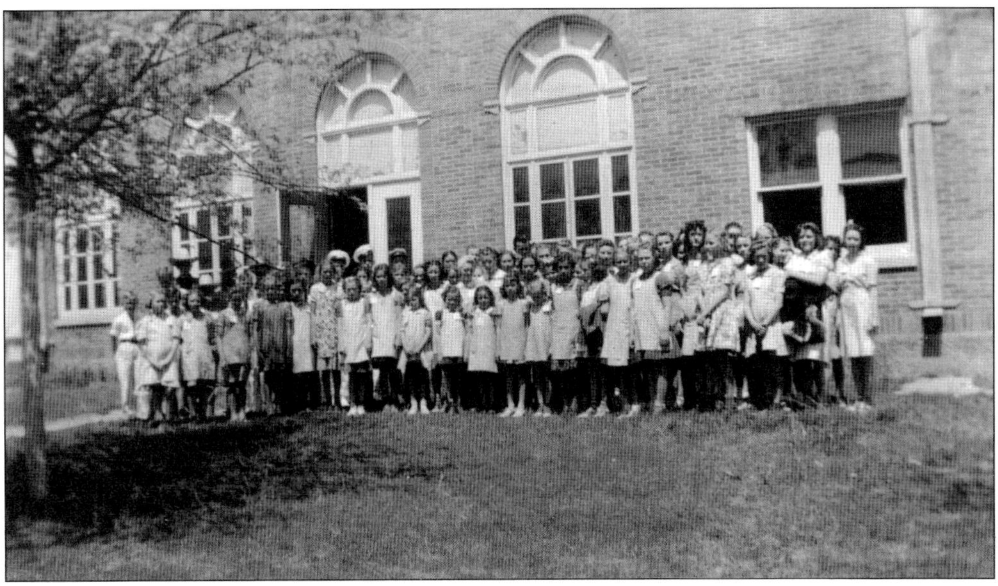

These 4-H members compete in the 1940 appropriate dress contest. Good hygiene and grooming were a major part of this contest as well as selecting the appropriate clothing for various occasions. Wool suits, best dresses, wash dresses, party dresses, and boy's work wear were just a few of the classes in the contest. County winners went on to compete at Oklahoma State 4-H Roundup.

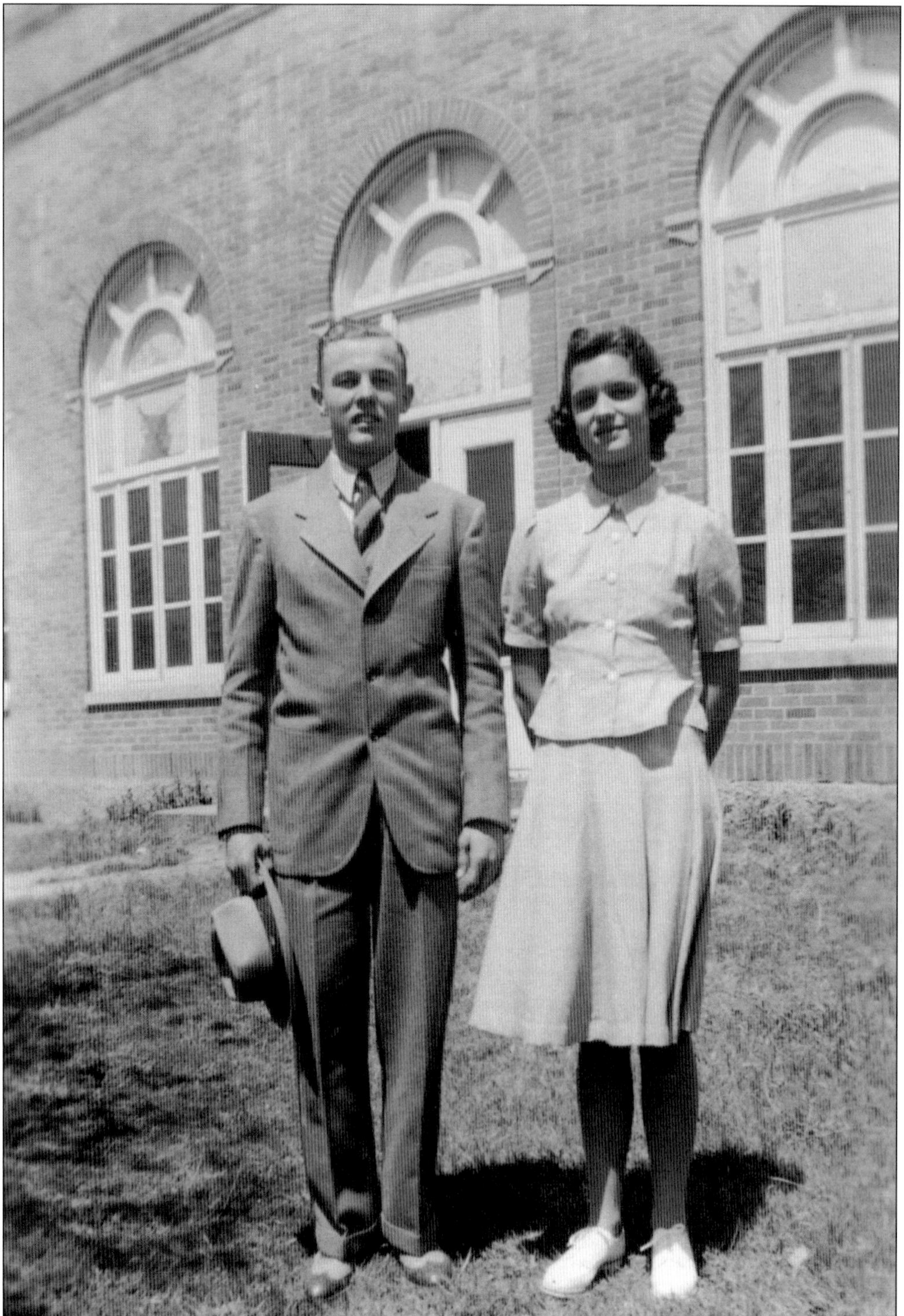

In this 1940 photograph, 4-H members Doris Rowe of Woodland and Max Pyeatt of Sulphur pose for the camera. Each was selected as champions in their appropriate dress divisions.

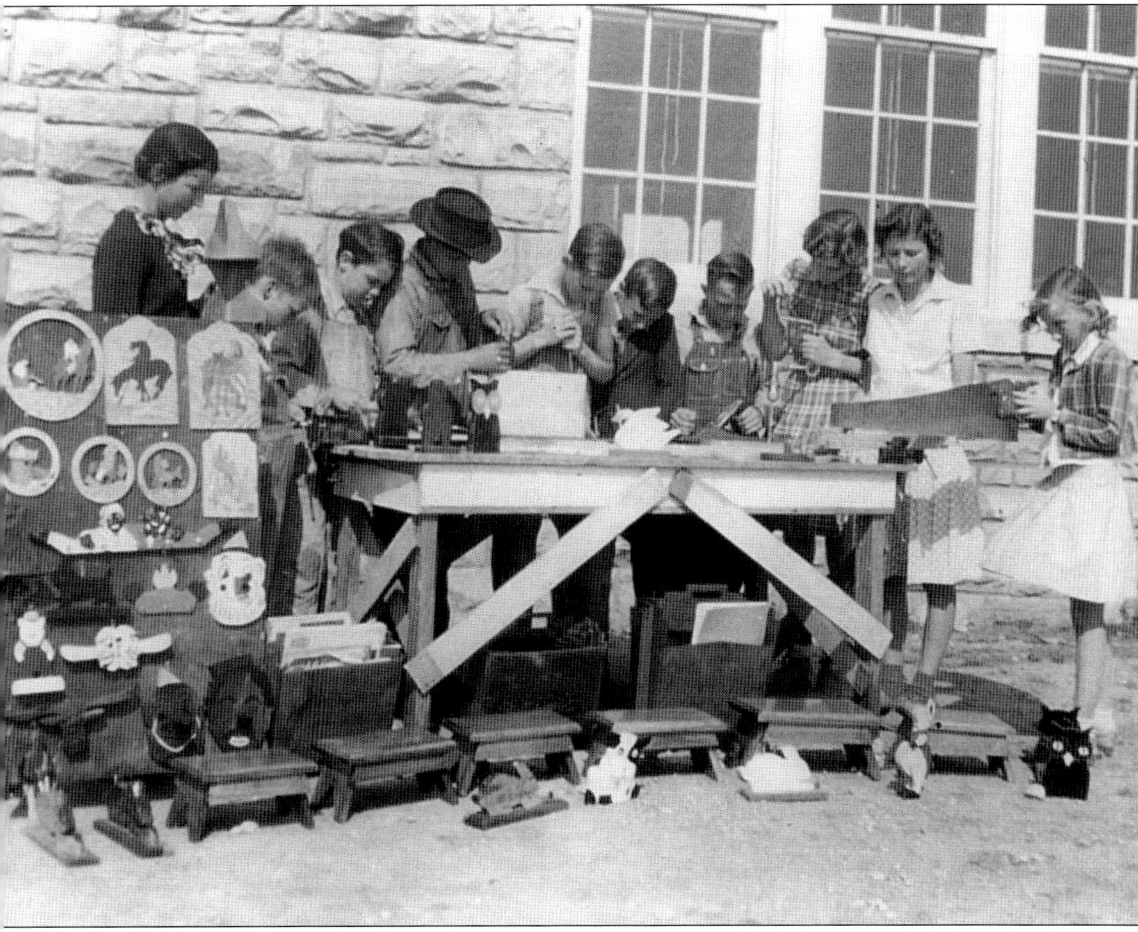

Members of 4-H learn how to build things for the home through the 4-H woodworking project. Work adult volunteers in 4-H were called coaches. This photograph shows stools, magazine racks, bookends, and items for the walls, all made by 4-H members. This photograph was taken at the Woodland School.

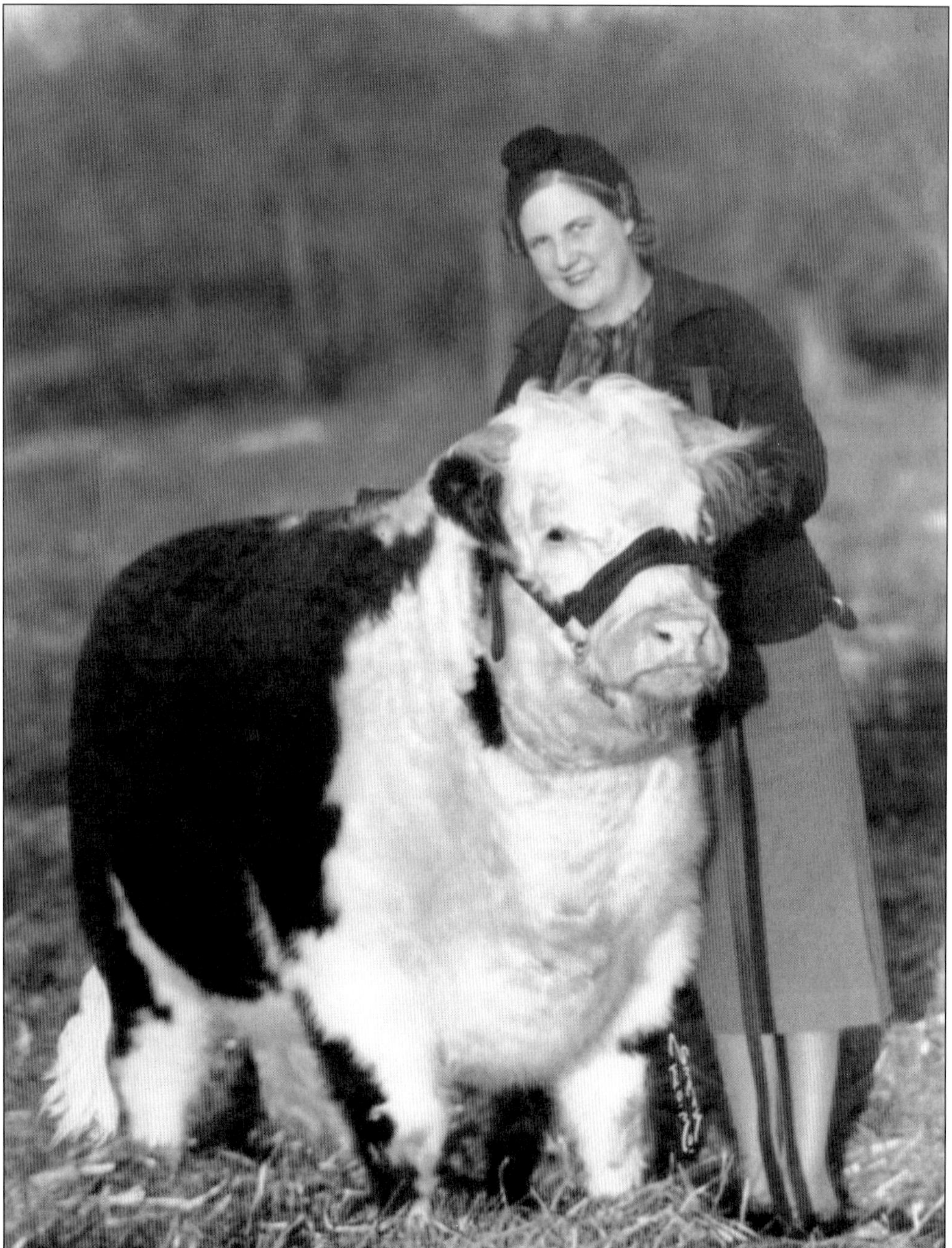

Mrs. Tom McClelland, wife of Turner Ranch manager, poses with one of the prized Hereford bulls. Turner Ranch was often referred to as "Hereford Heaven," and it would sell cattle all over the country.

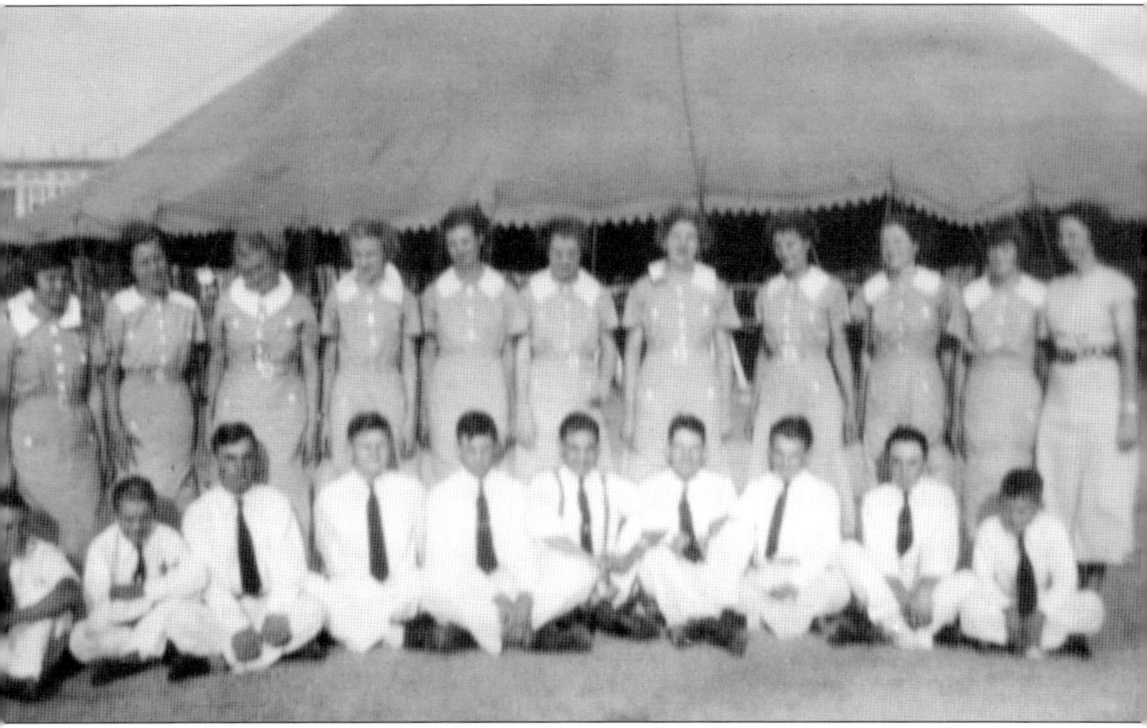

This picture of 4-H delegates was taken at the Oklahoma State 4-H Roundup in June 1941. Delegates would meet in the 4-H Clubs and Student Activities Building (constructed in 1938) on the A&M campus in Stillwater. Today, the building is known as Gallagher-Iba Arena, named as a tribute to longtime basketball innovator and coach Henry Iba.

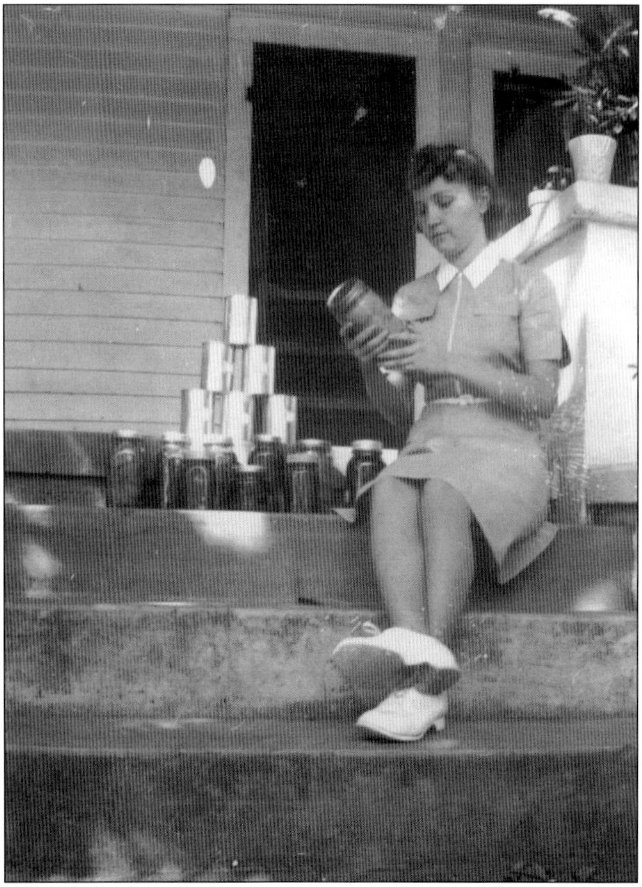

These are a few of the 122 quarts of fruits, vegetables, and meat canned by Maude Hill in her sixth year of 4-H Club work. Maude placed first in her sixth-year canning project and also placed sixth in her emergency meal exhibit at the county fair.

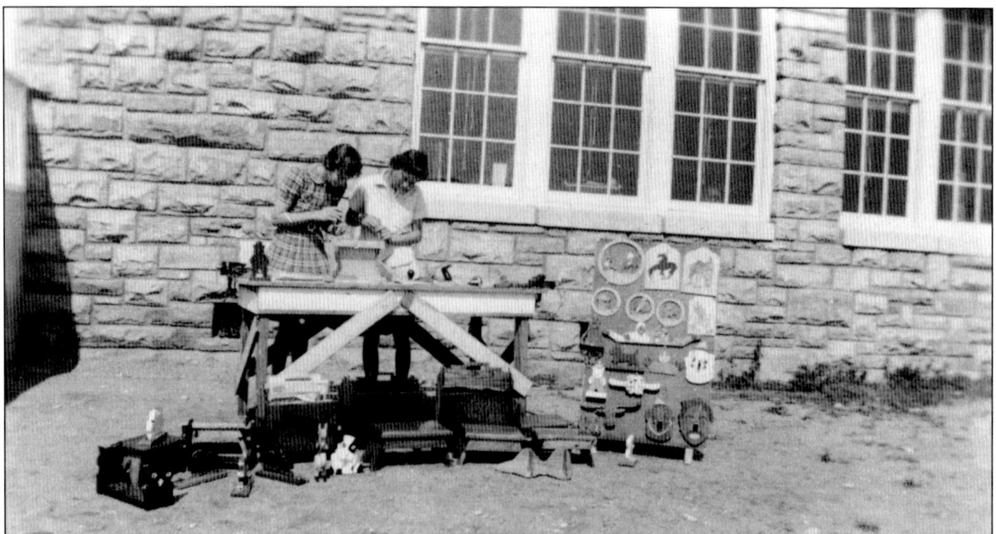

Edith Hager (left) and Pauline French, both of the Gilsonite 4-H Club, present a demonstration on building a footstool from a wooden apple box. Gilsonite was a community located south of Sulphur, near Buckhorn.

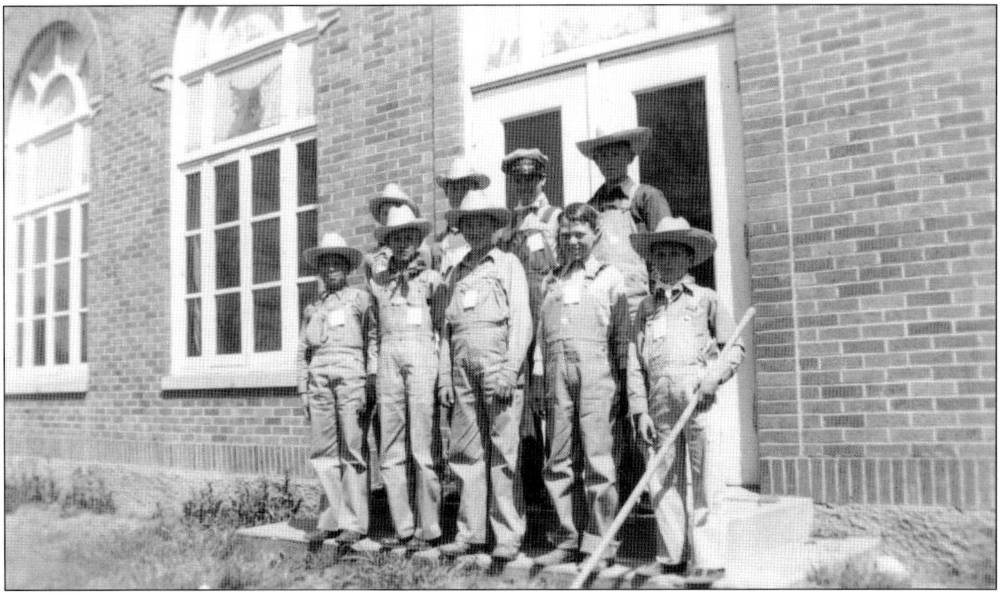

A work dress class for boys under the age of 16 years poses on the courthouse lawn after being judged.

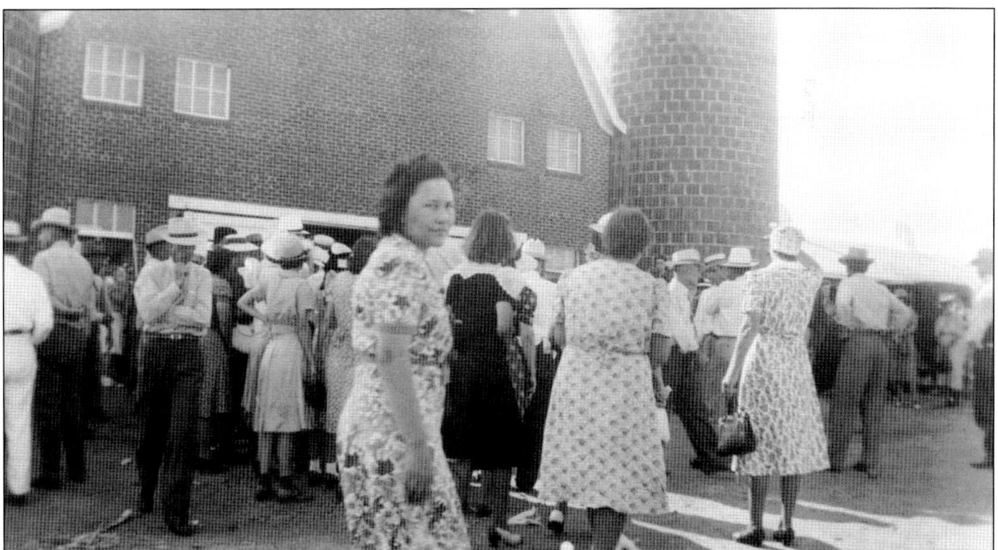

Murray County men and women are touring the A&M dairy barn while attending the state Farm Congress in Stillwater in 1940. New ideas and information from the congress were brought back home to be used for improvements.

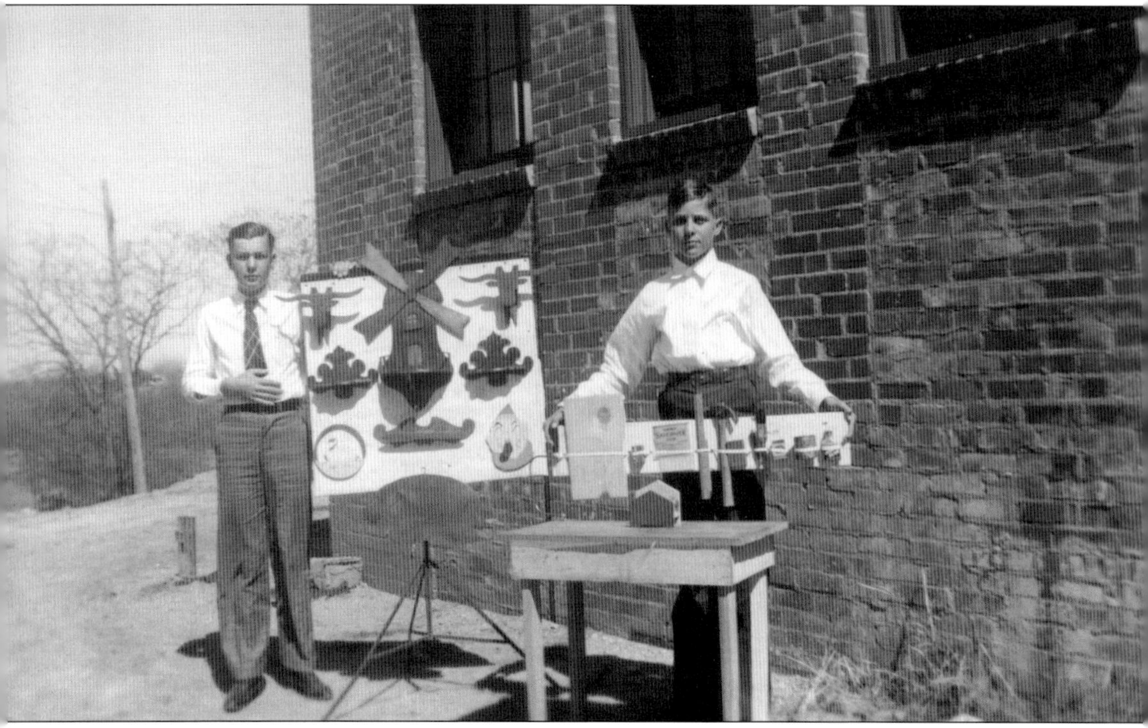

Kirby Khykendall (right) and Carl Rowe, both of the Woodland 4-H Club, present a demonstration on handicraft at the Murray County 4-H Demonstration Contest. Members of 4-H still compete today in public speaking by using demonstrations as a method for introducing the major points members want to present.

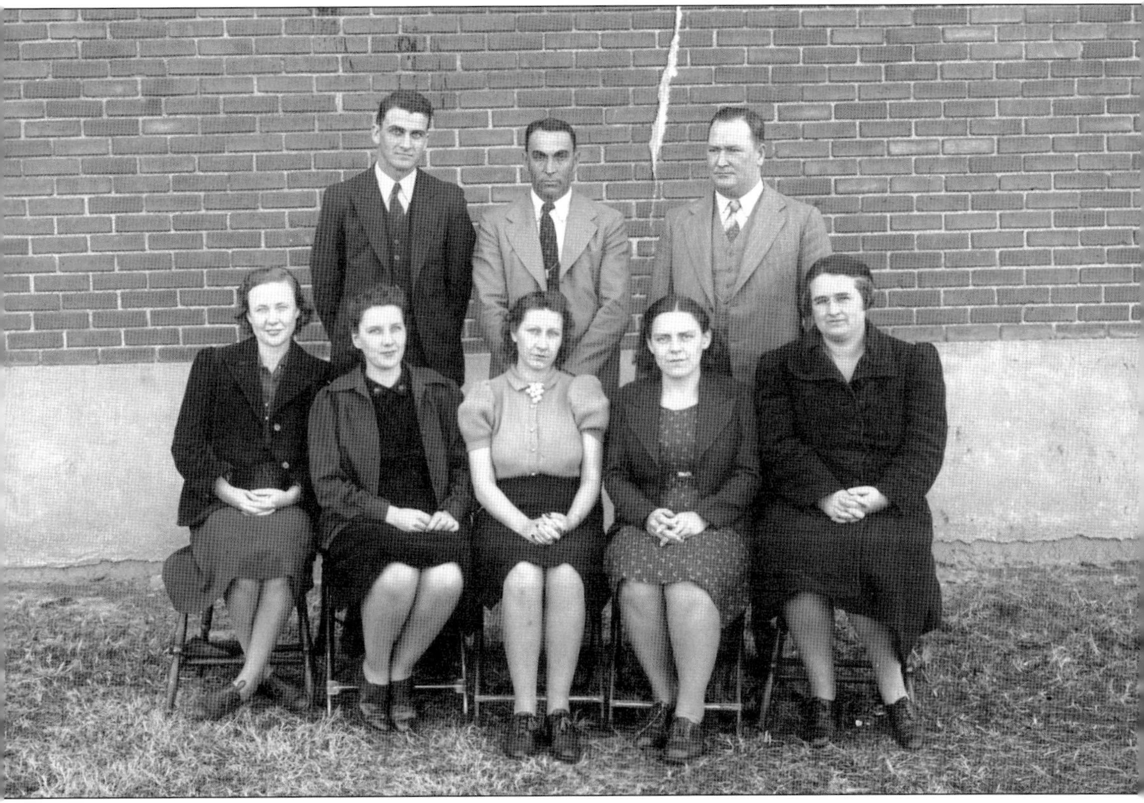

The Hickory teaching staff in 1940, was made up of, from left to right, (first row) Gertrude Ozbirn Donoghue, Lucille Willard, Lorena (Ted) Nowlin, Wyneava Vale, and Mrs. Cable; (second row) Cecil Moore, Lee Brian, and Paul Hewatt.

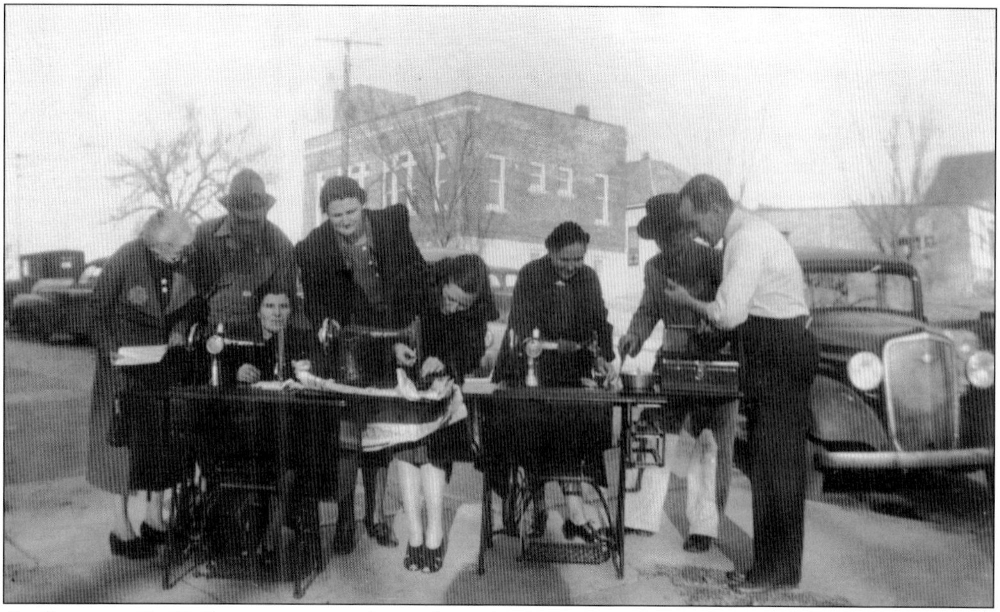

On January 10, 1941, a sewing machine clinic for farm women was held at Convention Hall in Sulphur. Farm women would bring their sewing machines to the clinic and learn how to take it apart, clean, make repairs, and put back together. An engineer from the A&M campus would present the clinic.

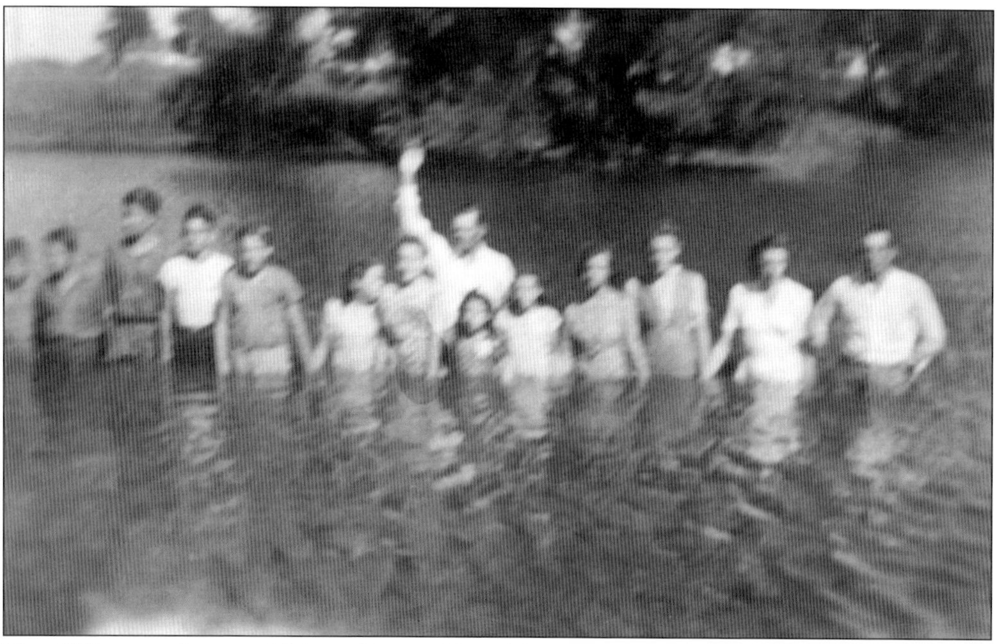

This 1945 image depicts a Hickory Baptist Church baptism in Hickory Gin pond. A large cotton gin was once located in Hickory, close to the railroad track for easy shipping of the cotton bales. (Loyce Gerth.)

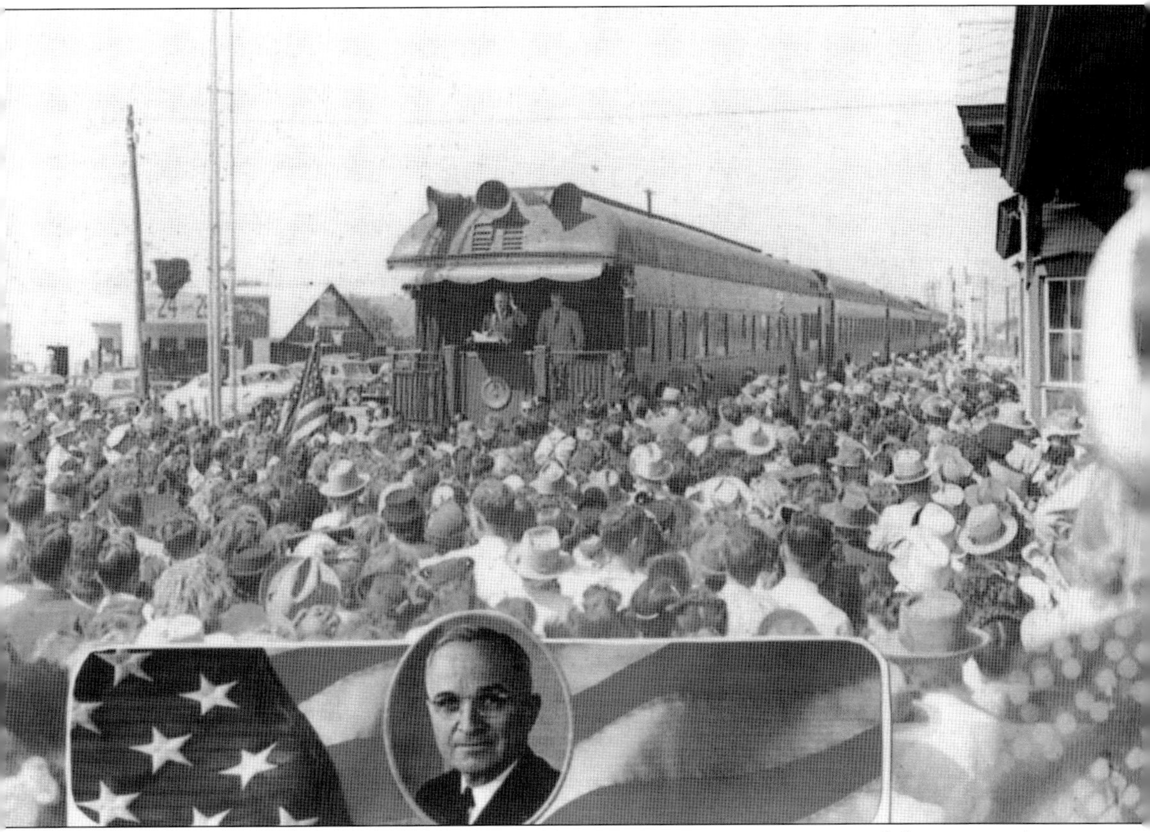

In 1948, the train stopped in Davis for Pres. Harry S. Truman, Democratic candidate, to speak to the crowd regarding his run for reelection. The Truman/Barkley ticket carried Murray County and the State of Oklahoma, and Truman went on to win the election with 49.6 percent of the nation's vote. The opponent was Thomas E. Dewey, a Republican from New York. (Davis Museum.)

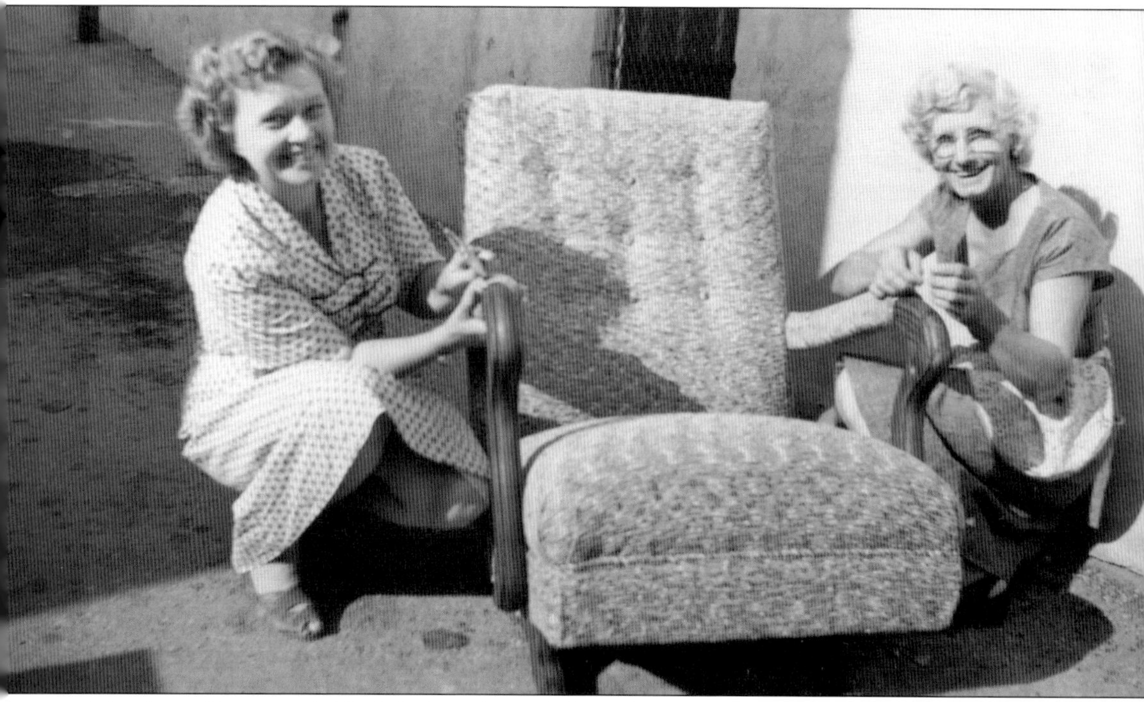

Mrs. Louis Danyeur (left) of the Fairshine Club works to reupholster her chair during a county workshop. Mrs. Chaffin, also of the Fairshine Club, assists her. Reupholstering furniture was one way of stretching the family's budget.

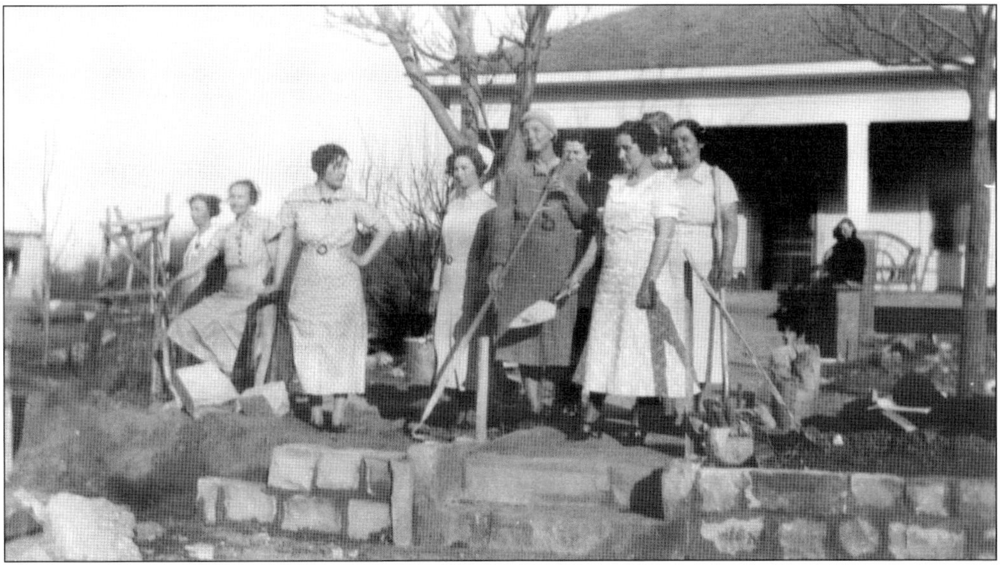

Murray County Home Demonstration Club members are working to build a rock retaining wall. Members would gather at members' homes to assist each other with yard improvement. Entire communities were improved with this type of club work, including church and school yards.

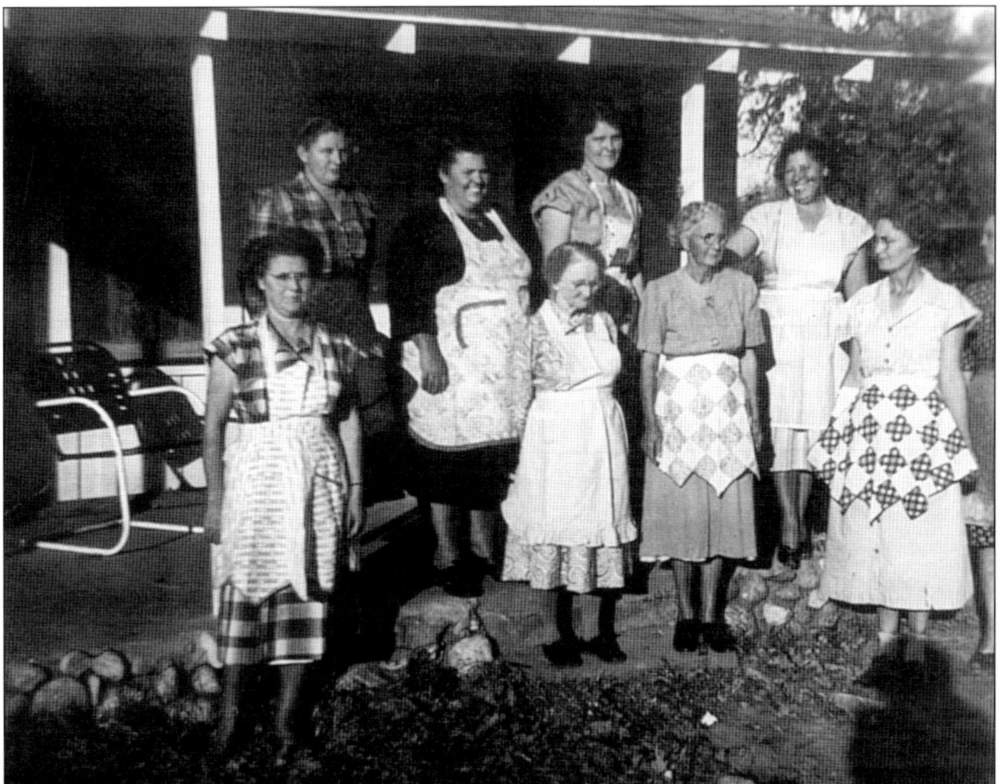

Club members pose wearing their newly sewn aprons. From left to right are Gladys Jobe, unidentified, Lorene Cast, Granny Barry, Zona Cagle, Granny Arms, Bea Barry, Flora Lewis, and unidentified. This meeting took place at the home of Gladys Jobe on Buckhorn Road, south of Sulphur.

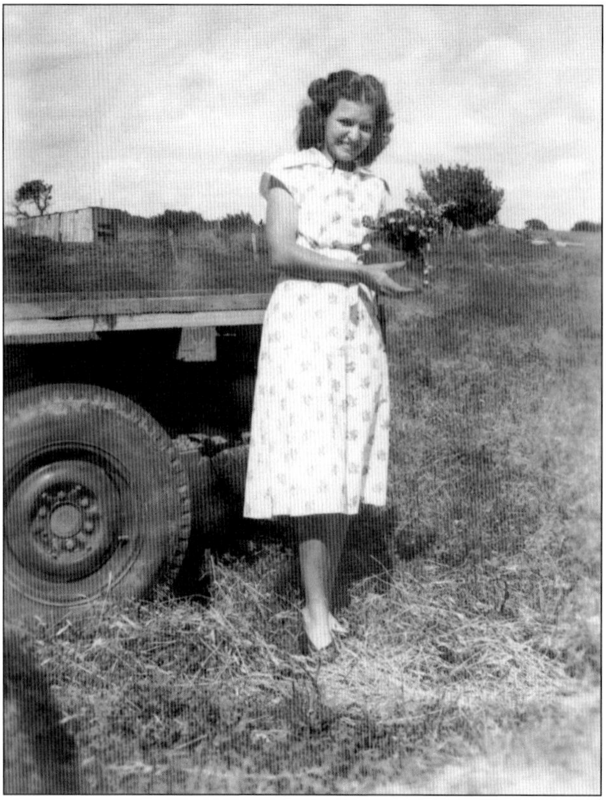

Maxine Moore Lannom, wife of Bill Lannom, poses beside the farm truck with her wild onion plants. Maxine is currently a 60-plus-year member of home demonstration club work and is still involved with the county fair and extension activities. Maxine is 87 years of age and very active in her community. Her coconut pie recipe is famous throughout the county, and some of her pies have sold for as much as $500 in community auction fundraisers. (Johnnie Mobly.)

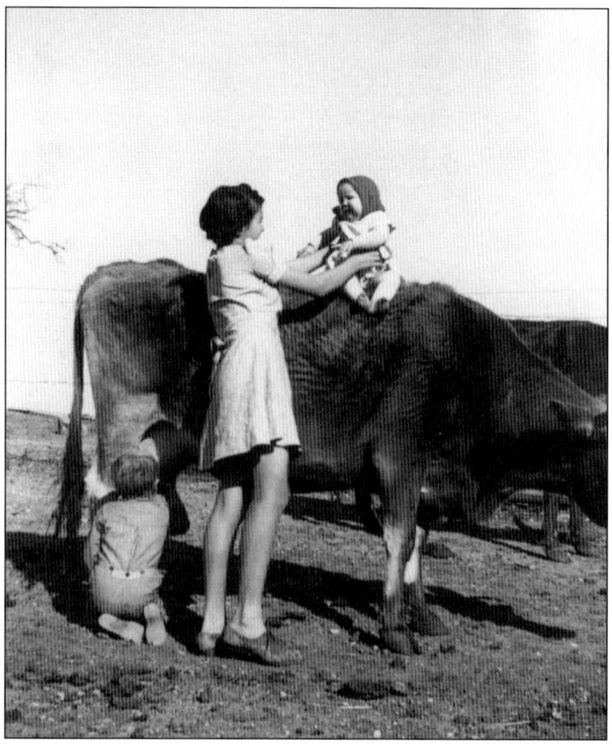

Farm kids Dorothy (Crawford) Brown holds little sister Ruth (Crawford) Pope on the back of the milk cow while little brother Jack Crawford tries to milk it in 1940. (Ruth Crawford Pope.)

Alma Crawford waters her rafter, or flock, of over 500 turkeys. Her daughter Ruth had to walk the turkeys every day to the cornfield where they would catch and eat grasshoppers. The Crawford farm was north on Sunshine Road and is home today to Ruth Crawford Pope who runs cattle and bales hay on the family farm. (Ruth Crawford Pope.)

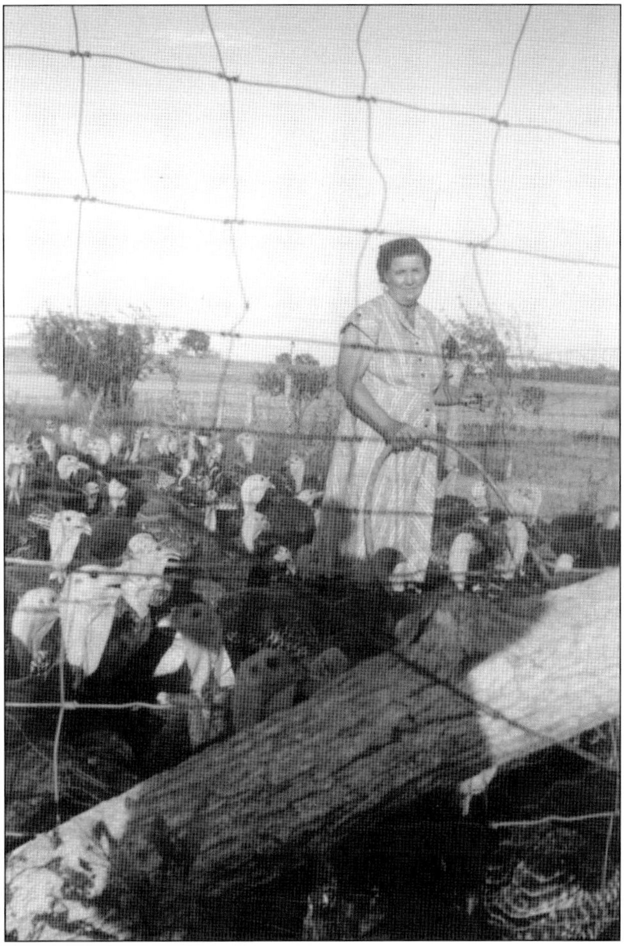

Ed Crawford inspects his bulldozer before heading out to work. Crawford built many area lakes, several roads, and cleared many acres of Murray County land with his equipment. (Ruth Crawford Pope.)

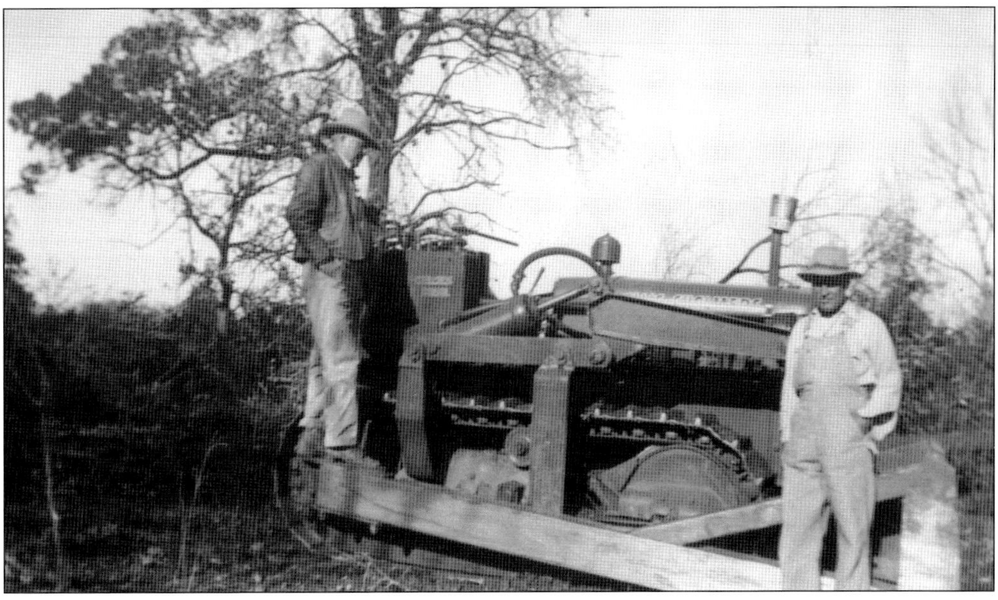

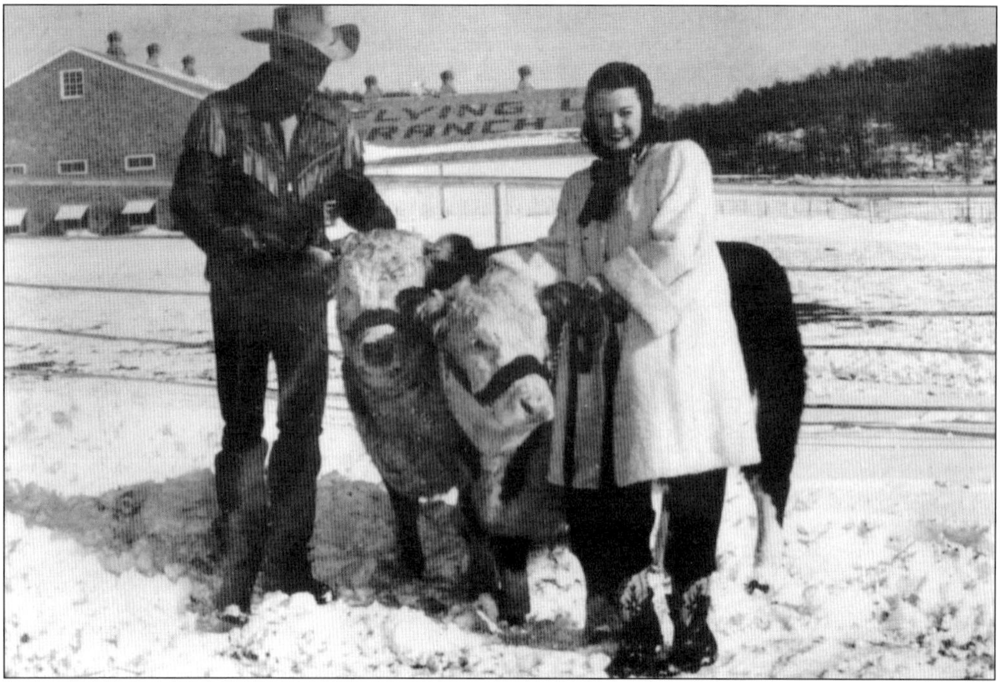

Roy Rogers and Dale Evans were married on December 31, 1947, in Davis, Oklahoma, on the Flying L Ranch. While shooting the movie *Home in Oklahoma*, they developed a friendship with ranch owners and returned to be married on the ranch. Art and Mary Jo Rush were best man and matron of honor. The marriage was Rogers was his second and the fourth for Evans, and this successful marriage lasted 51 years until Rogers's death in 1998. Dale Evans died at the age of 88 in 2001. (Davis Museum.)

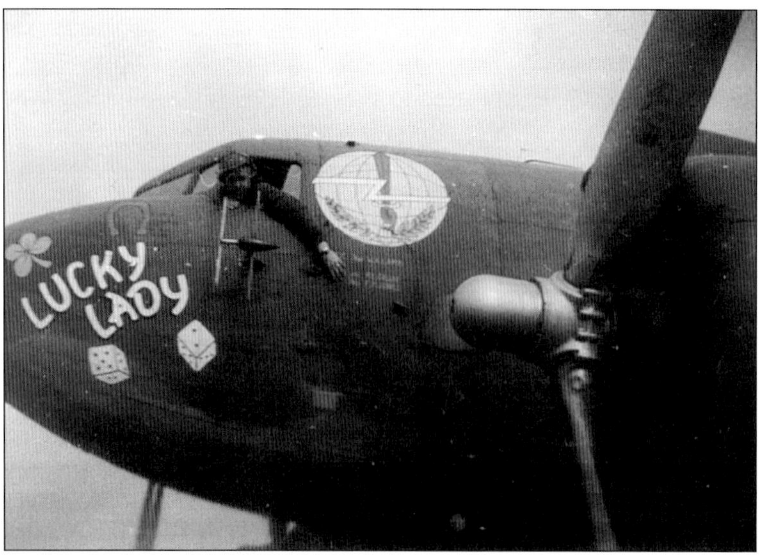

F.M. "Pete" Jones is shown at age 22 in 1943. As a member of the 7th Troop Carrier Squadron 10th and 12th Air Force, he was stationed in Italy flying as a team member with the *Lucky Lady*. His mother raised Pete, the youngest of four children, on a farm north of Sulphur. His father, F.M. Jones died at age 41.

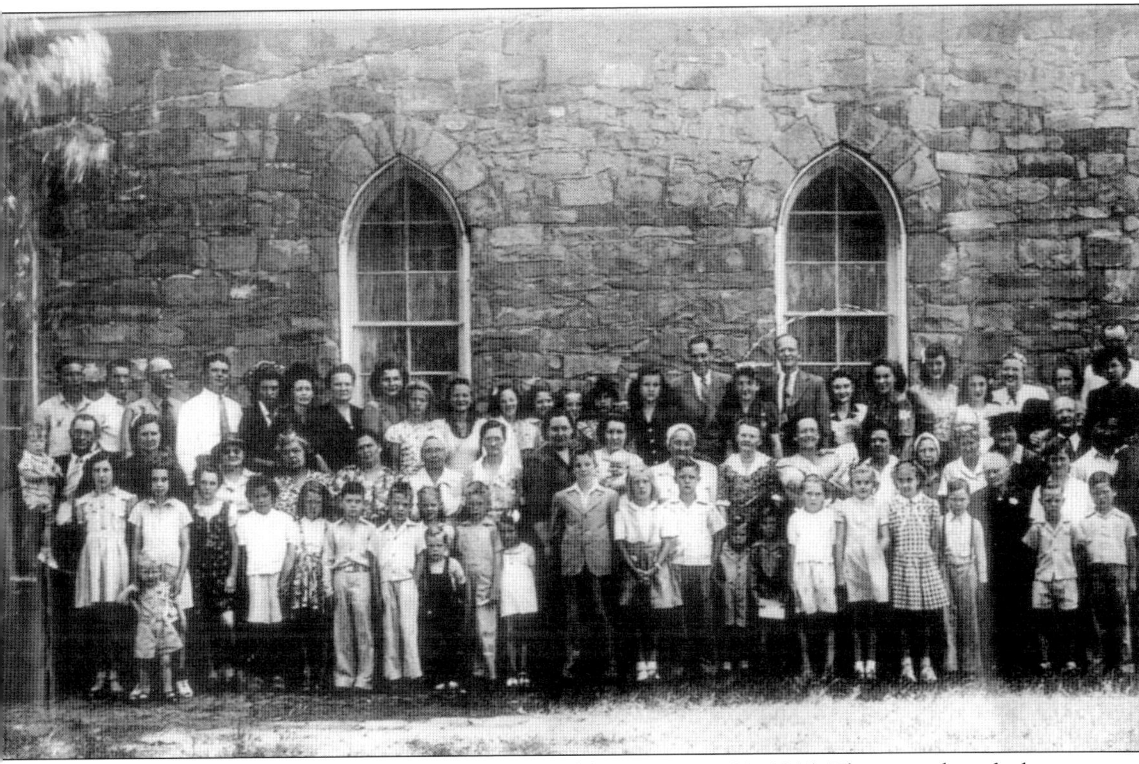

Dougherty Baptist Church members are pictured here on May 20, 1945. They are identified as, from left to right, (first row) Evelyn Hunter, LaNell Scott and Conger baby, unidentified, Edith Newby, Cordie Giddens Hankins and granddaughter, Garman M. Baldwin, Scottie Scott, Oma Lee Hendricks, Don L. Hendricks, Gary Neil Morgan, Janie Morgan, Aaron Coll, Twannah Lance, Bud Edmonson, two unidentified persons, Patsy Lance, Norma Jean Tomlinson, Shirley Brubaker, unidentified, Mrs. Thornton, Tom Edmondson, George Newby (boy behind Tom Edmondson is Giddens grandson); (second row) Lawrence, Jess Hunter holding Earl Hunter, Zora Hunter, Mrs. Samples, Mrs. Giddens, Helen Payne, Mrs. Payne, Alma Morgan, Radie Scott Brubaker, Bug Scott Conger, Mrs. Bullard, Mrs. Brubaker, Oma Hendricks and Rickie, Mrs. Lawrence, Mrs. Saunders, unidentified, Ruby Howell, Lee Howell, Bruce Gibson, Mr. Bullard, and Dolph Morgan; (third row) Leamon Bullard, Earl Tomlinson, Mr. Brubaker, Ray Roberts, Pauline Giddens Hankins, Nellie Brubaker Samples, Mrs. Coll, Loliss Tomlinson, Mildred Saunders, Irene Saunders, Alma Roland, R.I. Hendricks, Margaret Jones, Mary Jane Newby, Joyce Baldwin, Brother Rounds, Joe Morgan, Brother Robinson, Hazel Brubaker Robert, Leta Scott, Becky Hendricks, Mary Lance, Ina Lee Bullard, Wanda Brubaker, Eva Yvonne Hunter, and Ford Montgomery. (Judy Hale.)

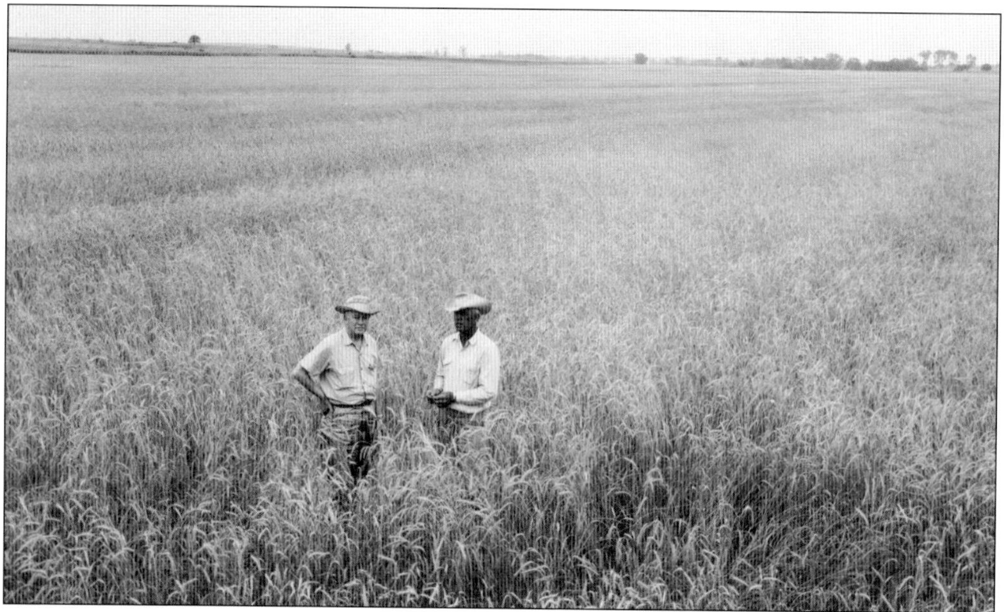

Gov. Roy J. Turner (left) and Hubert Little, Turner Ranch farm manager, look over the pasture grasses on the Turner Ranch. Turner was elected as Oklahoma's 13th governor and served from January 13, 1947, to January 8, 1951. He established the Turner Ranch in the 1930s. He died of a brain tumor in 1973. (Ron Little.)

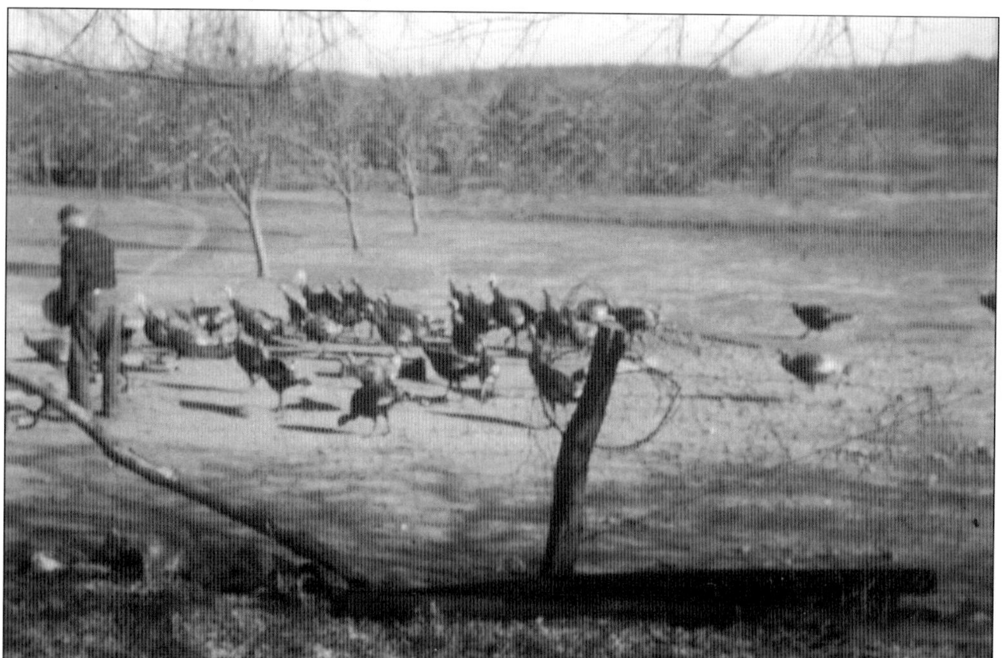

George Bela Aaron feeds his rafter of turkeys. The Aaron farm was south of Sulphur, just off Buckstitch Road. Aaron raised the turkeys to sell during the Thanksgiving and Christmas seasons. His daughter Johnnie remembered hanging the turkeys by their legs on the clothesline, then cutting their heads off. Aaron would deliver the dressed turkeys to families across the county. (Johnnie Aaron Mobly.)

Four

The 1950s and 1960s

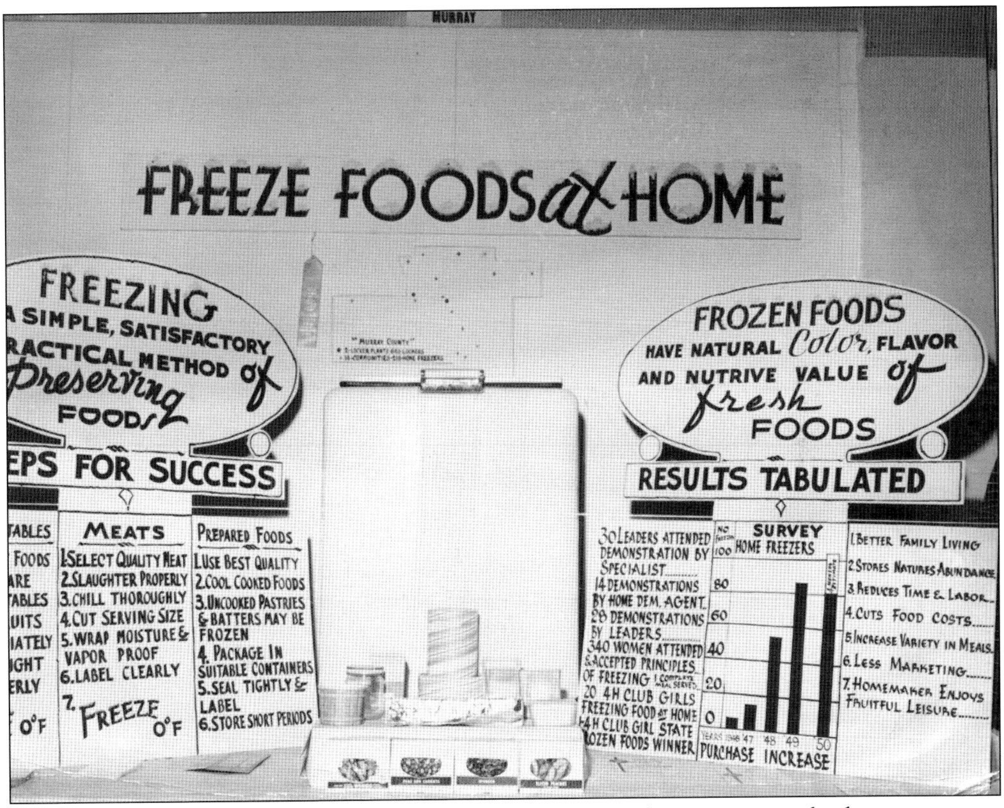

In the mid-1900s, individual families did not have their own freezers to store food; it was custom for rural families to take their meat to the local meat locker. When they needed meat, they would visit the locker and take home only what was needed. Lockers were located in both Sulphur and in Davis. In 1946, there were 7 freezers sold in the county; in 1947, there were 18 sold. The year 1948 saw a rise to 58 freezers sold, 1959 recorded 85 sold, and in the first four months of 1950, there were 82 sold. This home demonstration club exhibit on frozen foods won fifth place at the state fair in 1950.

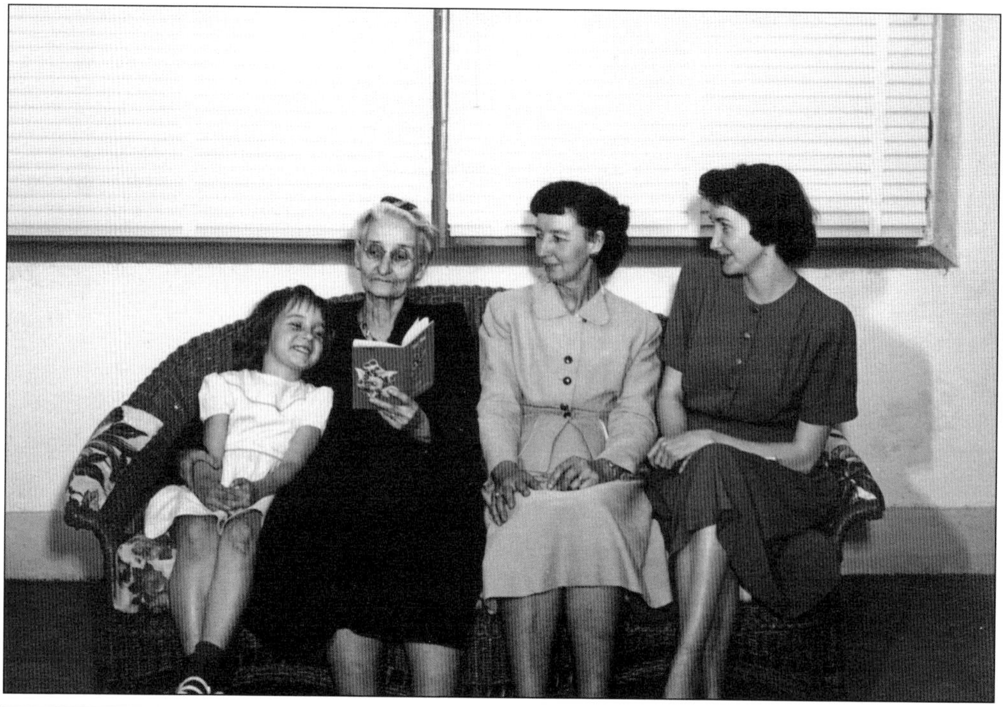

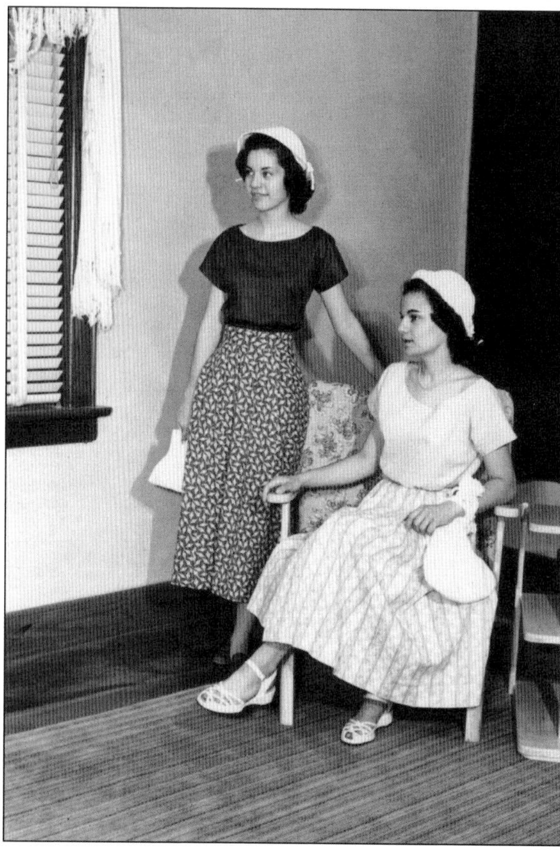

Pictured are four generations of extension club work in the Joy Home Demonstration Club. From left to right are great-granddaughter of Mrs. Smith, Susan Scruggs; Mrs. C.L. Smith; her daughter Mrs. C.C. Scruggs; and her granddaughter Mrs. E.D. Scruggs.

These 4-H members of 1950, Kitty (left) and Glenna Grant, are dressed for their cotton clothing demonstration, which placed first in the county contest and sixth in state competition. The Grant girls were very active 4-H members from the Woodland club.

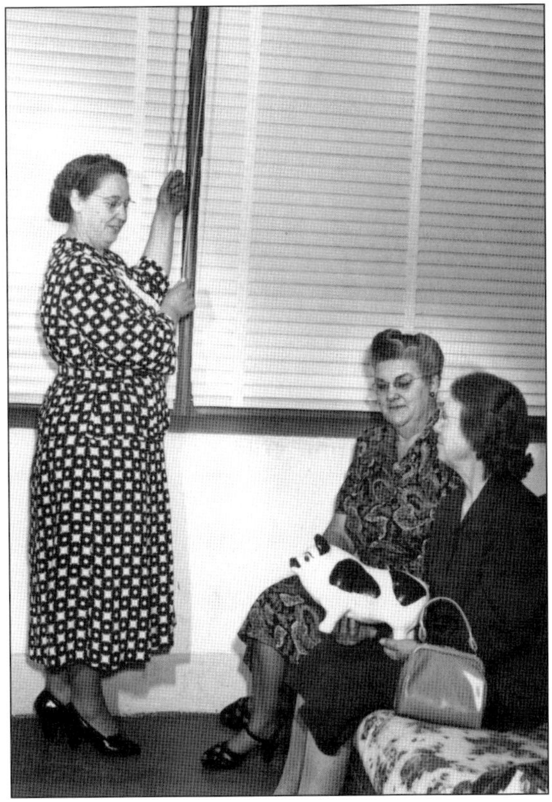

The Joy Extension Homemakers Club raised $276.92 with its pig project. They used these funds to purchase Venetian blinds for the Joy School auditorium, blinds for the Joy School club room, and blinds for one classroom as well as renovation of furniture, painting the floor, and repainting the woodwork of the club room. The club room was a classroom that was set aside by the school for the home demonstration club to use for meetings. Mrs. Dee Tompkins (standing), club president, shows the new blinds to Mrs. C.M. Thomas (seated left), project chairman, and Mrs. Sam Harrison, who donated the pig.

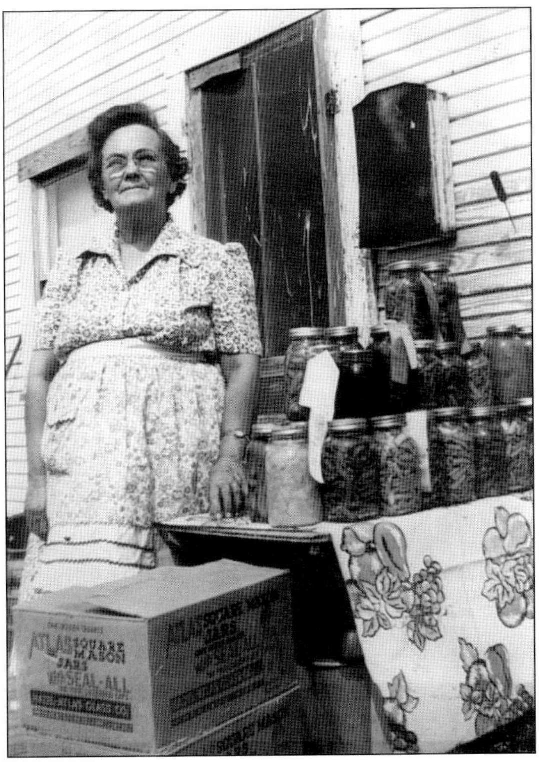

Anna Julie Arms, a 50-plus-year member of the Red Oak Home Demonstration Club, poses with some of her canning. Mrs. Arms's daughter Maxine Lannom is currently a 60-plus-year member of the Murray County Home and Community Education Club (the name of the organization today) and continues to work with the county fair and other extension projects at the age of 91 years. (Maxine Lannom.)

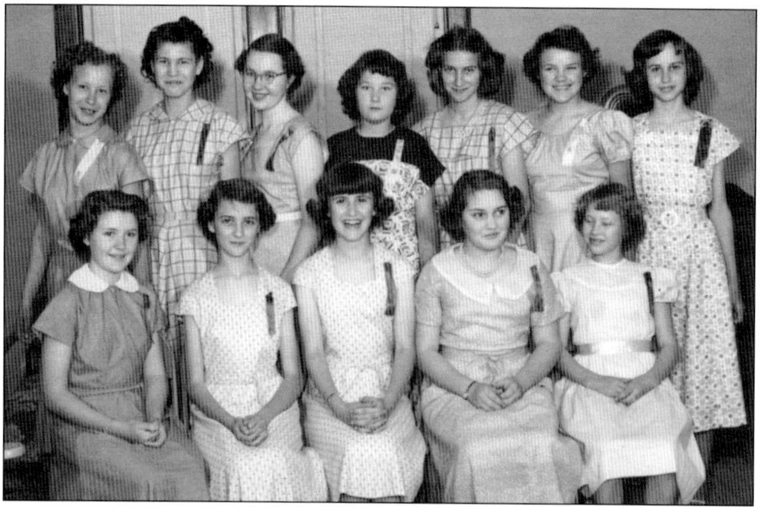

These 4-H girls pose for the camera in 1951 during the annual 4-H dress revue. They each made their dresses in the 4-H sewing project. Note the ribbons pinned to their dresses.

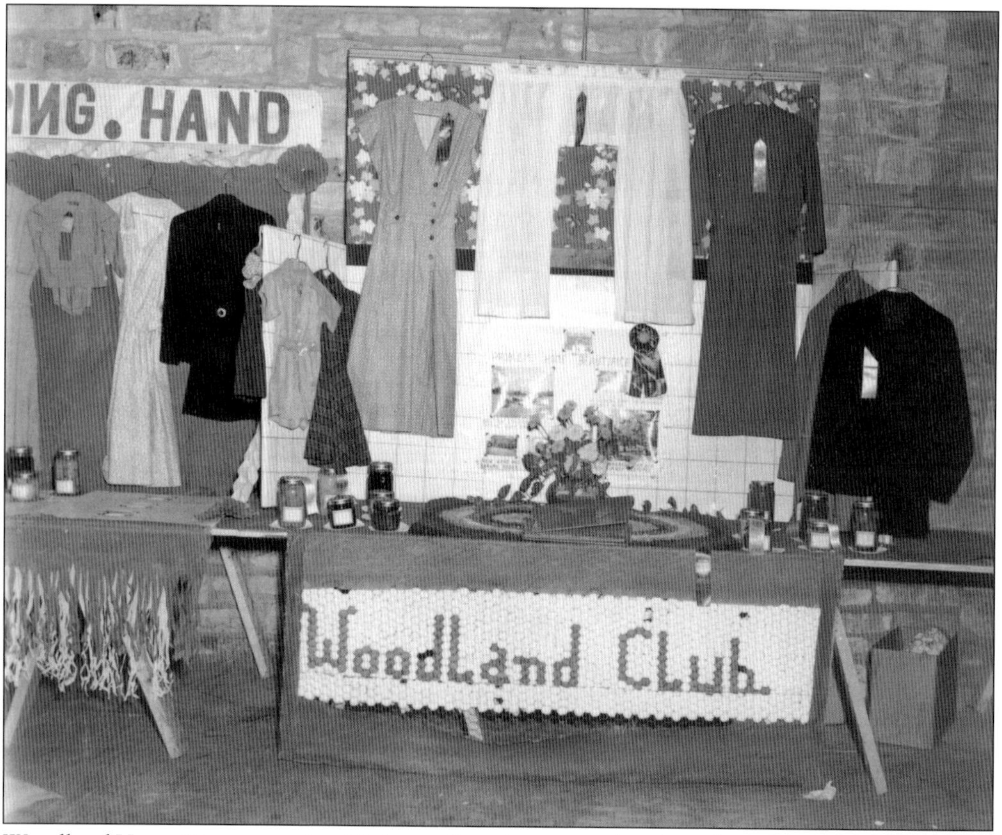

Woodland Home Demonstration Club won first place on its booth at the 1951 county fair. During these years, the fair took place at the Armory Building in Sulphur, which was built by the Works Progress Administration. The display was built by using sawhorses with a sheet of plywood on top. For many years, C.M. Mays of Mays Lumber Company in Sulphur donated the supplies to build the displays. After Mays's death, the store closed, and the historic lumber yard office building was moved north of Sulphur to the grounds of the Murray County Antique Tractor and Implement Club, where it is being preserved.

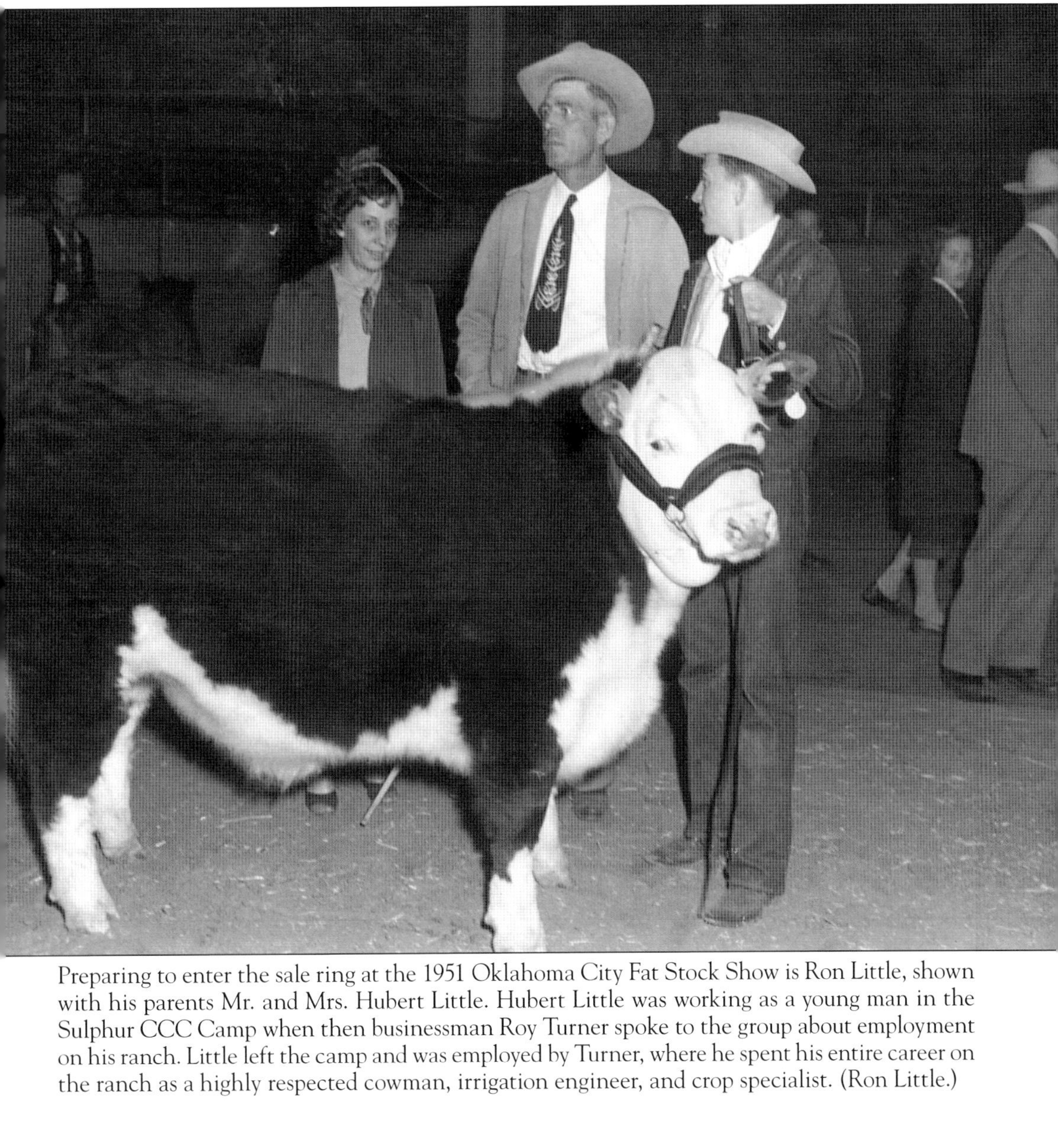

Preparing to enter the sale ring at the 1951 Oklahoma City Fat Stock Show is Ron Little, shown with his parents Mr. and Mrs. Hubert Little. Hubert Little was working as a young man in the Sulphur CCC Camp when then businessman Roy Turner spoke to the group about employment on his ranch. Little left the camp and was employed by Turner, where he spent his entire career on the ranch as a highly respected cowman, irrigation engineer, and crop specialist. (Ron Little.)

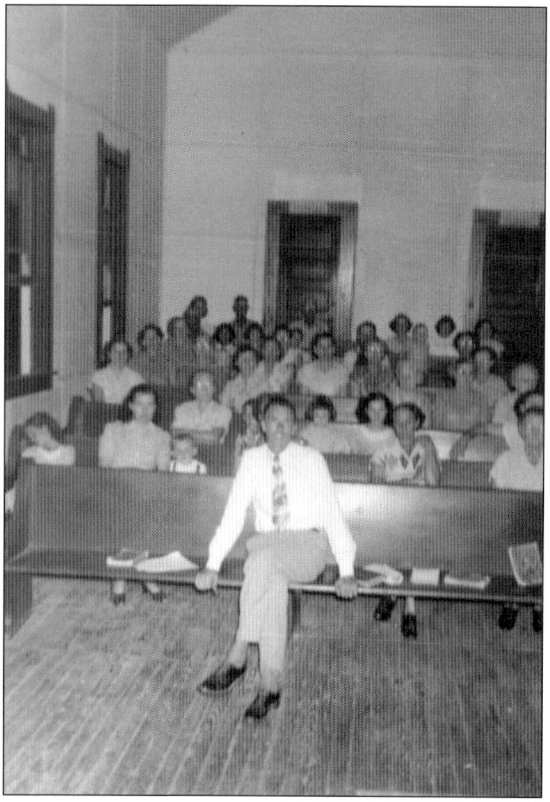

Hickory Baptist Church members are shown here in 1953. (Loyce Gerth.)

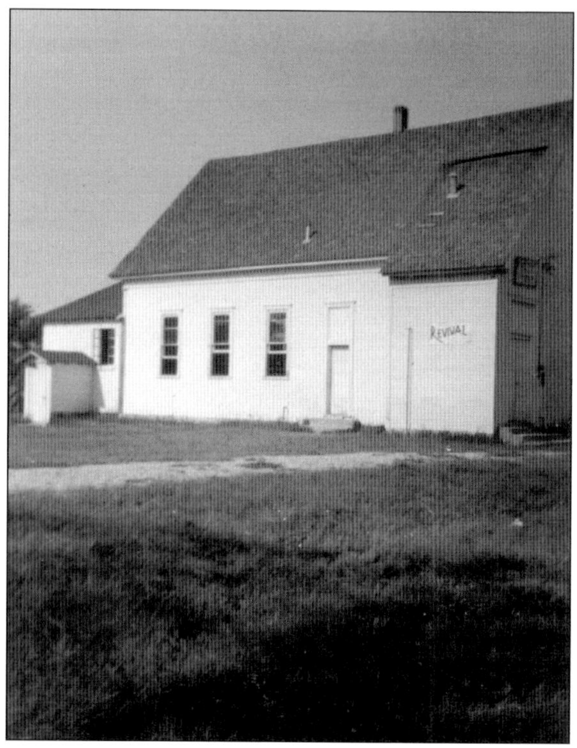

The Hickory Baptist Church is pictured here as it looked in 1953. The building was constructed in 1911 and was used until 1960. Many families attended church, were married, and said goodbye to their loved ones in this building during its 49 years of service. (Loyce Gerth.)

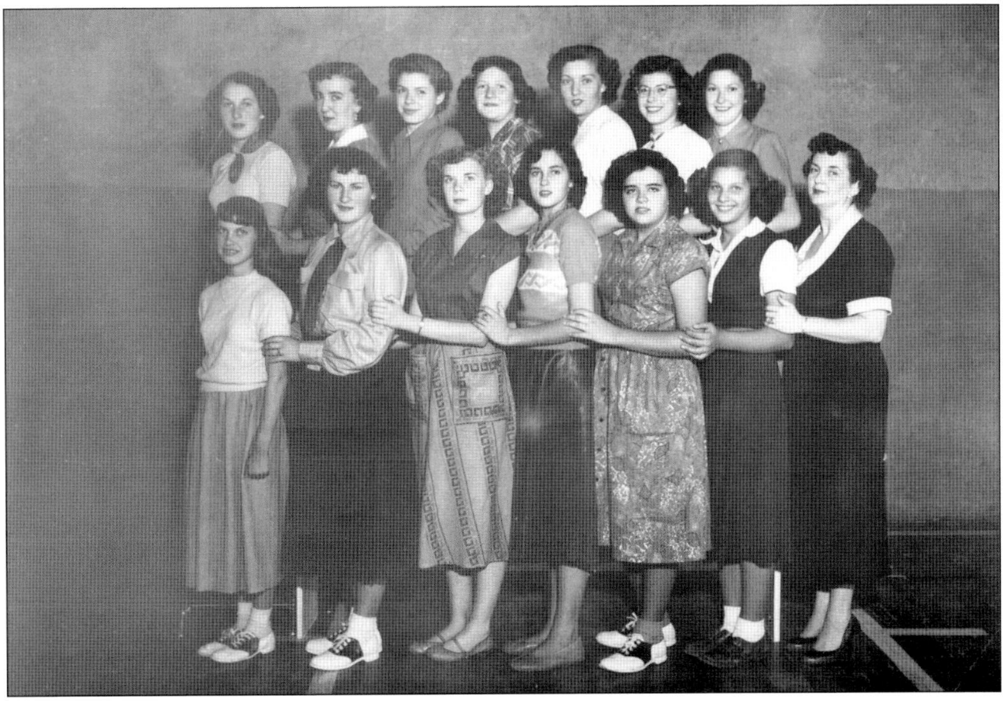

The Hickory High School glee club of the 1952–1953 school year poses in this photograph. The club would perform at special events and activities in the Hickory community. (Loyce Gerth.)

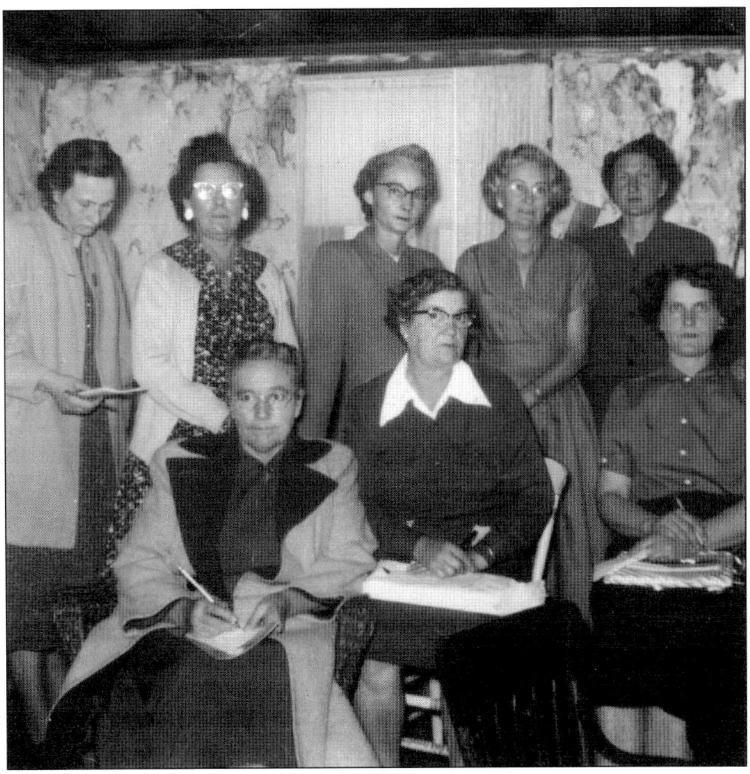

Here, 1954 Helping Hand Home Demonstration Club members prepare for a meeting. From left to right are (first row) Mrs. Hale, Annie Richards, and Zona Cagle; (second row) Mary Lea Pierce, Mrs. White, Jean Schooling, Allie Binderim, and Bonnie Fox.

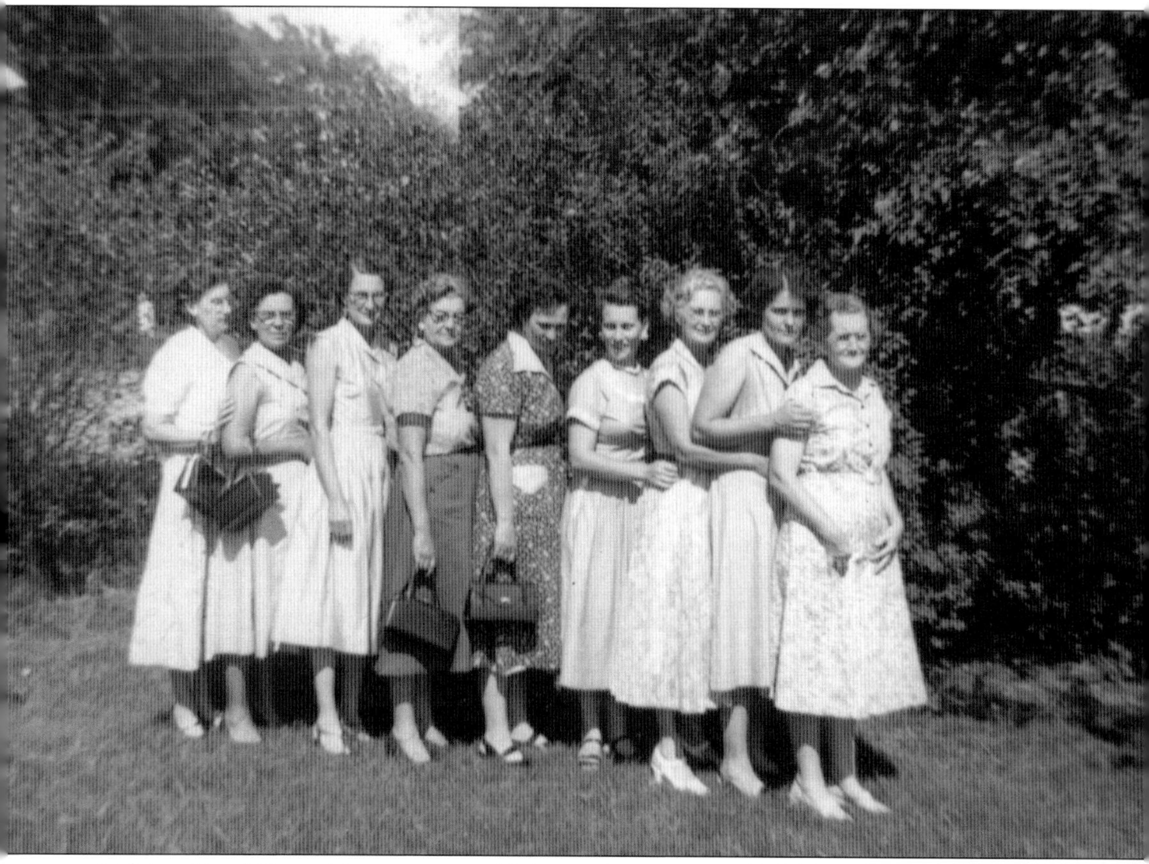

Helping Hand Home Demonstration Club members pose in 1955. From left to right are Flora Lewis, Mrs. White, Bonnie Fox, Annie Richards, Mary Lea Pierce, Wanda Jo Caldwell, Allie Binderim, Zona Cagle, and Charlee Duncan.

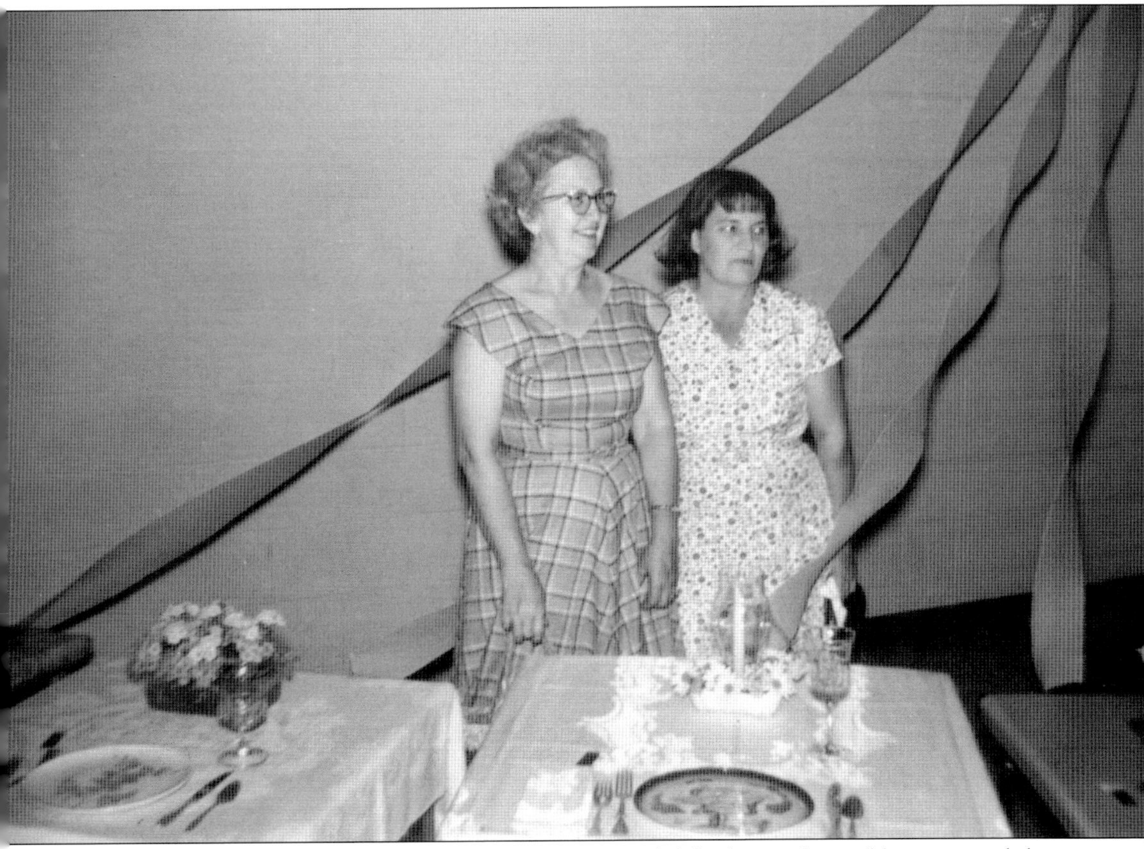

Ann Brittin (left) and an unidentified member of the Joy club look over their table-setting exhibit at the 1956 county fair. Ann's son Donald Brittin was a successful 4-H member who later honored his mother with the Ann Brittin Award, which is presented annually at the Murray County Fair to two outstanding artists. (Don Brittin.)

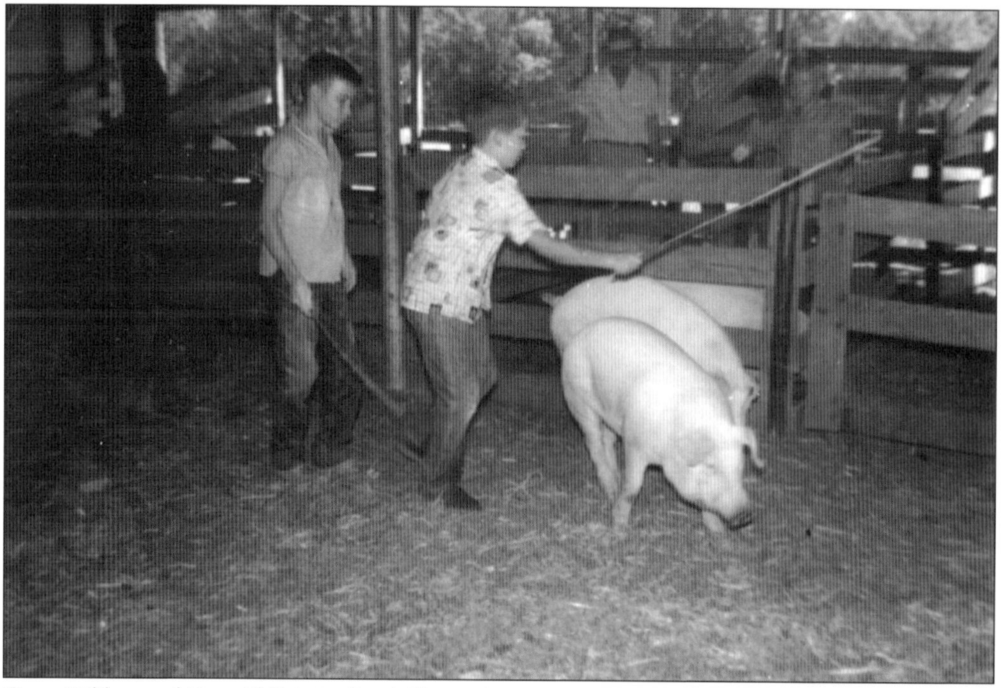

Gene Niblett and Donald Brittin, Joy 4-H members, participate in the 1956 county fair with their Chester White Gilts. Both of the mothers of these young boys were active members in the Joy Extension Homemakers Club. (Don Brittin.)

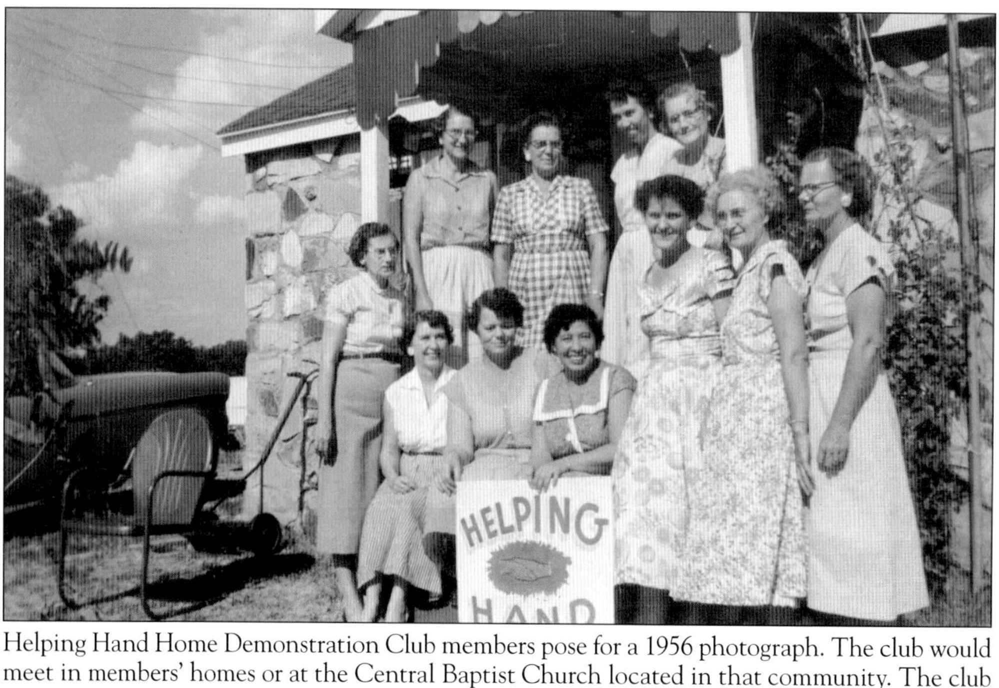

Helping Hand Home Demonstration Club members pose for a 1956 photograph. The club would meet in members' homes or at the Central Baptist Church located in that community. The club is still meeting on a monthly basis and is involved in many extension activities.

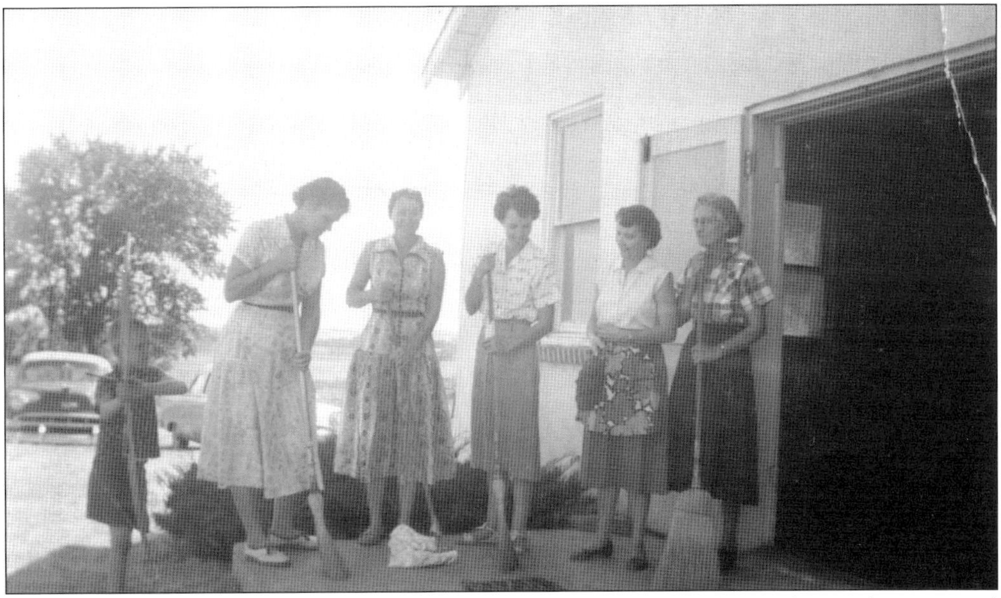

Home demonstration clubs changed many things in Murray County. Their volunteer hours started Sunday schools, organized rural church services, cleaned school yards, provided hot lunches to school children, and assisted their neighbors whenever needed. Here, Helping Hand members clean the steps during their annual deep cleaning of the Central Baptist Church, located south of Sulphur. From left to right are Cary Fox, son of Bonnie and A.C. Fox; Zona Cagle; Bonnie Fox; Ollie Lowrance; Lydia Schooling; and Allie Binderim.

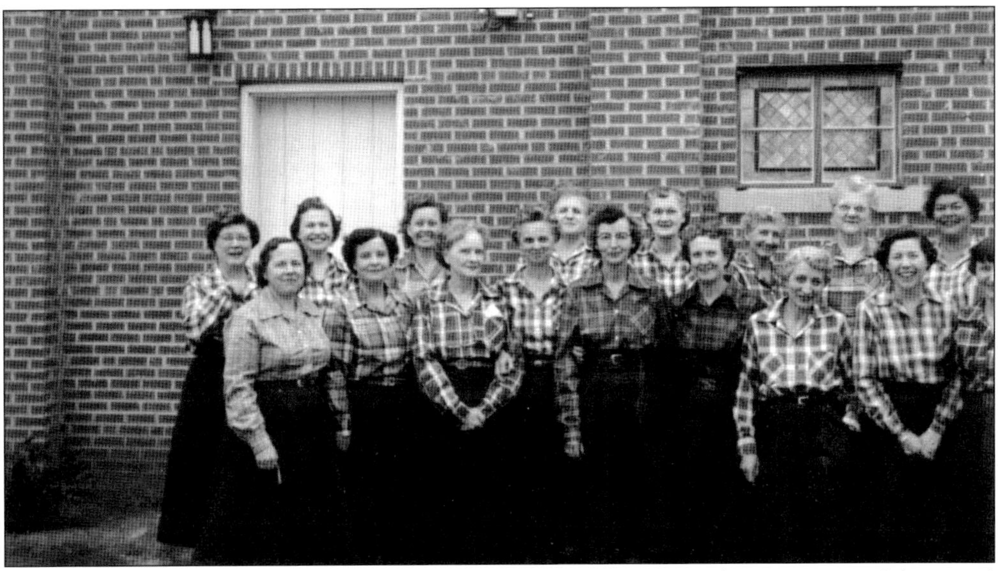

The 1957 Murray County choral group was organized with the home demonstration club council and the Federated Music Clubs. Mrs. Tom Howell of the Woodland club was director of the chorus. Officers for the group were Mrs. Pete Amason, of Sulphur, president; Mrs. C.M. Thomas of Joy, vice president; Mrs. Howard Gibson of Joy, secretary-treasurer; Mrs. Brann Montgomery of Woodland, librarian; and Mrs. Lester Hawkins of Davis, business manager. Mrs. Bob Massey of Davis was the accompanist. Other members were Mrs. Mat Wolf and Mrs. C.C. Scruggs, both of Joy; Mrs. H.L. Kennedy and Mrs. T.H. Hays, both of Davis; and Mrs. Bill Featherstone of Sulphur.

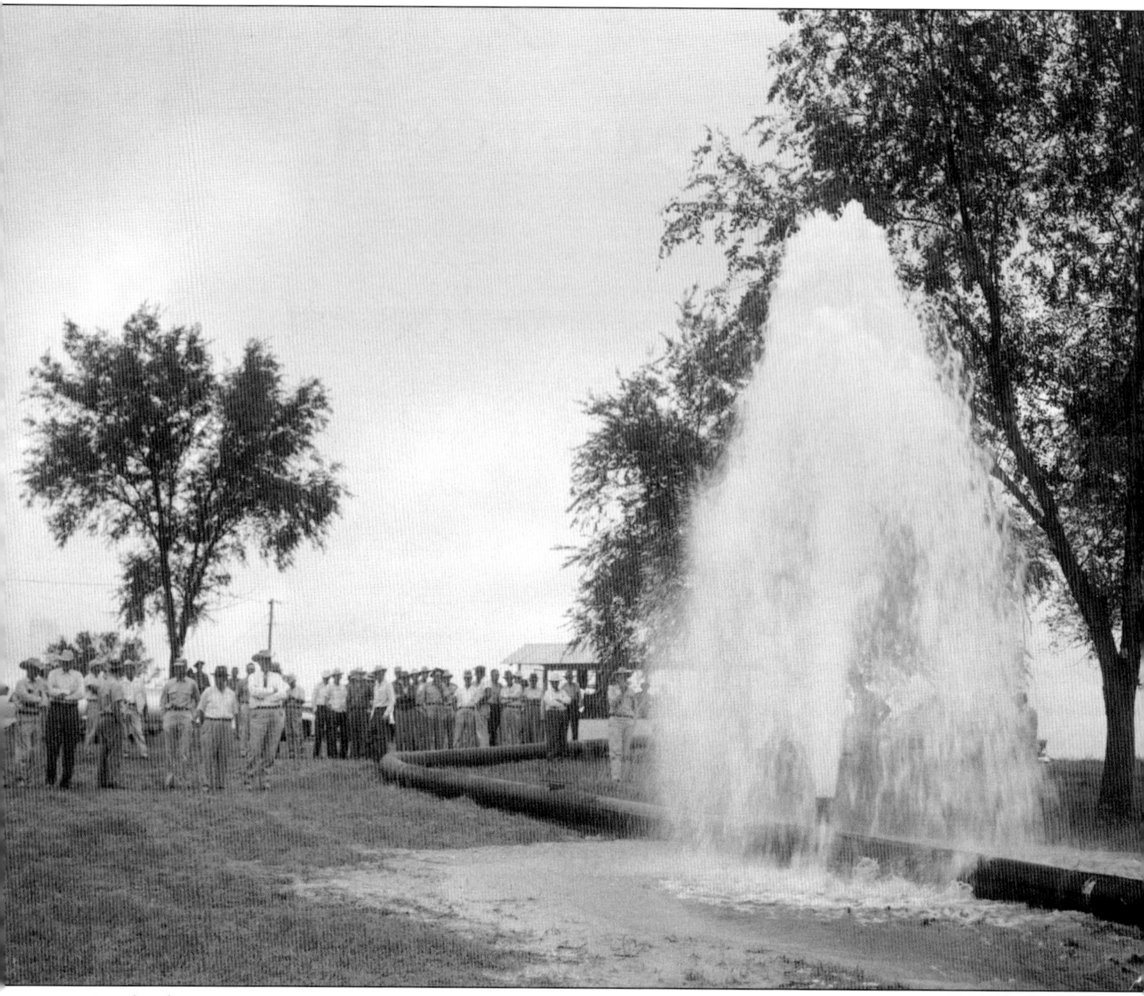

In the late 1950s, an artesian well was cased on the Turner Ranch, and it was farm manager Hubert Little's job to design an irrigation system and cattle watering system using the water. (Ron Little.)

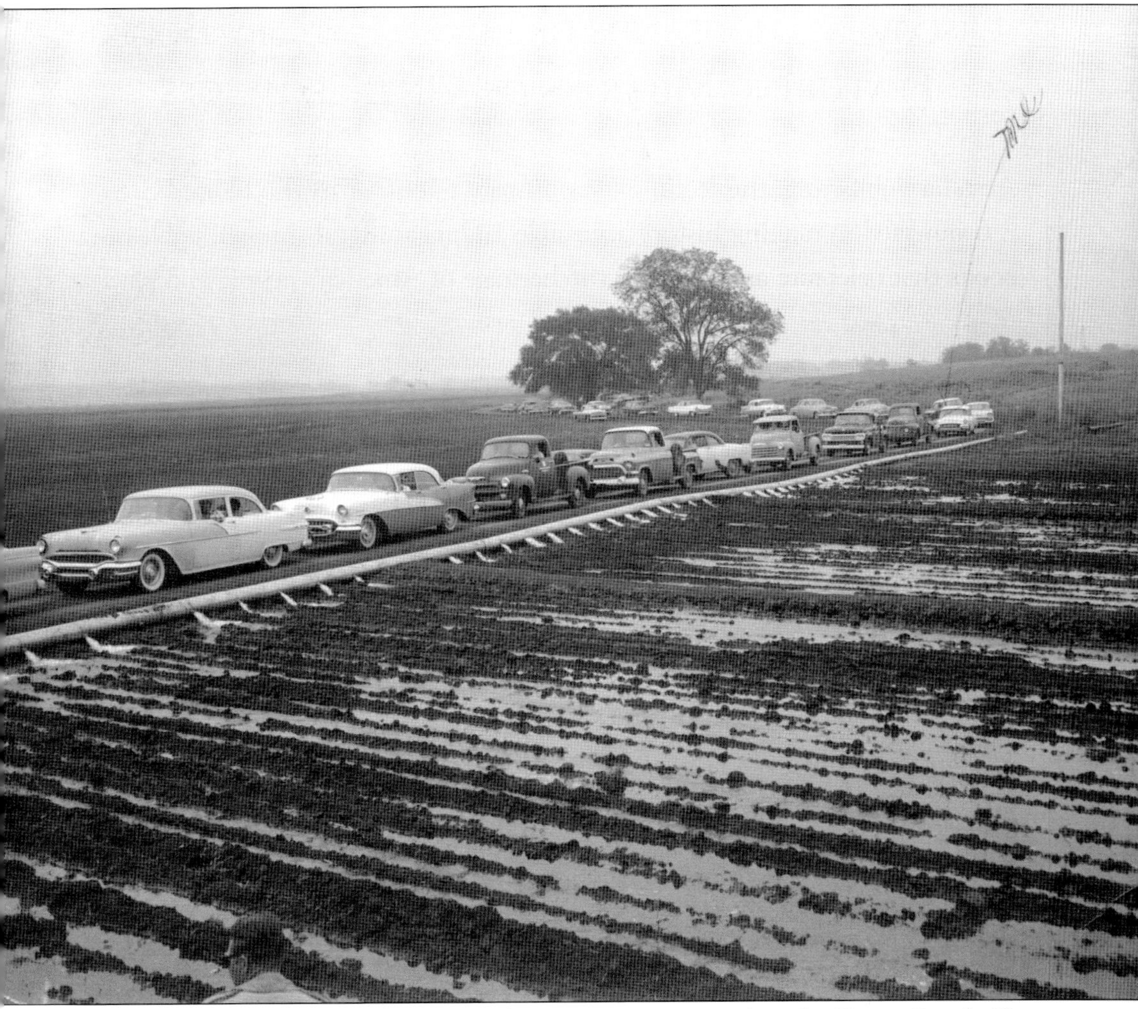

Using the artesian well water, the crops and pastures were irrigated on the Turner Ranch. Here, a caravan of cars on a tour of the ranch stops to observe the design of using the excess water. (Ron Little.)

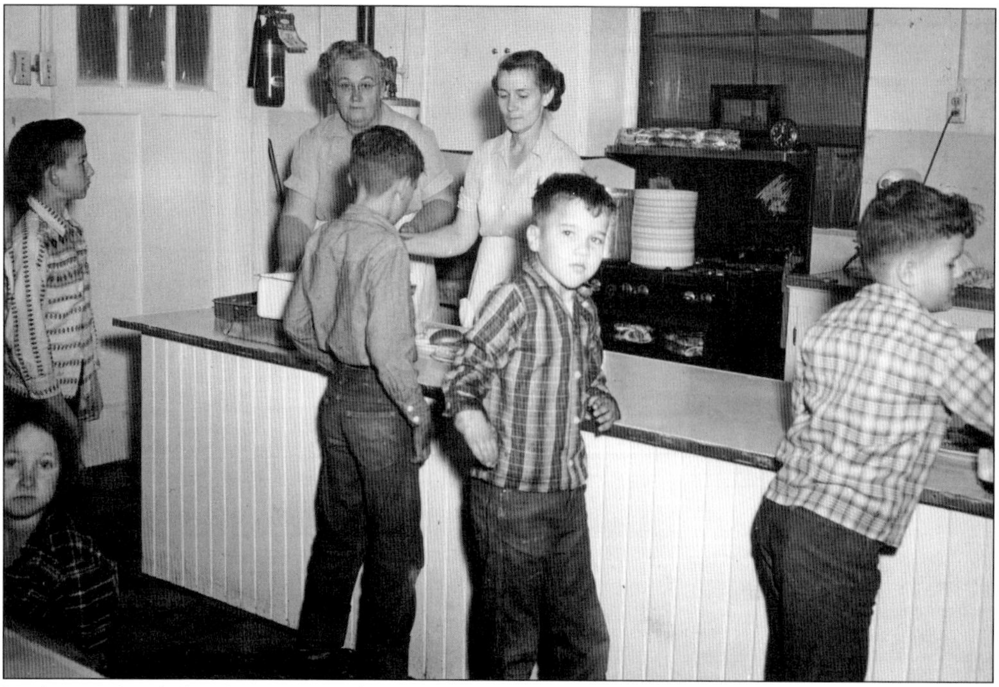

Hickory School's lunchroom was photographed during the 1958–1959 school year. Cooks Annie Hayes (left) and Maybelle Clary serve lunch to schoolchildren. The two center children are identified as Gary and Terrell Prather, and the other children in the photograph are unidentified. (Loyce Gerth.)

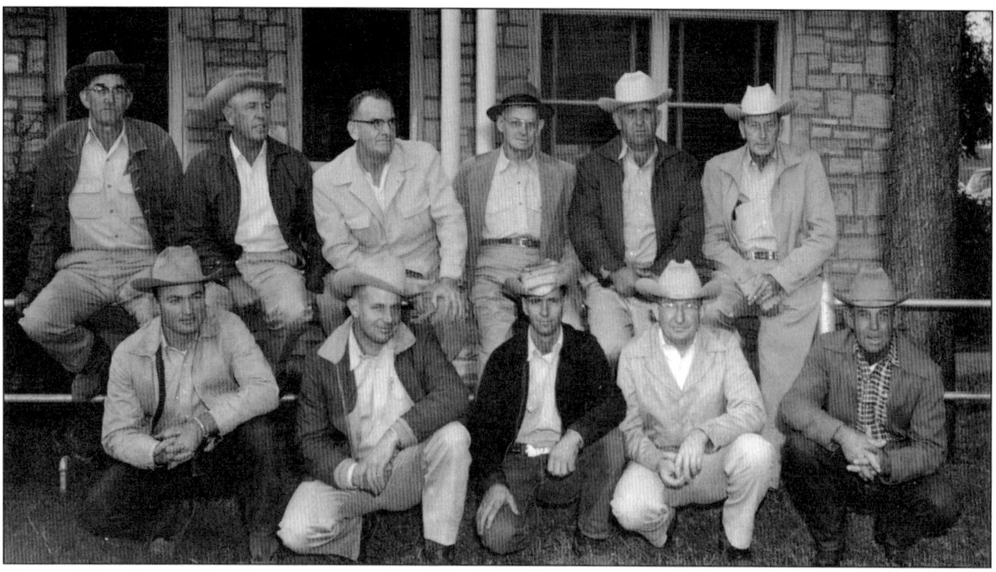

Turner Ranch employed many specialists. Pictured here are, from left to right, (first row) Tom Harris, Frank Wilson, Bernie Baker, Dr. G.T. Easley, and unidentified; (second row) Louis Gepart, Hubert Little, John Spradlin, John Blenken (who brought the first Hereford cattle to America), Walter Bond, and Jim McClelland. At one time, there were 18 houses on the ranch for ranch hands and their families. The Turner Ranch was often referred to as Hereford Heaven Ranch. (Ron Little.)

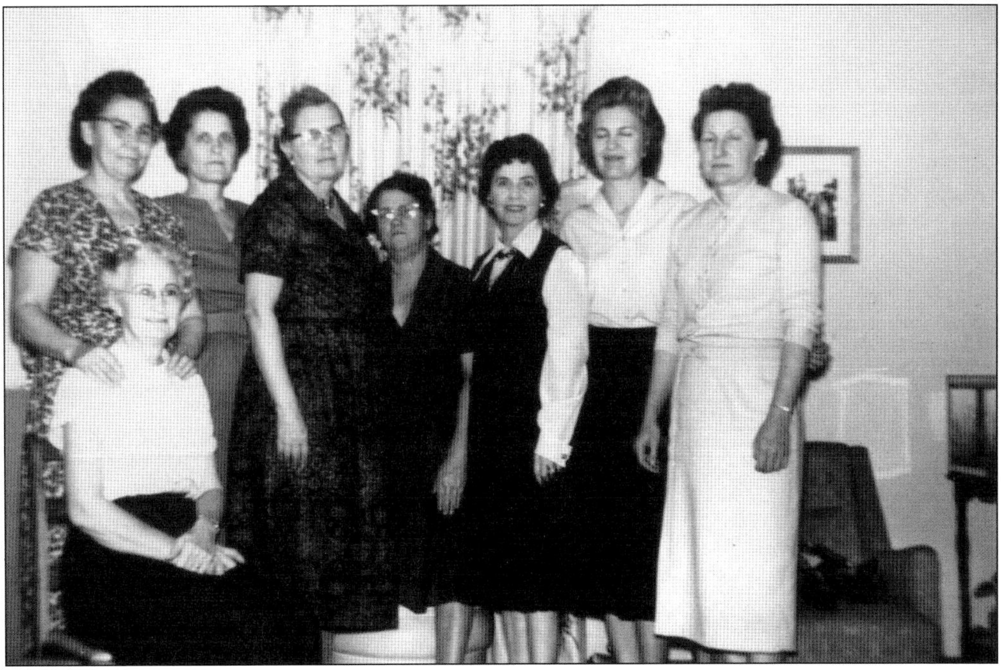

Smiling for the camera in the 1960s are, from left to right, Allie Binderim, Ruth Thompson, Zona Cagle, Corda Mann, Adell Tinney, Lydia Schoaling, Pearl Lowrance, and Bonnie Fox.

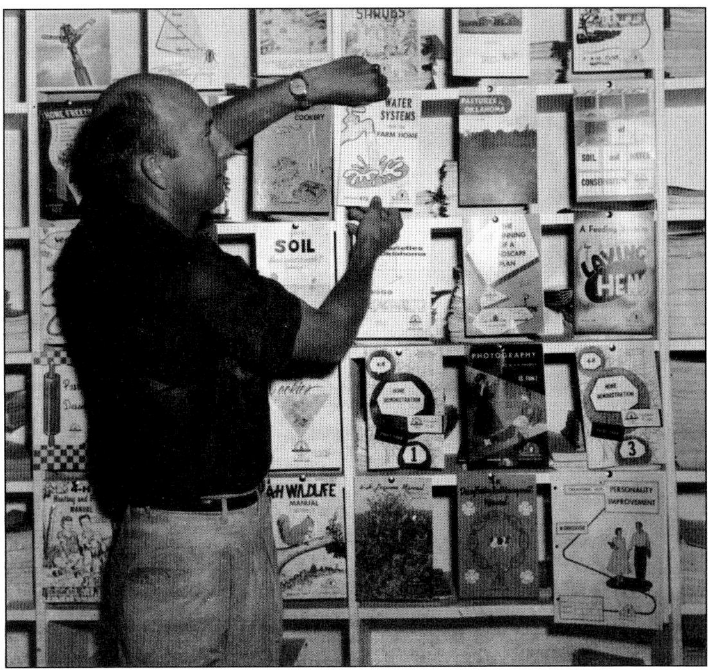

Extension agent George Seals organized *Extension Bulletins*. Seals served Murray County for many years, and upon his retirement, he made his home in Bartlesville, Oklahoma.

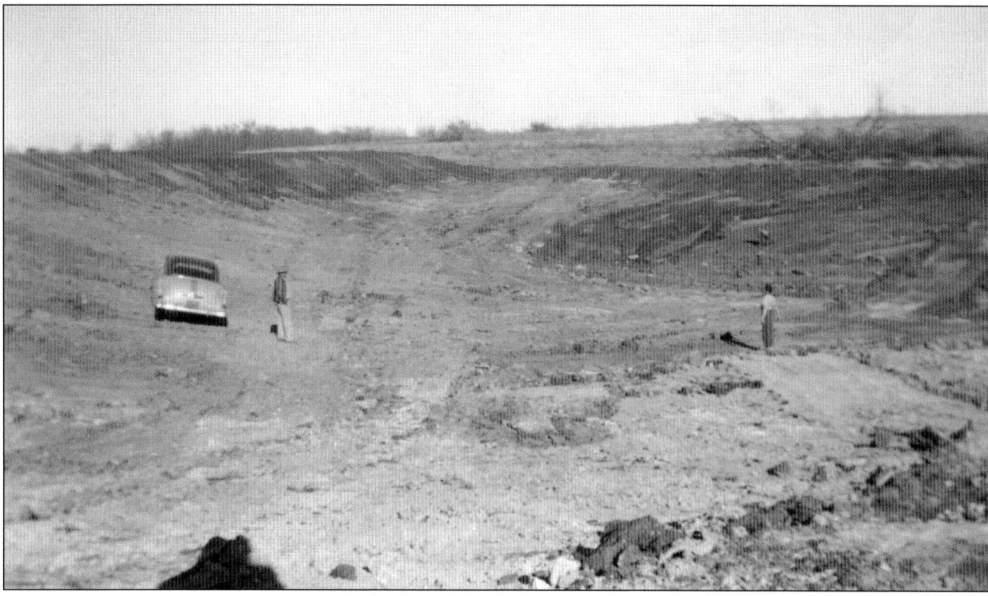

Ed and Alma Crawford are seen standing in Rock Creek No. 13 or Rock Creek No. 14 flood-control lake. Ed operated the heavy equipment that built the lake. Lake No. 13 was 11 acres in size and Lake No. 14 was 34 acres. These two flood-control lakes were built in 1961 and are located on today's Rocky Hughes farm north of Sulphur. (Ruth Crawford Pope.)

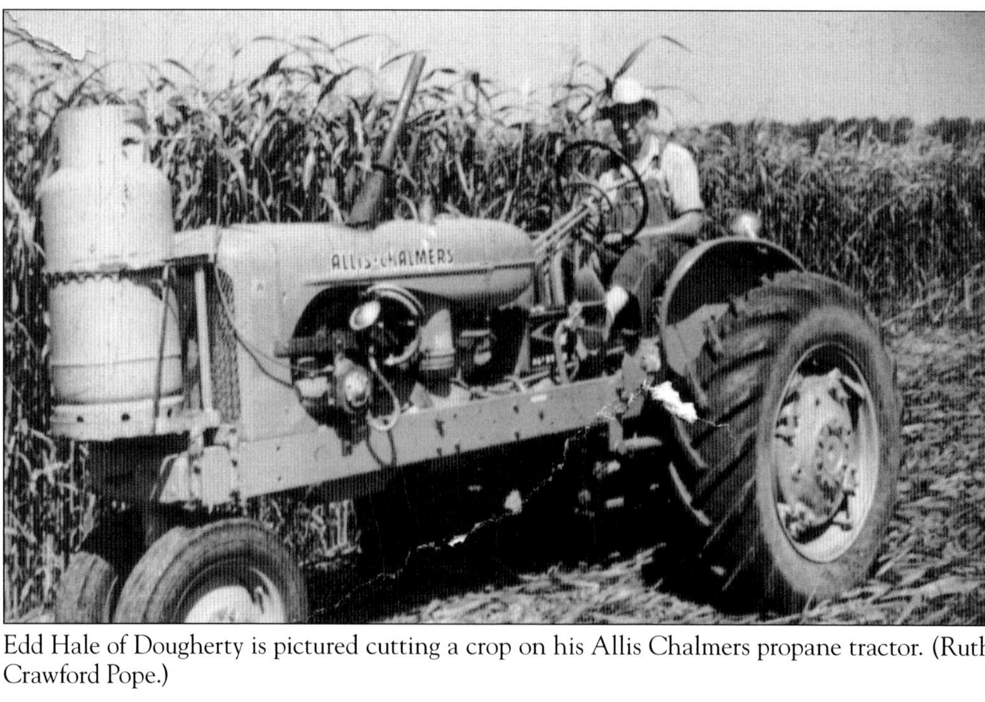

Edd Hale of Dougherty is pictured cutting a crop on his Allis Chalmers propane tractor. (Ruth Crawford Pope.)

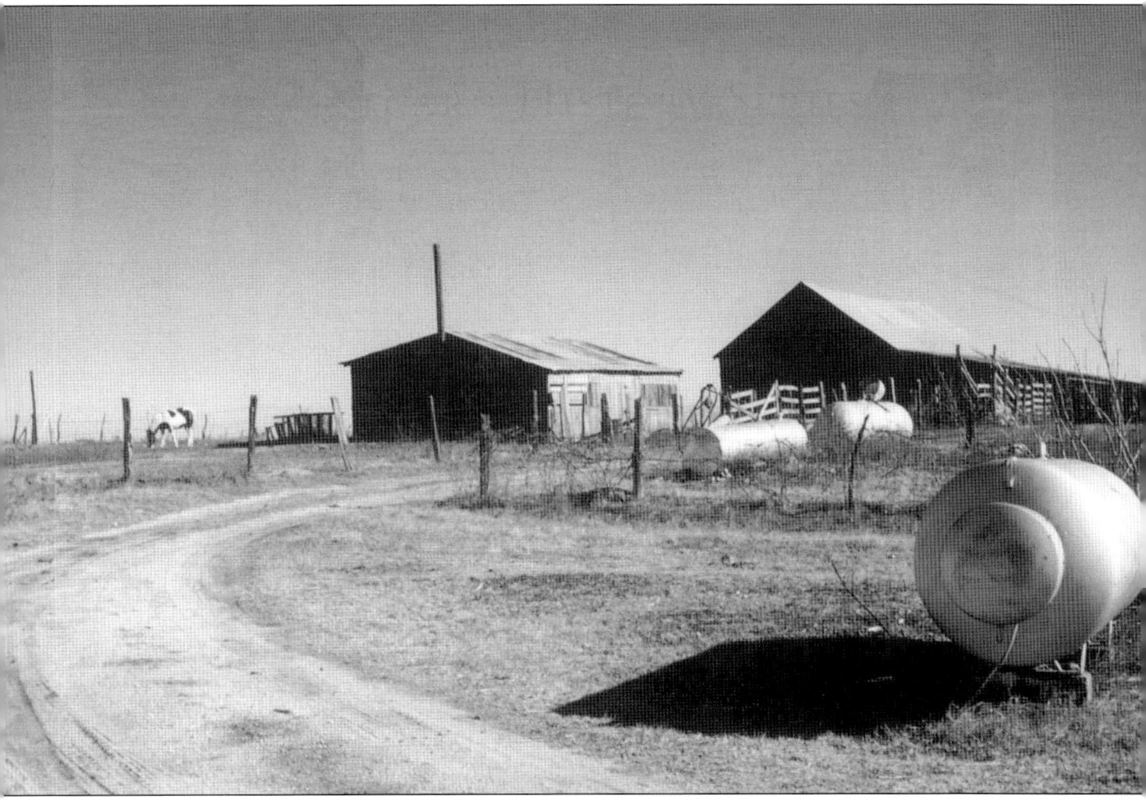

The original Mobly Dairy Farm located north of Sulphur. This farm was first owned by Charles Mobly and, later, belonged to his son Bob Mobly. Bob played several important roles in developing agriculture in Murray County. He was elected in 1958 to serve on the Agriculture Stabilization and Conservation Service where he served for 16 years. He was instrumental in helping establish the rural water districts and served on the board of directors for 17 years. He played a major role in helping establish the Young Farmers group and in organizing early-day farm parades. His wife, Johnnie, continues to be very involved with home demonstration work, being a charter member of the Oaklawn club. As a club member, she served in many leadership roles on the local, district, and state levels. One of her outstanding accomplishments was serving as the first female on the Murray County Fair Board, serving in that position for 50 years. She still lives on the farm and has been a member of extension club work for over 60 years. Son Gary Mobly and grandson Chad Mobly manage the land and cattle on the farm today. Daughter Beverly Mobly Runyan served as the Murray County Extension Office secretary for over 20 years before retiring in 2013. (Johnnie Aaron Mobly.)

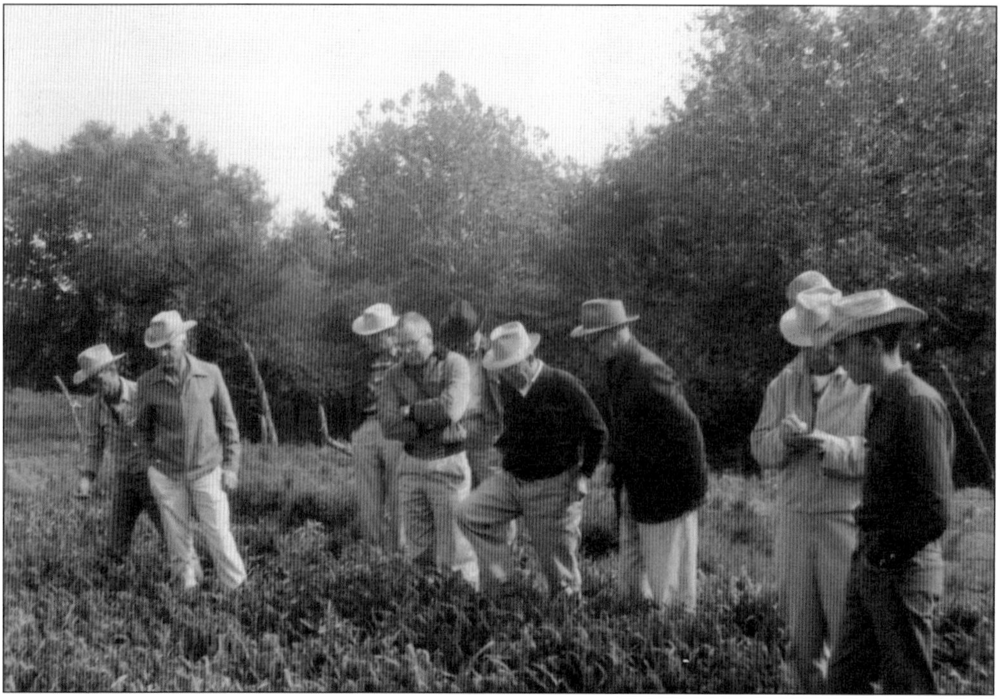

Murray County farmers and ranchers look over a pasture demonstration in 1963. Demonstrations are still used as a teaching method by extension and research.

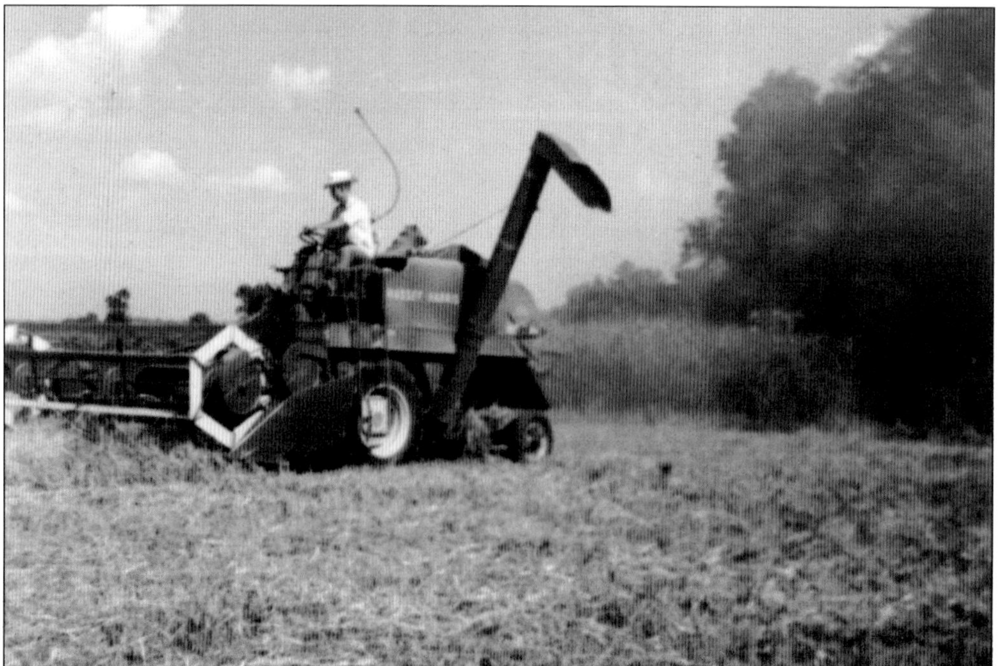

Combining the 1965 wheat harvest is Don Brittin on the family farm in the Joy community. The Brittin family was very involved with extension work through the home demonstration club and the 4-H program. (Don Brittin.)

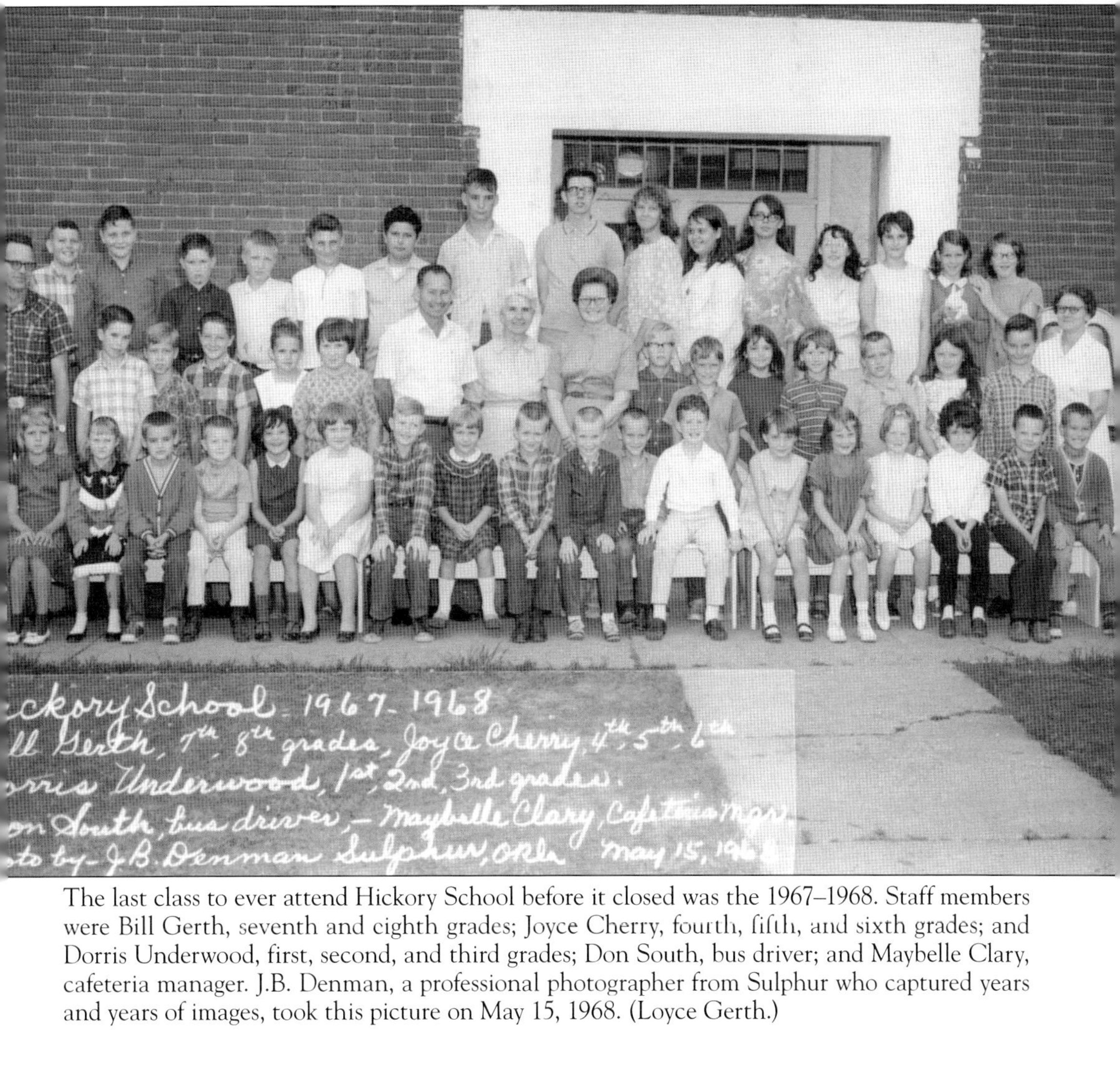

The last class to ever attend Hickory School before it closed was the 1967–1968. Staff members were Bill Gerth, seventh and eighth grades; Joyce Cherry, fourth, fifth, and sixth grades; and Dorris Underwood, first, second, and third grades; Don South, bus driver; and Maybelle Clary, cafeteria manager. J.B. Denman, a professional photographer from Sulphur who captured years and years of images, took this picture on May 15, 1968. (Loyce Gerth.)

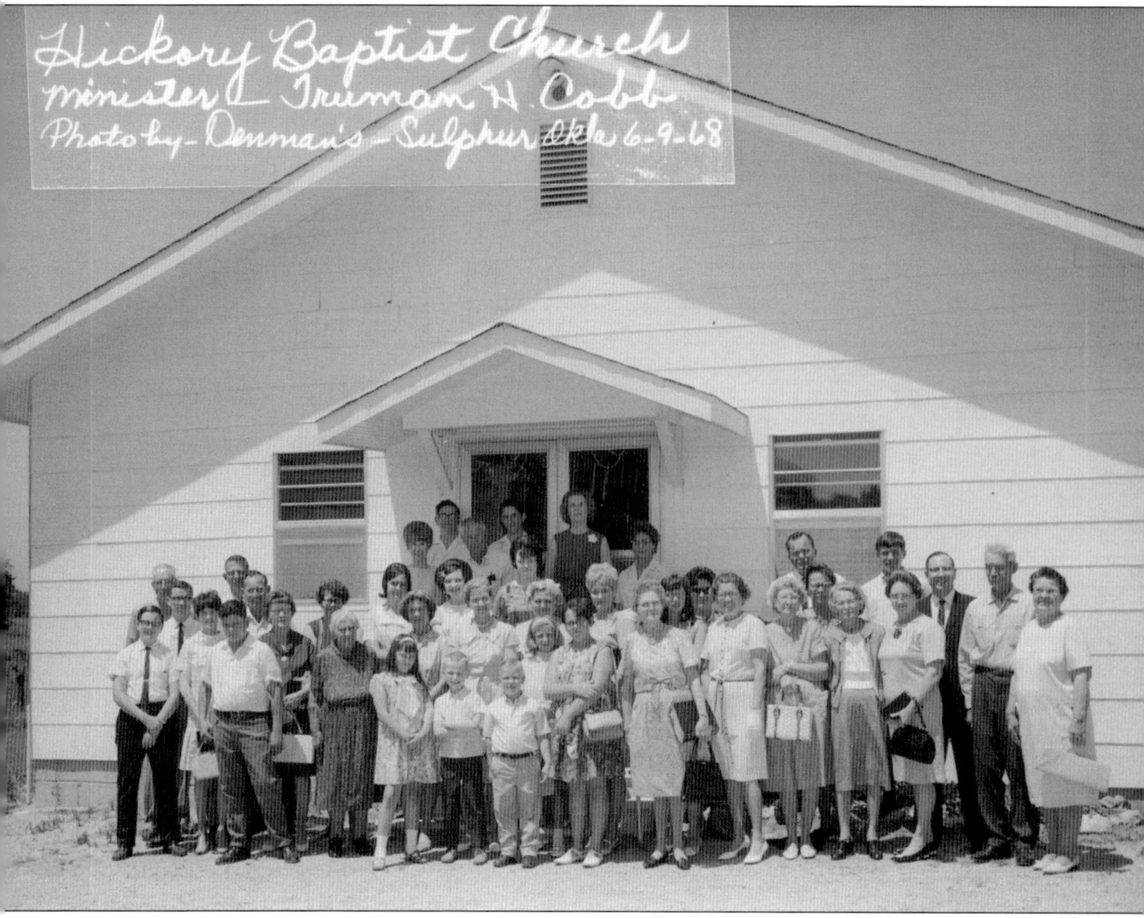

This photograph showing the Hickory Baptist Church was taken on June 9, 1968. The minister at the time was Truman H. Cobb. (Loyce Gerth.)

Howard Hanni came to Murray County in 1959 and became an agriculture fixture in the county. He was raised in Beckham County where he was very active as a 4-H member. He later attended Oklahoma A&M College, graduating with a degree in agriculture education. He and his brother Warren were partners in the H&H Ranch, located south of Davis. (Naomi Hanni.)

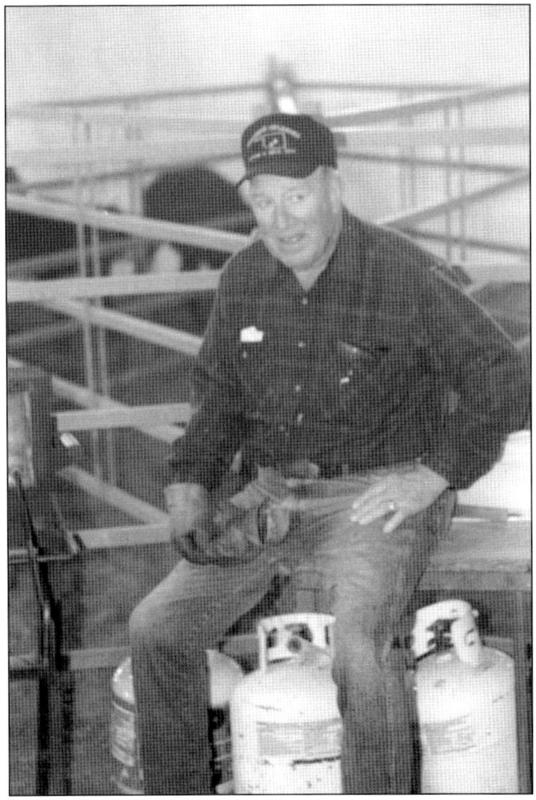

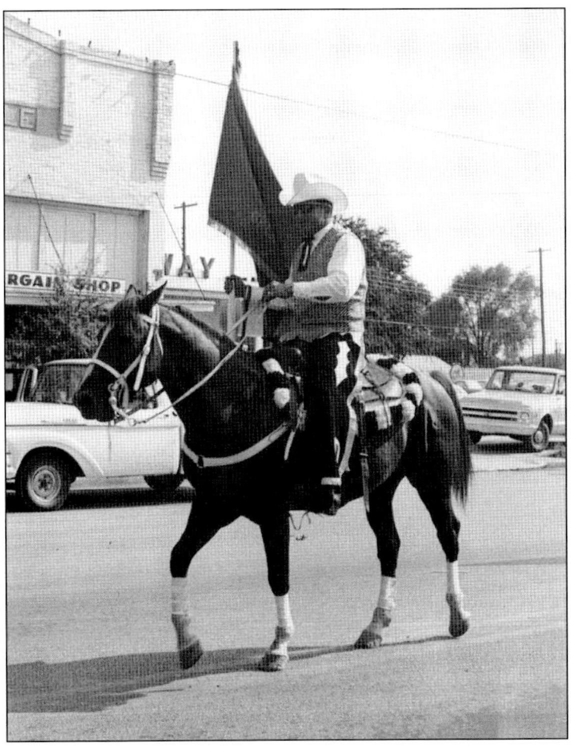

Howard Hanni rides in a parade as a member of the Davis Range Riders. Howard's wife, Naomi, and several other women handmade the saddle blankets the club used for parades. (Naomi Hanni.)

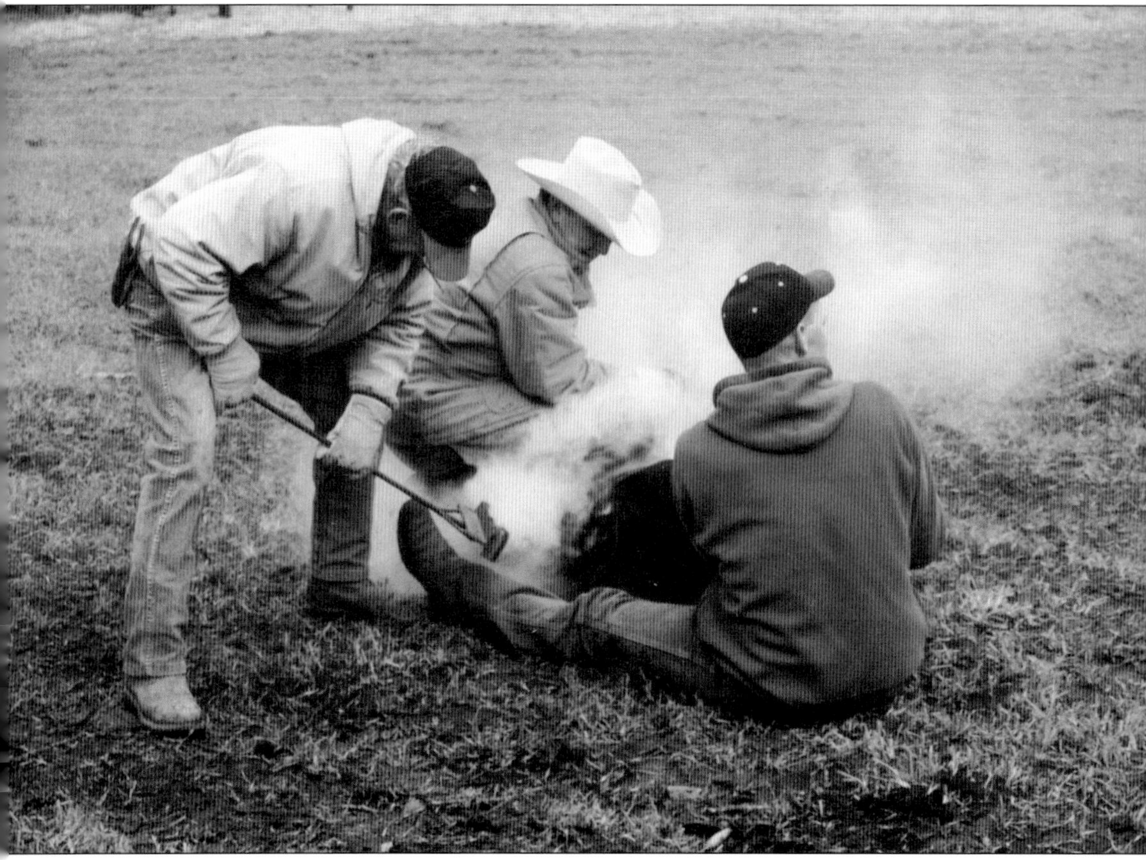

Local cowboys assist Howard Hanni (holding the branding iron) with branding a calf. The Hanni brand was a circle with "HH" inside. Today, cattle are freeze branded or ear tagged for identification purposes. (Naomi Hanni.)

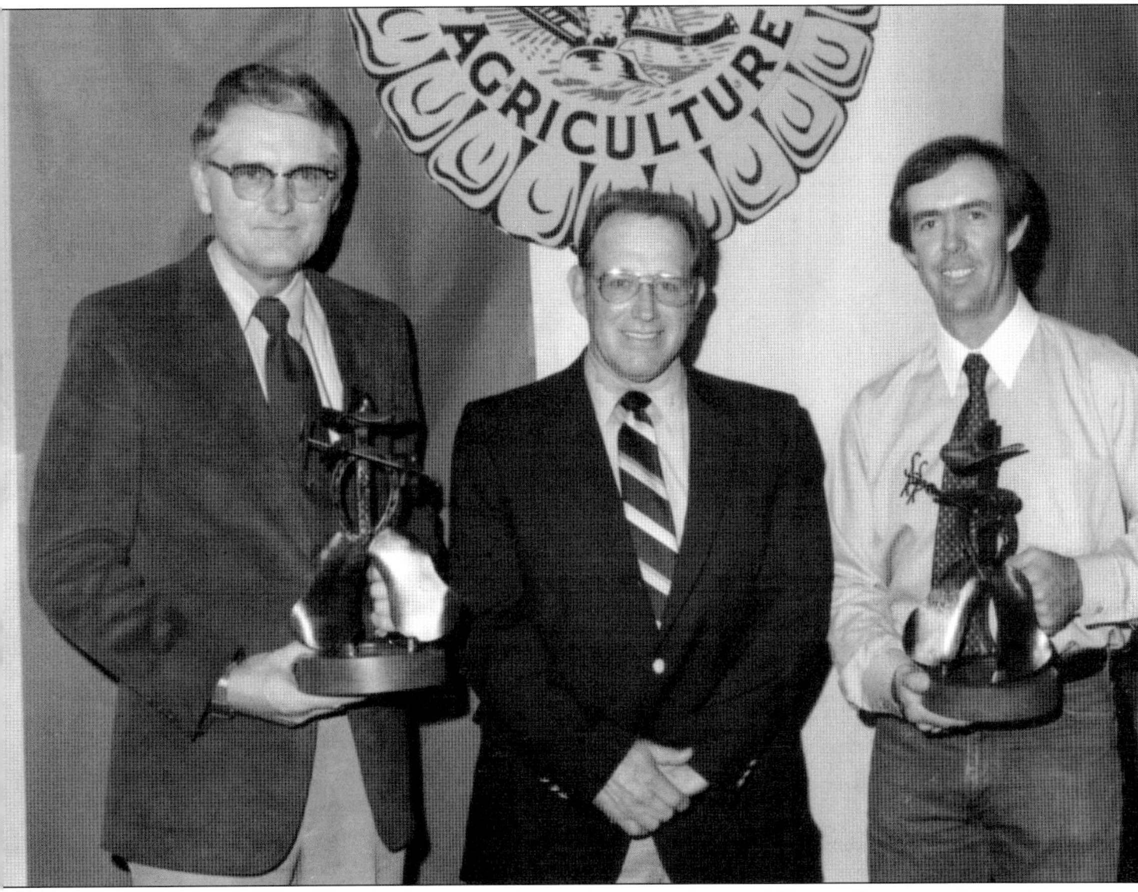

The Davis Public School has had an agriculture education class and Future Farmers of America organization for many years yet has had only five teachers in charge of the program. The first instructor was Warren Hanni (not pictured); followed by Mavis Hutchins (left); Howard Hanni (center); Steve Ratchford (right), a former student of Howard Hanni; and today, Howard Hanni's grandson Trevor Thomasson (not pictured). (Naomi Hanni.)

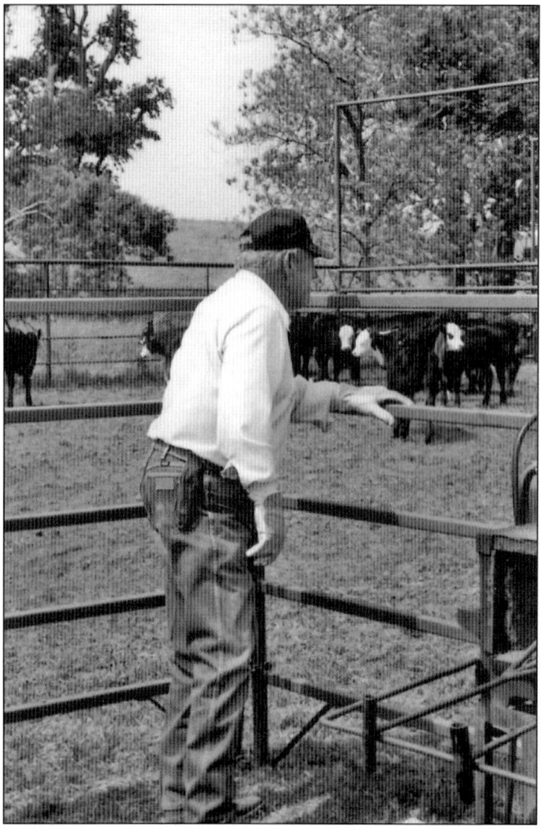

Howard Hanni spent his 33-year teaching career instructing young people regarding the importance of agriculture and the skills associated with living off the land. His ranch is still in operation, with his wife, Naomi, managing. (Naomi Hanni.)

Howard Hanni was an expert welder and taught hundreds of young men and women how to use the welding equipment to make projects. Here, he heats brands that he made to mark his cattle. (Naomi Hanni.)

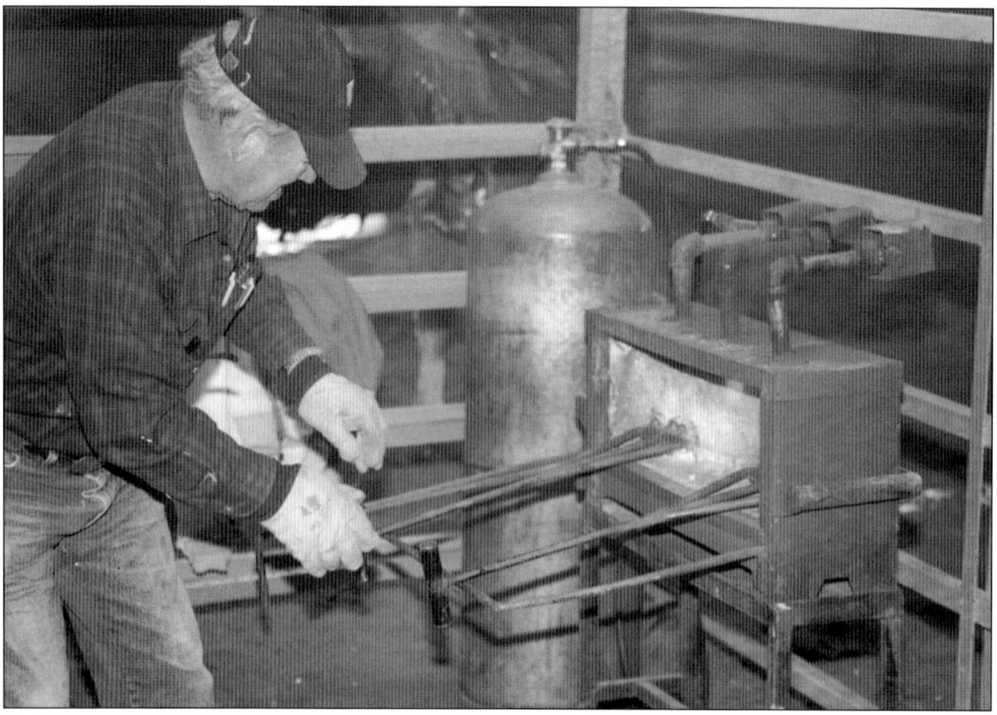

Five

Final Bits and Pieces

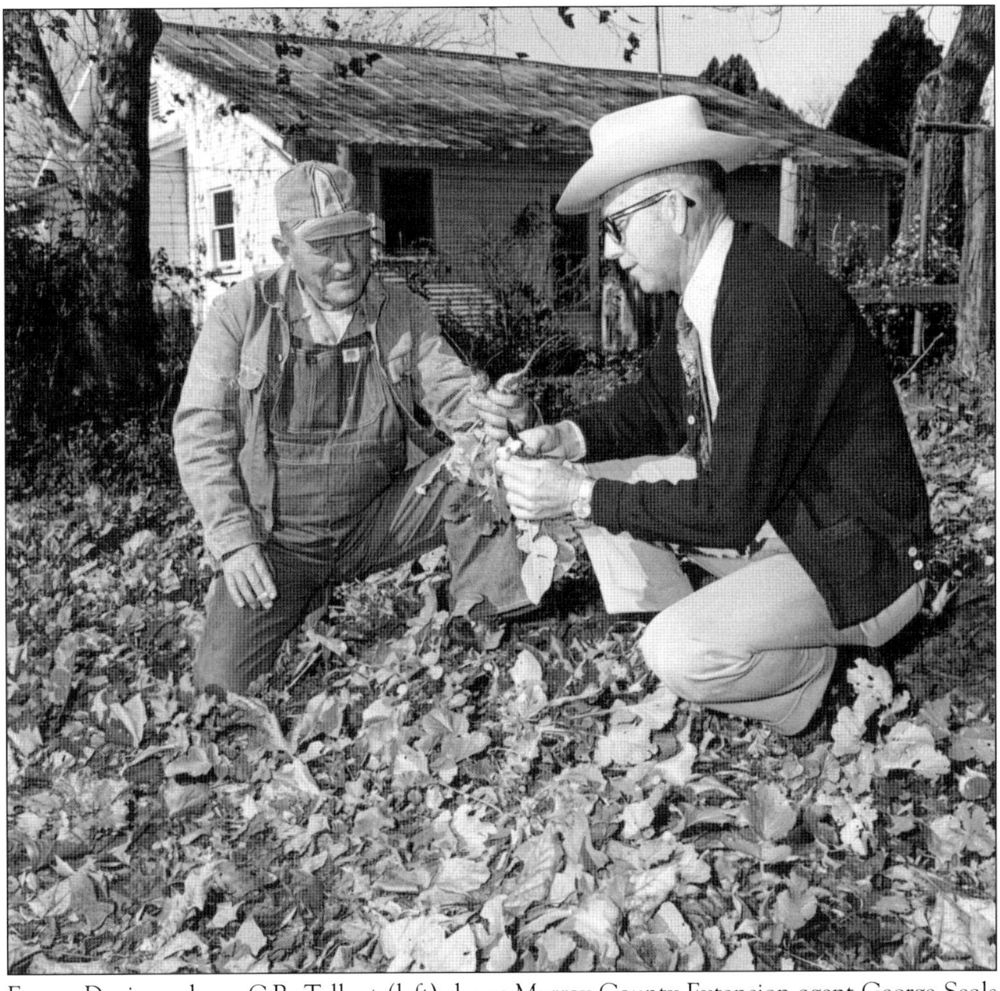

Expert Davis gardener C.R. Tallent (left) shows Murray County Extension agent George Seals the last of his 1974 garden, with radishes still crisp and sweet in late November.

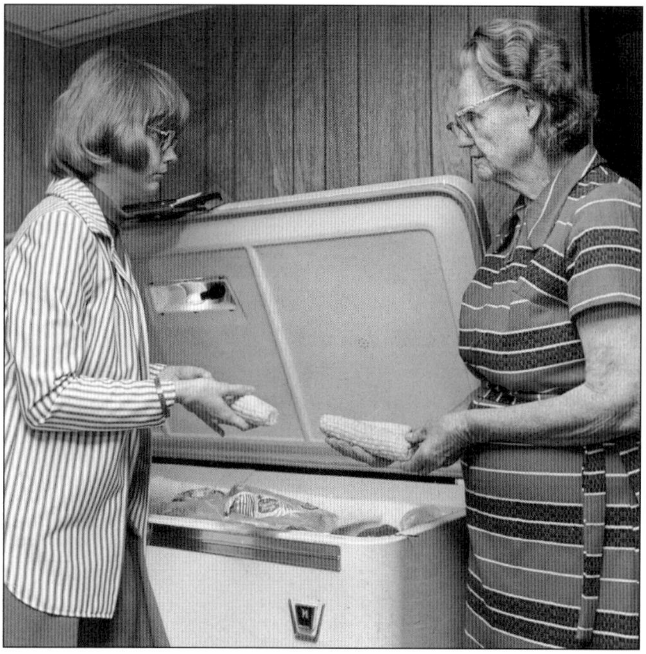

Mrs. C.R. Tallent of Davis shows Murray County Extension home economist Janice Curtis a package of roasting ears from her garden in 1974. Curtis served Murray County for several years before moving to Carter County to complete her career.

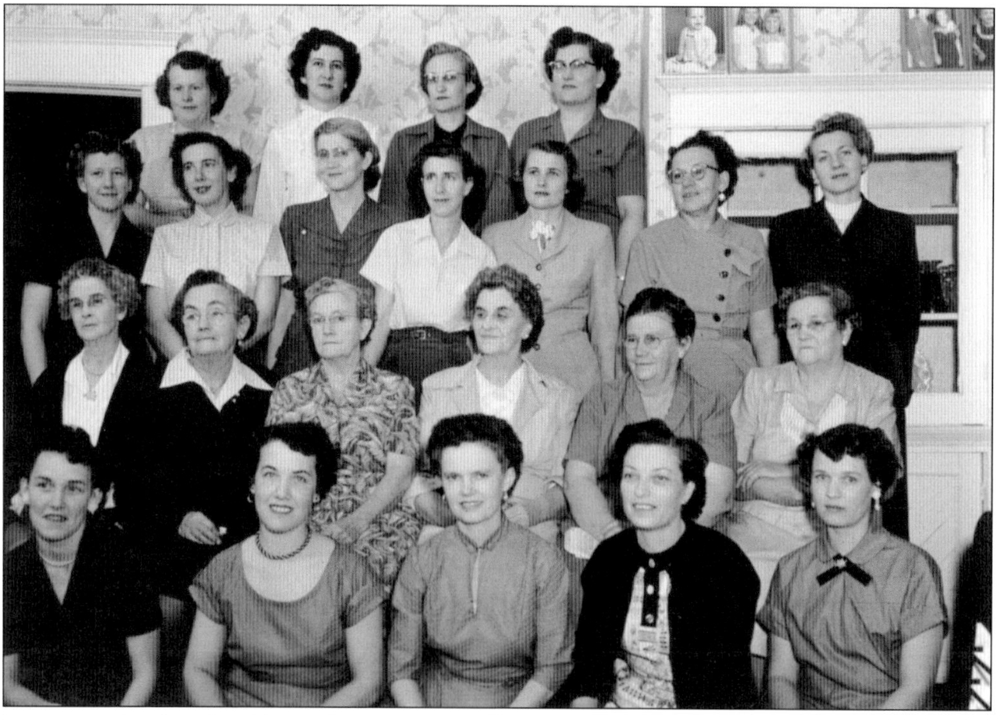

Pictured is the Red Oak Home Demonstration Club in the 1950s. Members are, from left to right, (first row) Mrs. Bagley, Mrs. Amos Arms, Mrs. J.E. Ballenger, Essie Ballenger, Mrs. A.R. Lannom, Mrs. West (seated), Johnnie Mobly, Maxine Lannom, Cletha Cleta Jaynes, Maudie Lansford, and Maxine Moore Lannom; (second row) Laverne Nichols, Virginia Akers, unidentified, Emily Palmer, Lucille Splawn, unidentified, and Irene Phelps; (third row) Shorty Ballenger, Clethel Chilcoat, Phyllis Lewis, and Ella Mae Stout.

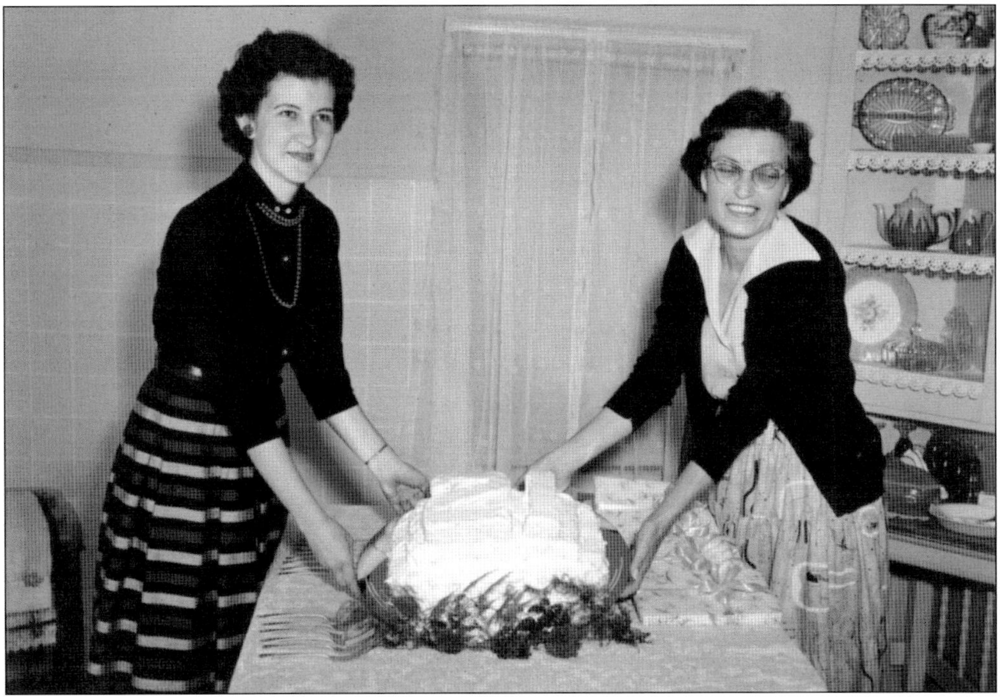

Clethel Chilcoat (left) and Maudie Lansford pose with a celebration cake in 1954. Records do not reflect the occasion. Lansford was a well-known local artist, and today, many of her paintings hang in homes and buildings across the county.

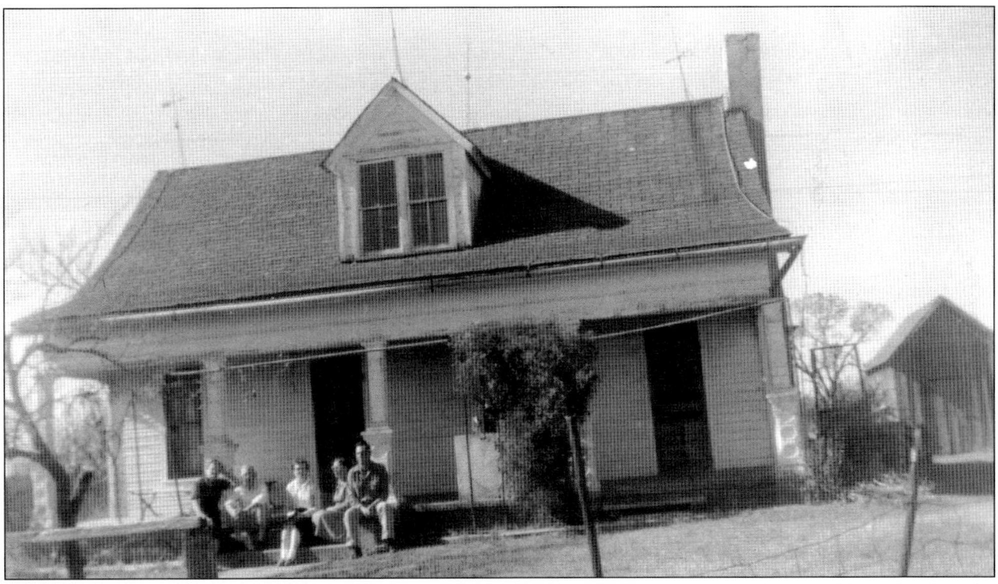

This image shows Perry Jones at home north of Sulphur. The Jones ranch is still in the family. It began with a 60-acre Indian allotment and has grown into over 3,200 acres today. Pete Jones, grandson of the original allotment owner, owned the ranch, purchasing most of the land after leaving the Air Force in the 1940s. Pete married Lawanda Brassfield from Davis, and they were married 61 years until his death in 2013 at the age of 91 years. The land was once home to a dairy, selling milk to Colbert Dairy in Ardmore. (Lawanda Jones.)

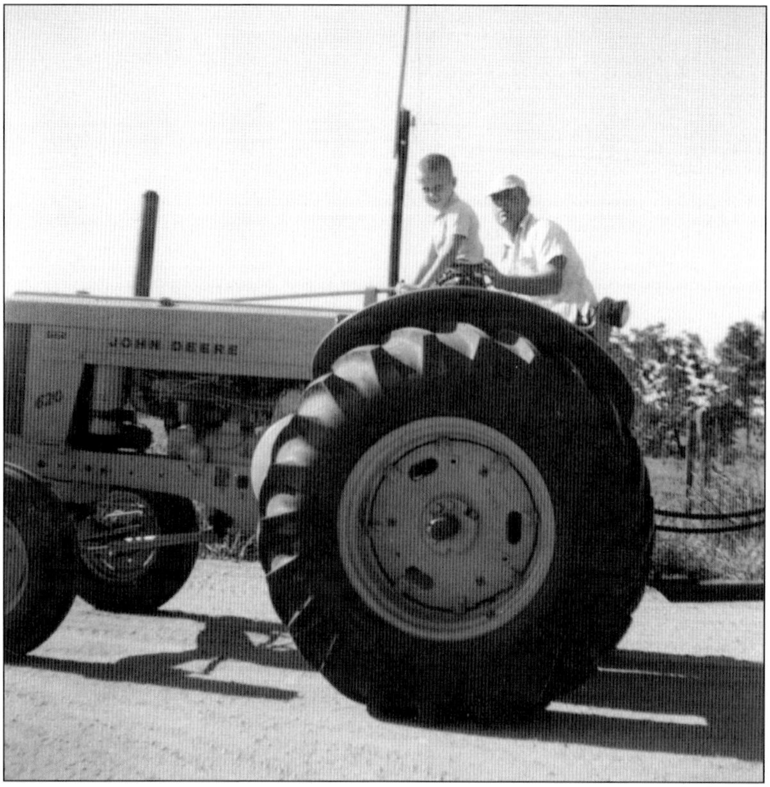

Pete Jones and son Fob (named after his grandfather) ride on Pete's first John Deere tractor. The tractor was a special edition because it was painted yellow instead of the traditional John Deere green. Fob is currently an attorney, practicing law in Sulphur. Pete raised cattle and foraged crops as well as worked as a rural mail carrier for Route 2 for 35 years before retirement in 1982. (Lawanda Jones.)

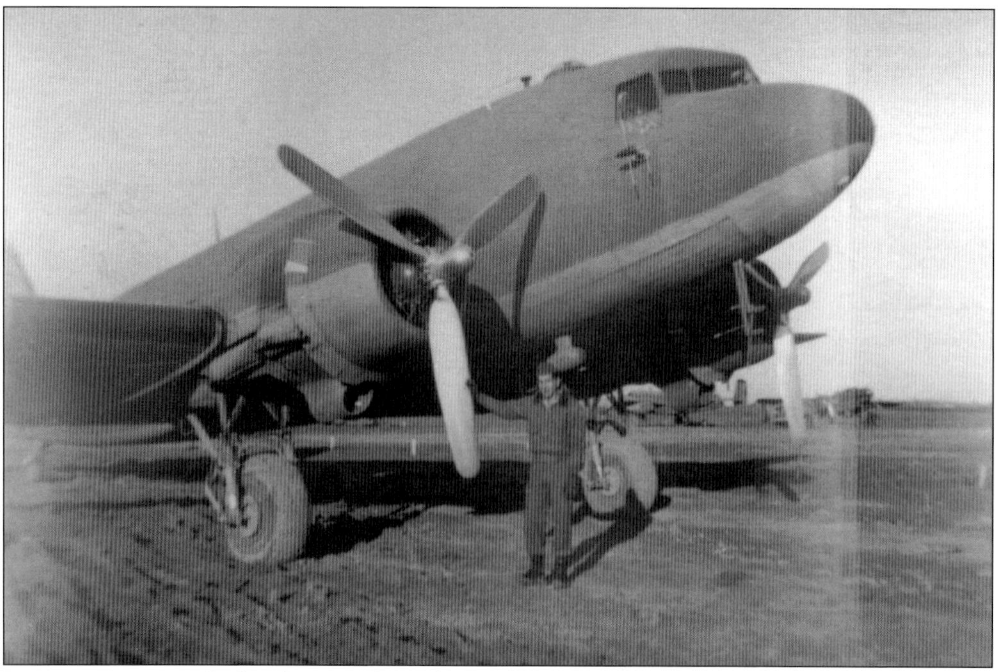

Pete Jones poses with the plane *Lucky Lady* in 1943 while stationed with the Air Force in Italy. Jones's job was to pack the plane with wounded soldiers in preparation for their flight to receive medical care. (Lawanda Jones.)

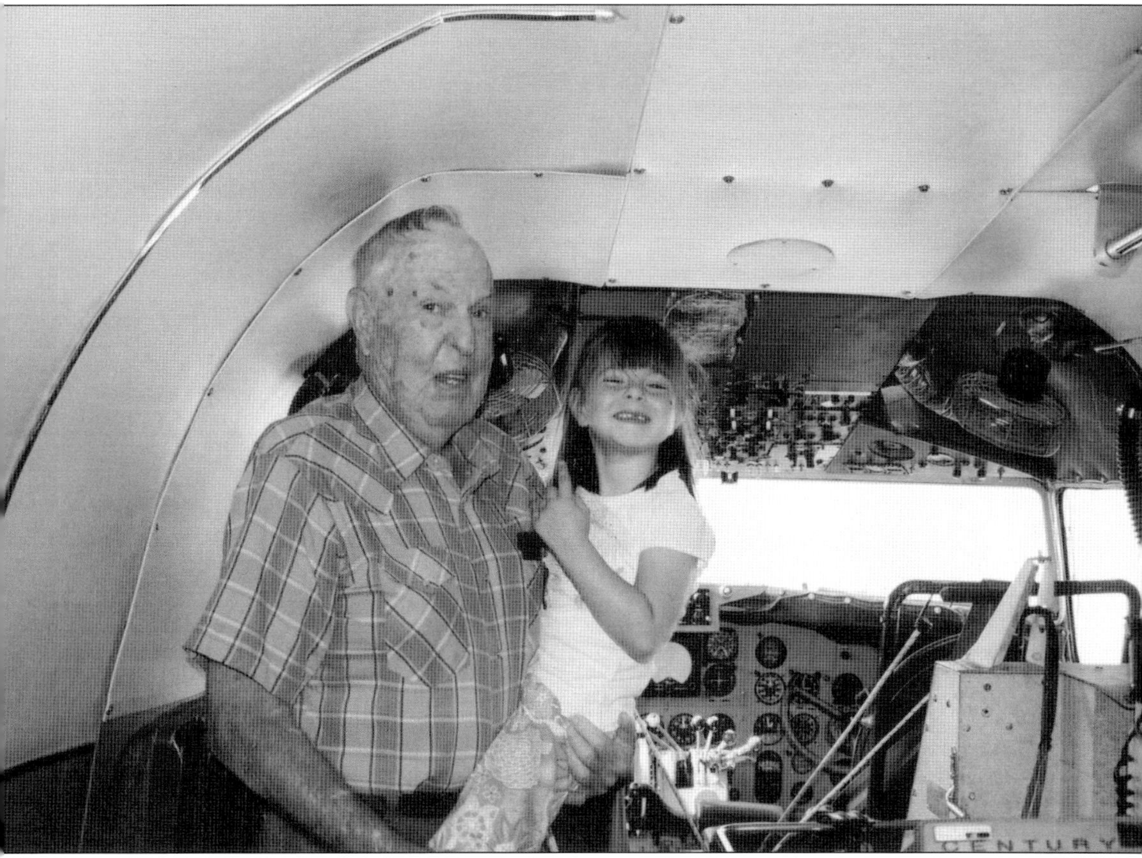

In 2007, an Air Force plane from the 1940s, exactly like the one Pete Jones flew with, came to the airport in Pauls Valley. Pete took his only grandchild, Meredith Jones, to tour the plane and was able to recall every detail inside and outside of the plane. It had been 65 years since he last flew in that make and model plane. (Lawanda Jones.)

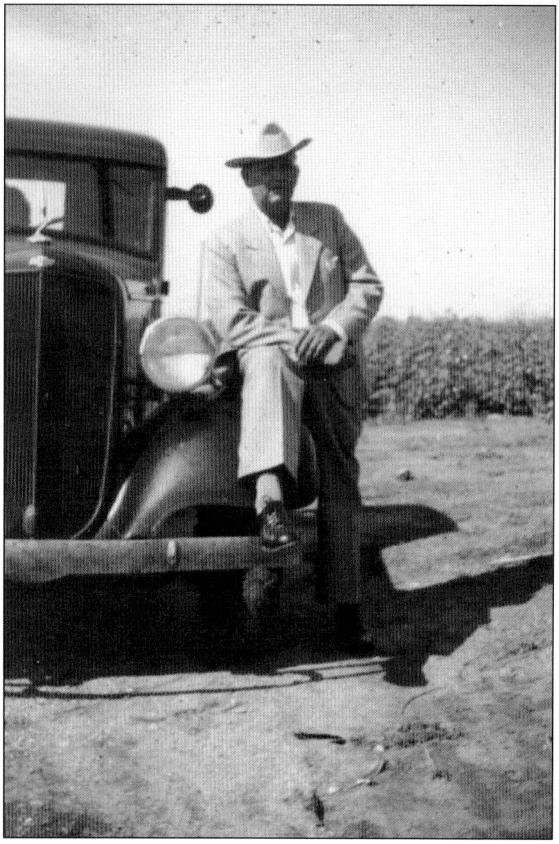

Frank Brassfield lived his entire life in Murray County where he and his wife farmed east of Davis. They were the parents of Lawanda Brassfield, who married Pete Jones from Sulphur. Lawanda still makes her home on the Jones Ranch north of Sulphur and is an active 60-plus-year member of the Oaklawn Home and Community Education Club, as it is known today. (Lawanda Jones.)

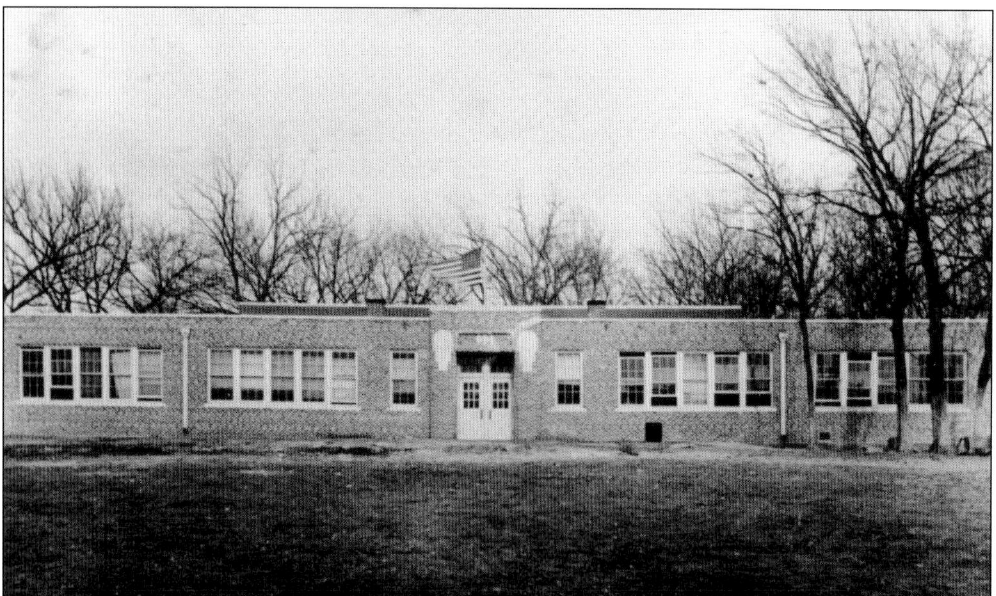

This is the Dougherty School as it looked in 1924. Even though the building is not used as a school today, it does continue to play an important role in the Dougherty community, where it serves as a meeting place for special events. (Judy Hale.)

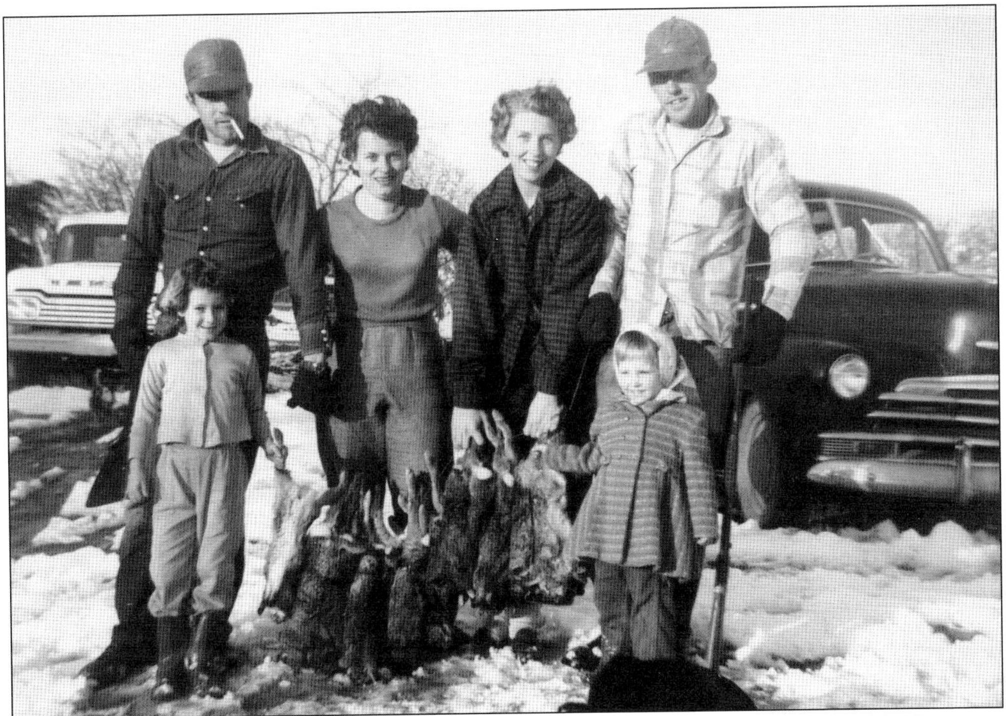

In January 1960, Mize brothers Richard and Don, along with their children go rabbit hunting. The Mize home place, located south of Sulphur, has been in the family for many years. Richard and Don's father, Shorty Mize, operated a dairy on the land for many years. After leaving the Korean War, serving as a paratrooper, Don returned to work the dairy. Since the dairy closed, sheep, chickens, and cattle have been raised on the land. Both Don and Richard still make their homes on the farm. The two brothers married cousins, and both couples have been married for 61 years. From left to right are Don (with daughter Teresa standing in front of him) and his wife Jearlene, alongside June and Richard (with daughter Brenda standing in front of Richard). The rabbits provided meals for both families. (June Mize.)

The Murray County Soil Testing Laboratory was set up in the extension office in 1952. The county agent would run tests for potash, organic matter, phosphorus, acidity, and free carbonates. The test results were then used for making recommendations on improving the soil. By 1959, a total of 2,033 tests had been conducted, and the charge was 50¢ per sample.

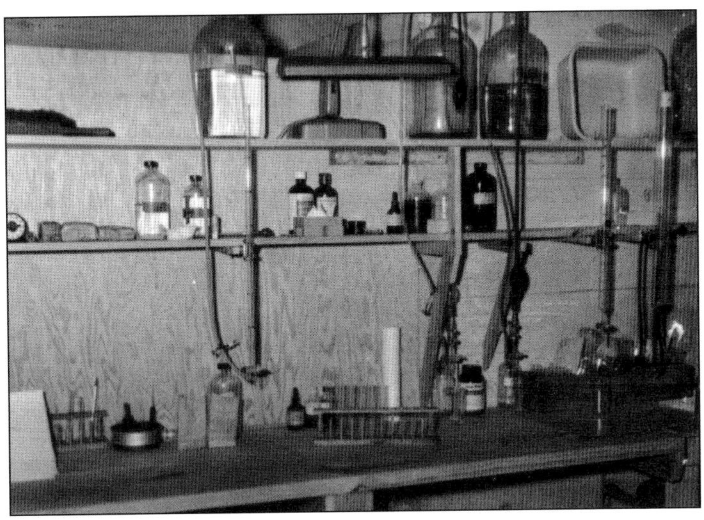

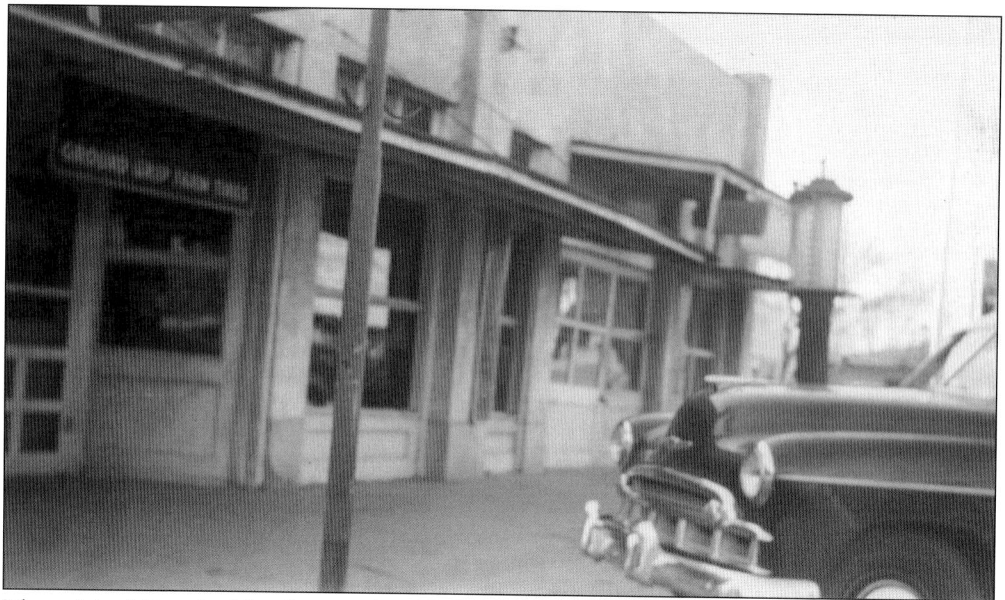

The original Crawford Implement Company was located at North Third Street in Davis. The business later moved south of Davis, and today, it is the P&G Laundry, owned by Ruth Pope, Ed Crawford's daughter. (Ruth Crawford Pope.)

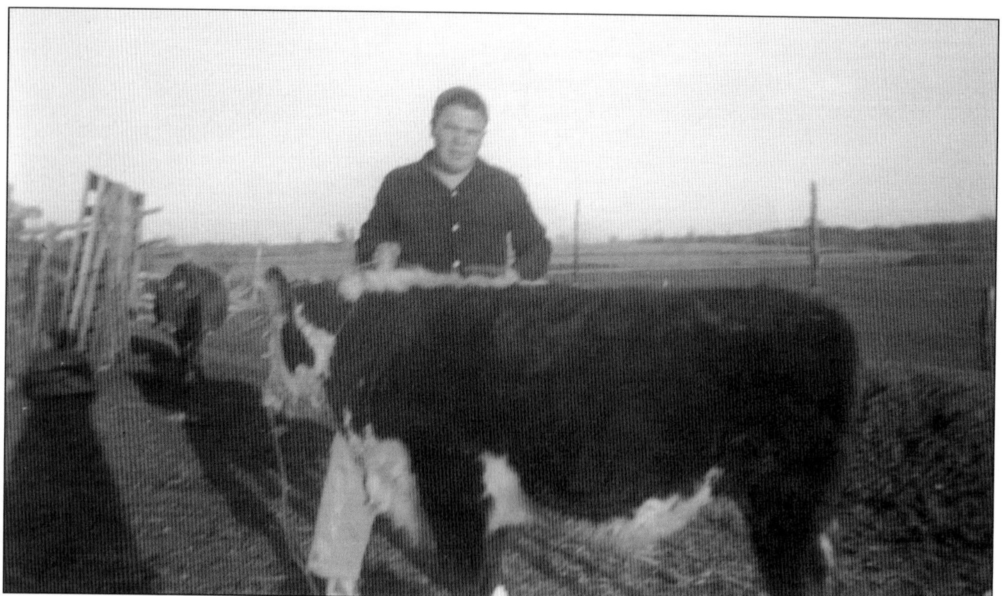

Jack Crawford poses with his show calf. The Crawford place was located north on Sunshine Road, east of Davis. (Ruth Crawford Pope.)

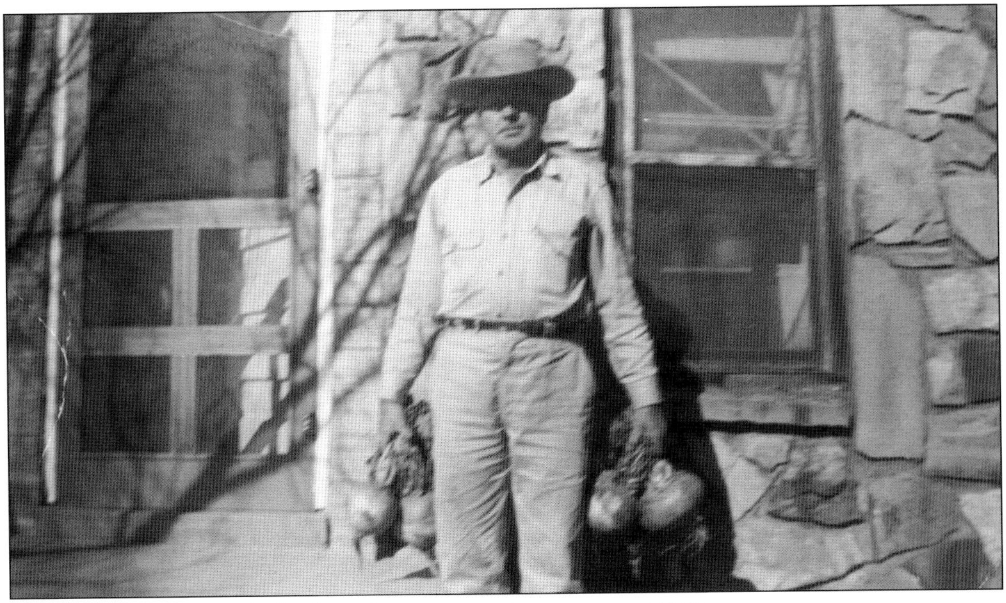

Ed Crawford poses with the huge beets grown in his garden. (Ruth Crawford Pope.)

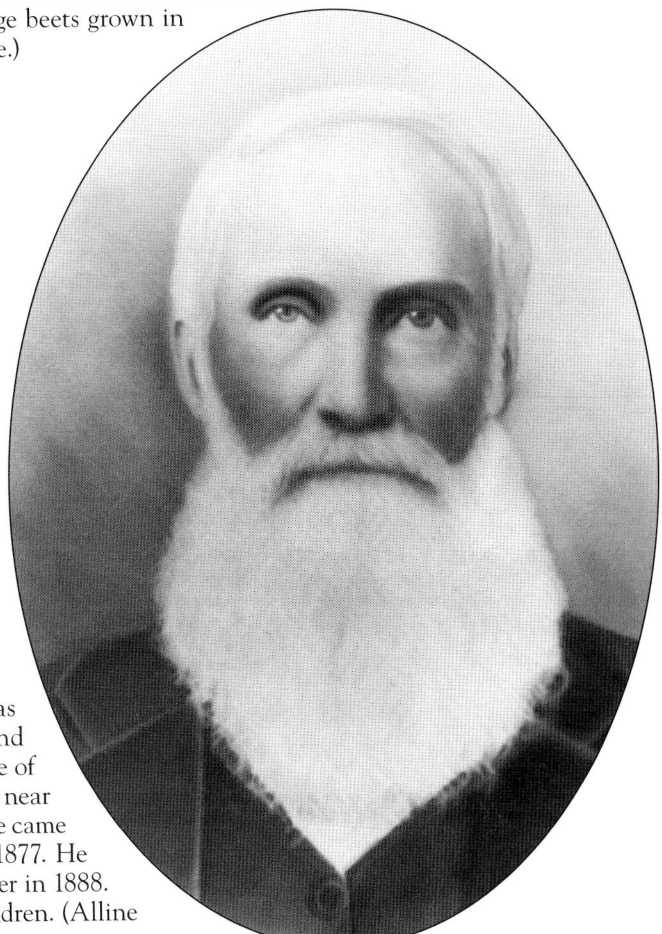

Jeremiah Vardaman Moss was born September 27, 1826, and died February 2, 1895, at the age of 72 years, 4 months, and 2 days near Fort Arbuckle. It appears that he came to the Fort Arbuckle area in 1877. He married Tinzey Isabel Chronister in 1888. They were parents to seven children. (Alline Moss Hilliard.)

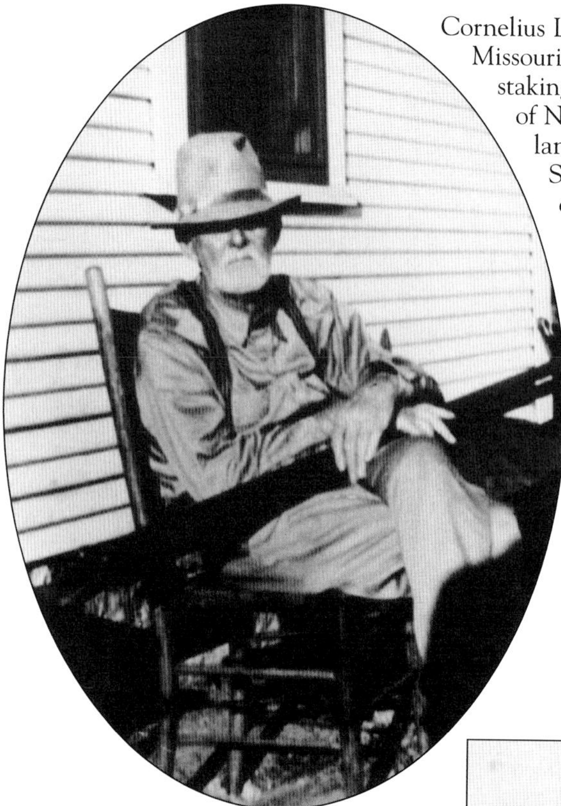

Cornelius Loyd Moss was born January 20, 1858, in Missouri and made the land run on April 22, 1889, staking his claim one mile east and one mile south of Norman, Oklahoma. He homesteaded the land for 14 months and then moved to the Sulphur area, where he made his home east of Sulphur. He died in 1948 at 90 years old. One of the Moss family descendants, Judy Moss lives in the original C.L. Moss two-story bungalow house. (Alline Moss Hilliard.)

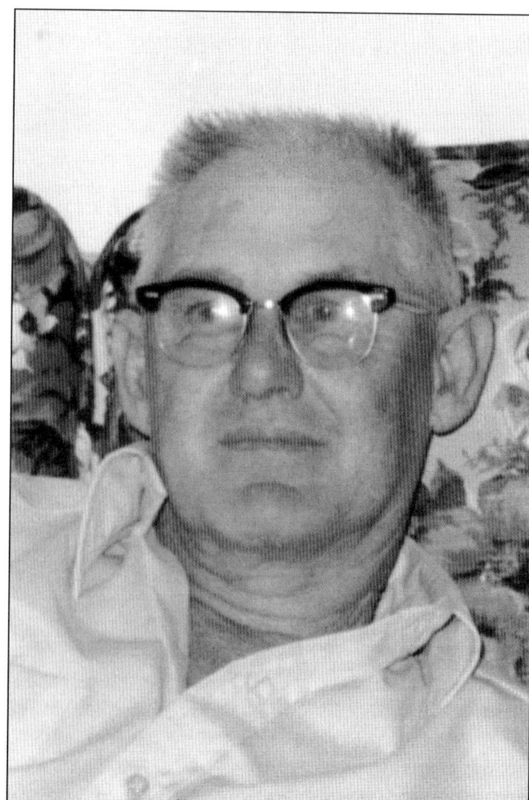

Calvin Moss, son of Cornelius Loyd Moss, and his wife, Letha, raised their 11 children—Judy, Alline, Patsy, Marilyn, Clyde, Mary, Jim, Deen, Jerry, Carol Sue, and Reba Kay—on the Moss place that has been in the family for over 100 years. (Alline Moss Hilliard.)

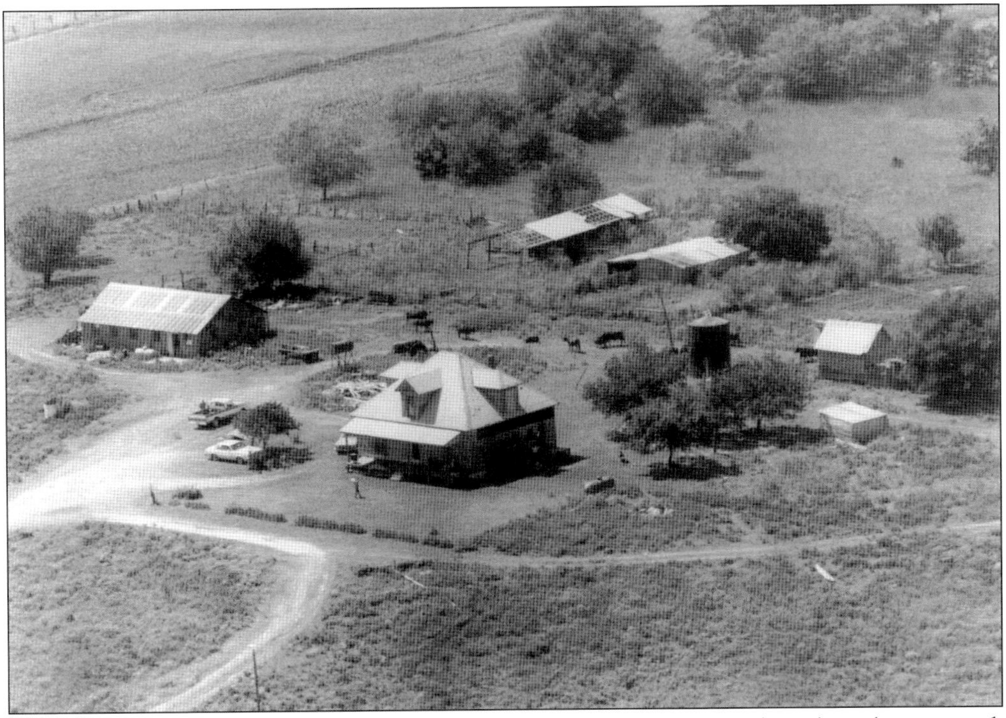

This aerial photograph shows the C.L. Moss home place. Many people have been born, raised, and died in this house. (Alline Moss Hilliard.)

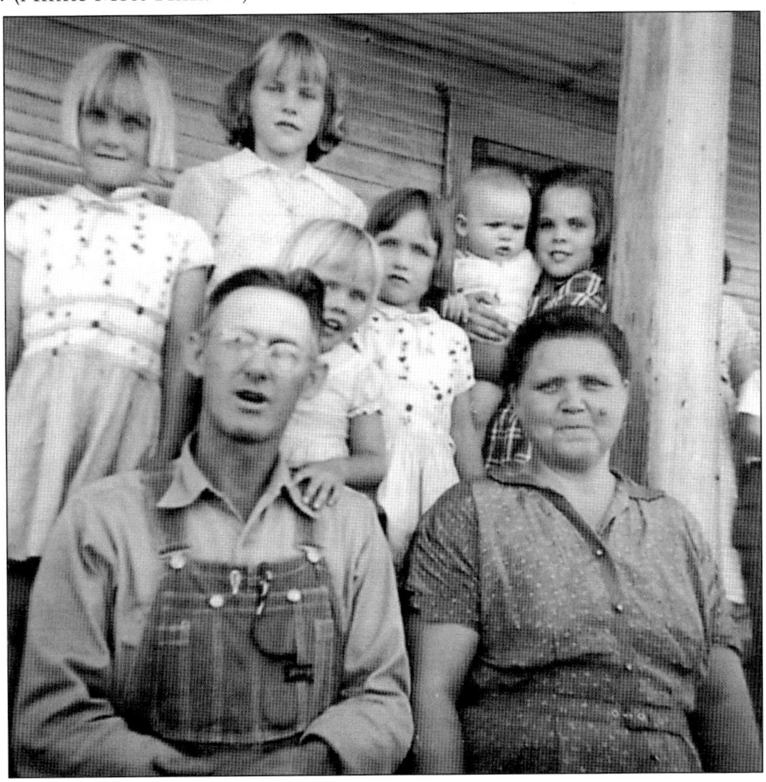

Calvin and Letha (Chambers) Moss pose with some of their children. Behind them, from left to right, are Judy, Alline, Patsy, Marilyn, baby Clyde, and Mary. (Alline Moss Hilliard.)

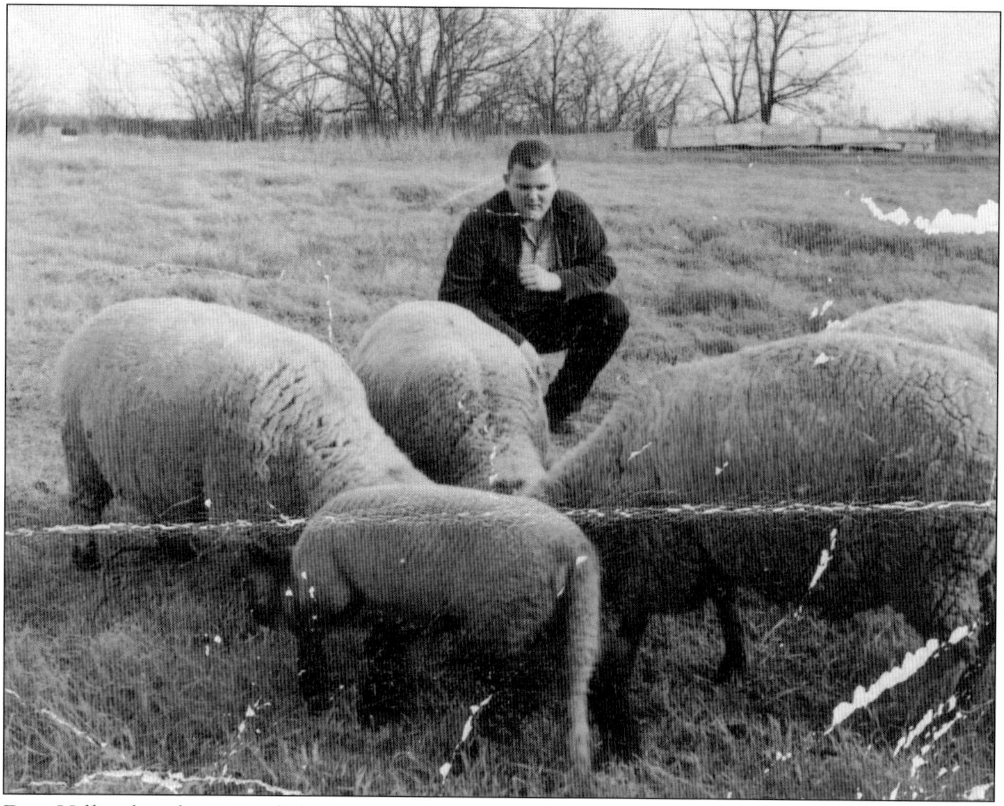

Don Hilliard is shown with his high school Future Farmers of America sheep project. Hilliard married Alline Moss, and they made their home across the road from the original Moss place. (Hilliard family.)

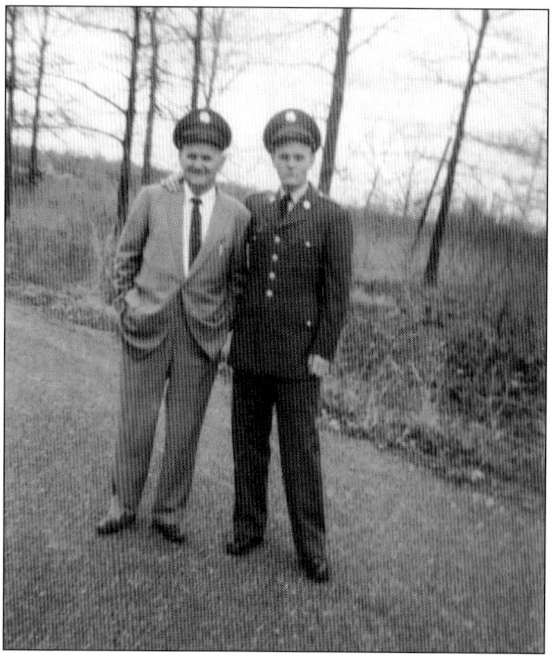

Don Hilliard (right) poses with his father, Buster Hilliard, while home on leave from the Army in 1962. Buster and his wife, Belle Maxine West, owned and operated a grocery store that once sat on the corner where the Vision Bank is currently located. The Hilliard children were Joe, Sue, Sherry, Don, and Danny, and the family lived in the back of the store. (Hilliard family.)

Big brother Don Hilliard holds little brother Danny. This photograph was taken in the living quarters in the back of their father's grocery store. (Hilliard family.)

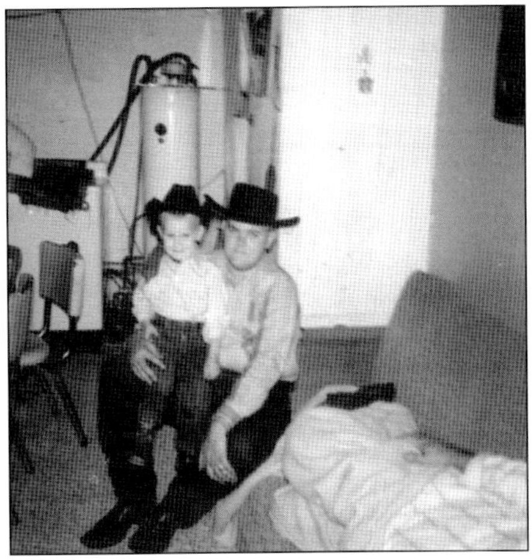

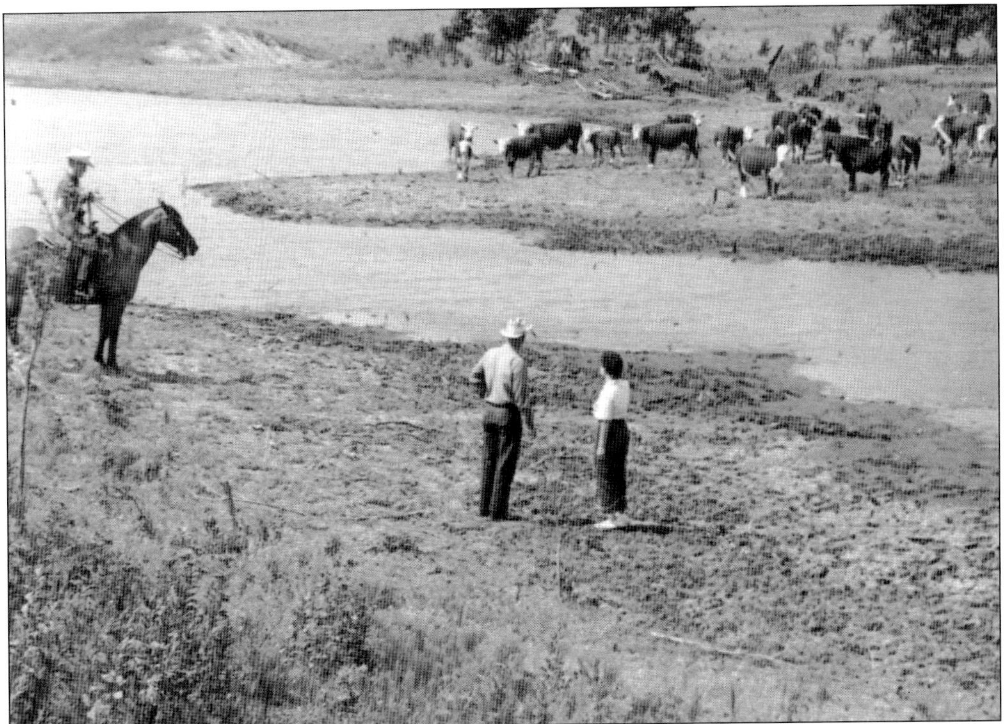

Two brothers, Arthur Herbert "Pete" Howe and Samuel Francis "Pamp" Howe married two sisters—Elmer "Pug" Blackwell and Mozelle "Slick" Blackwell—and as two dairy families in the Nebo community, they left their mark on the dairy industry in Oklahoma. Pamp and Slick had two children, Pat and Dorothy. Today, Pat, his wife Marilyn, and their son Patrick run a large cattle operation that covers hundreds of acres in Murray and Johnston Counties. Pete and Pug had three children: Steve, Karen, and Kay. Steve went on to operate his father's dairy for many years, winning many production and dairy cattle breeding awards on both the state and national levels. Steve and Pat have both raised their families on land that belonged to their fathers, and both still make their homes on Howe farms. This photograph is of Pat on horseback gathering cattle while his parents, Pamp and Slick, look on. Pete and Pamp Howe's father, Charles Francis Howe, was the original owner of the Nebo store, located somewhere close to the Nebo school right after statehood. (Pat Howe.)

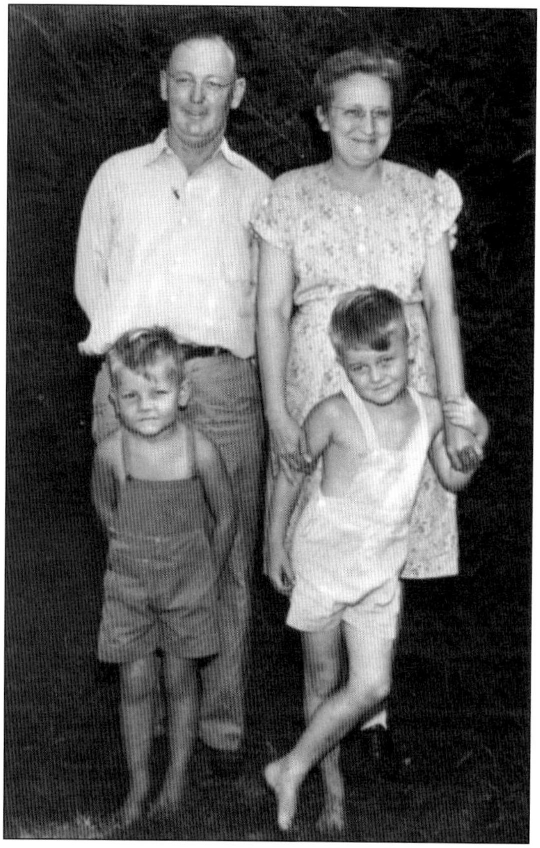

W.H. (left), also called Herbert, and Clifford (Walkup) Drake appear with their sons Tom (left) and Bob in this photograph. Herbert's father came to Murray County in 1924, and Herbert joined his father here in the 1930s, moving from the Oklahoma City area. (Drake Farms.)

Drake's Service Station was located in Davis and was operated by Herbert Drake for nine years before he purchased the Drake Motor Company. (Drake Farms.)

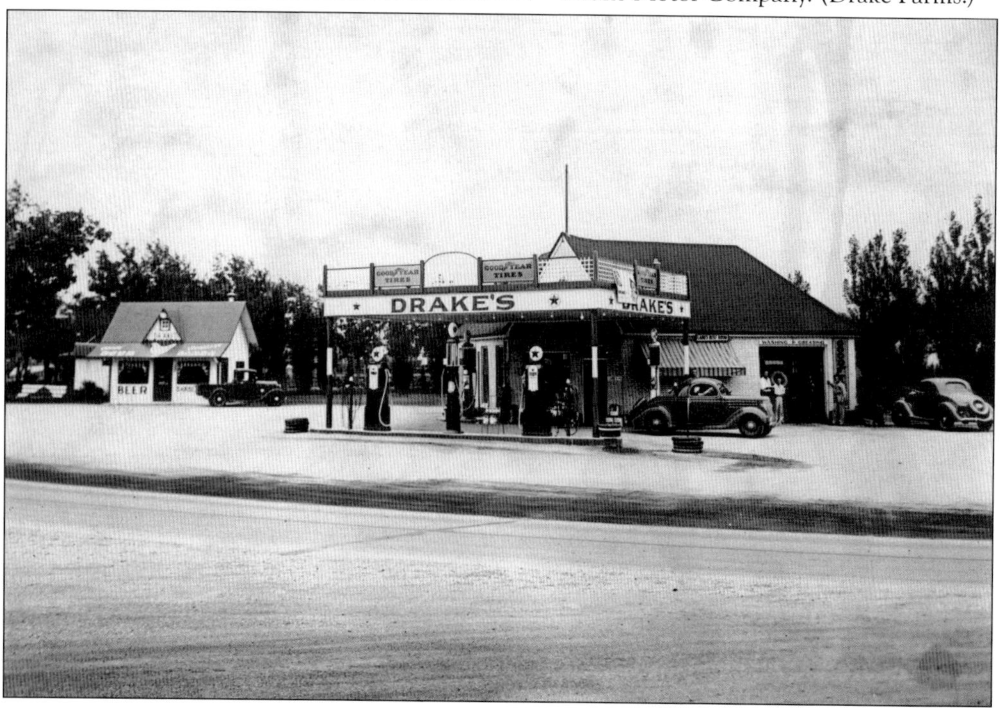

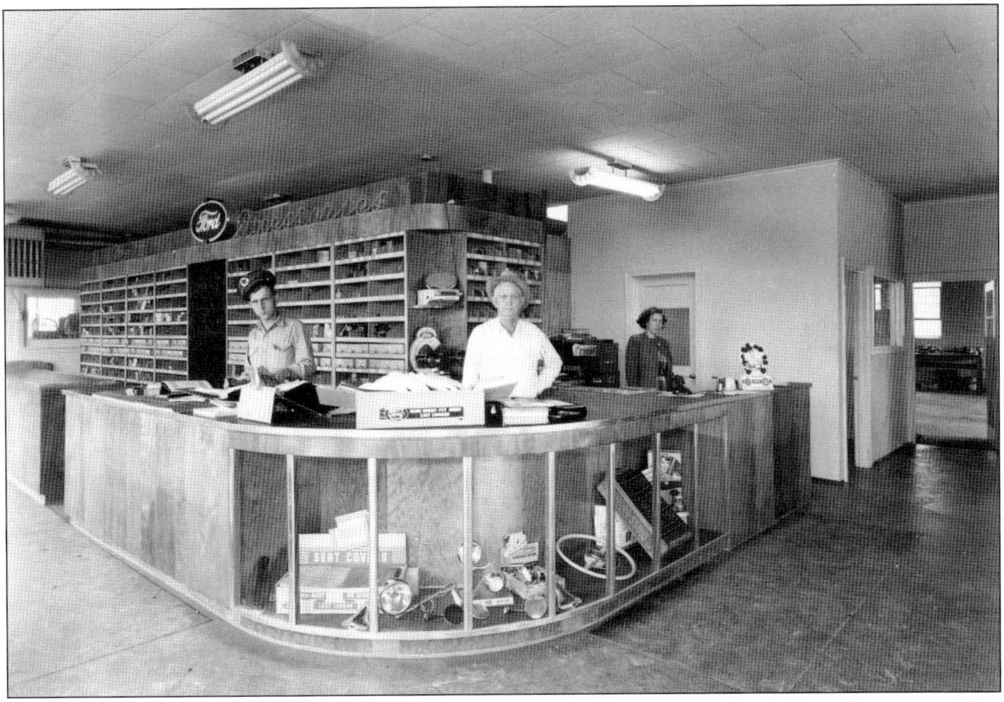

This photograph was taken inside the service department of the Drake Motor Company. The dealership sold Ford automobiles and opened in 1939. The woman in the photograph is Minnie Pullen. (Drake Farms.)

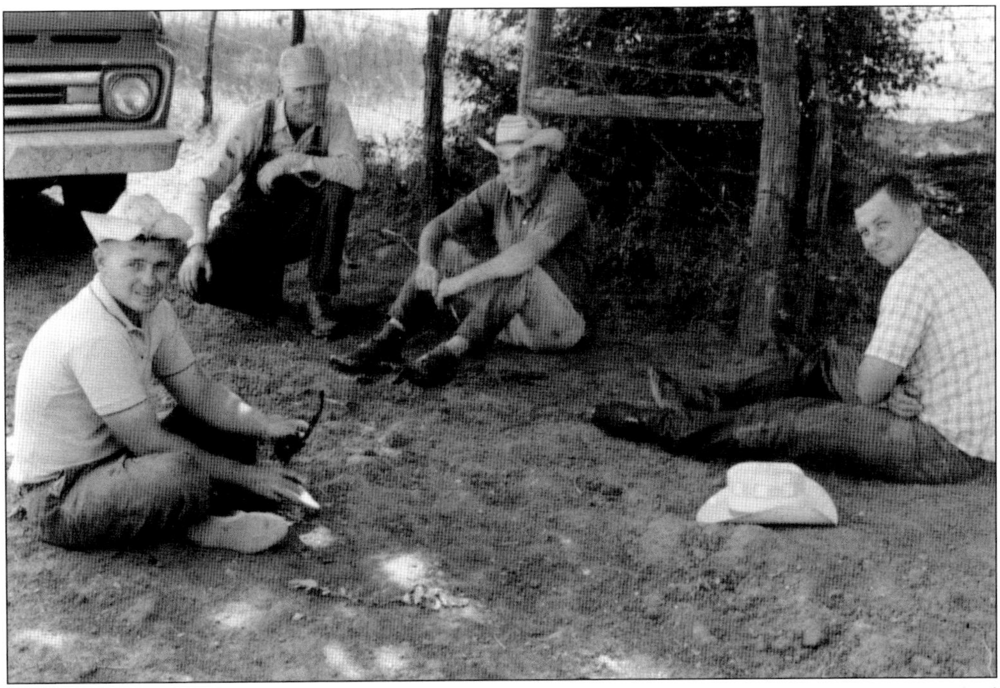

Cooling off in the shade in 1965 are, from left to right, Bob Drake, Glen Brownlee (who worked for the Drakes for 40-plus years), Jimmy Salter, and Tom Drake. (Drake Farms.)

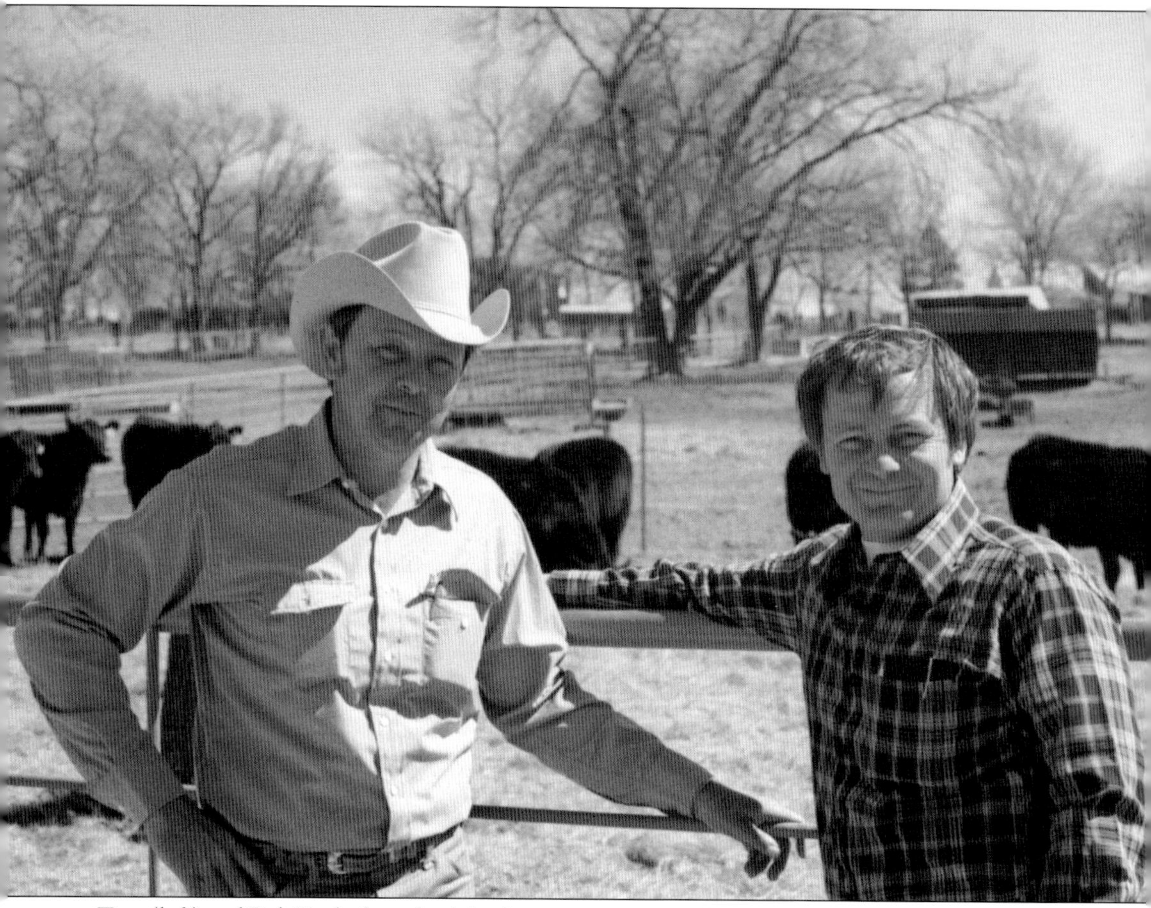

Tom (left) and Bob Drake have both had a major impact on Murray County agriculture. After the death of their father in 1964, Bob, Tom, and their mother formed Drake Farms in 1966. Working together they increased their land and cattle numbers, and Drake Farms became well known across the nation. Bob began his community service career in 1964 by serving on the farm bureau county board. Since 1964 to today, he has served as either board secretary or president. He served on the state farm bureau board for nine years, serving from 2002 to 2011. Bob served as president of the Oklahoma Cattlemen's Association from 1986 to 1988 and as National Cattlemen's Association national president in 1995. He is currently chairman of the National Grazing Lands Coalition serving in that role since 1997. Tom married Judy Morton from Sulphur, and Bob married Kay Blevens from Davis. In 2002, most of the land was sold to the Chickasaw Nation; Joe Tom Drake, Bob's son, manages the remaining farmlands and cattle. (Drake Farms.)

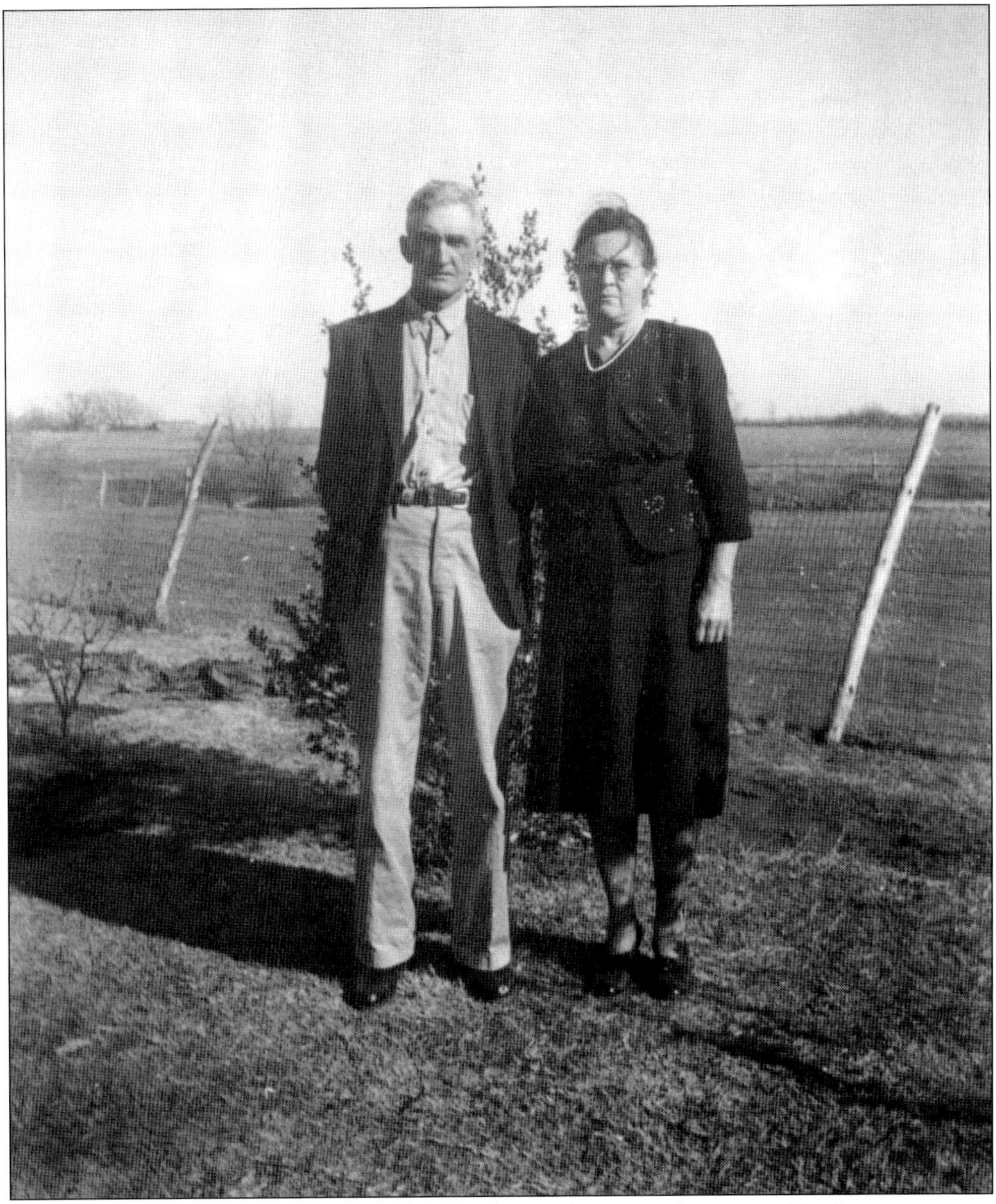

Tom Albright and Bessie Alice (Jayne) Albright are shown in this image. Tom's parents came from Rover, Arkansas, in 1905 and farmed the land owned by the Boss Tillery family. In 1943, Tom and Bessie purchased land and established their own farm and small dairy across the road from the Tillery place. Here, they grew oats, alfalfa, corn, and cotton. Tom and Bessie had eight children: six sons and two daughters. They were named Clyde, Dan, Tommy, Kirby, Joe, Ray, Irene, and Nadine. Five of the six sons served in World War II in some capacity. Today, son Joe and his wife, June, make their home on the original homesite, arriving back in Murray County upon Joe's retirement after 50 years of service with the US Department of Agriculture.

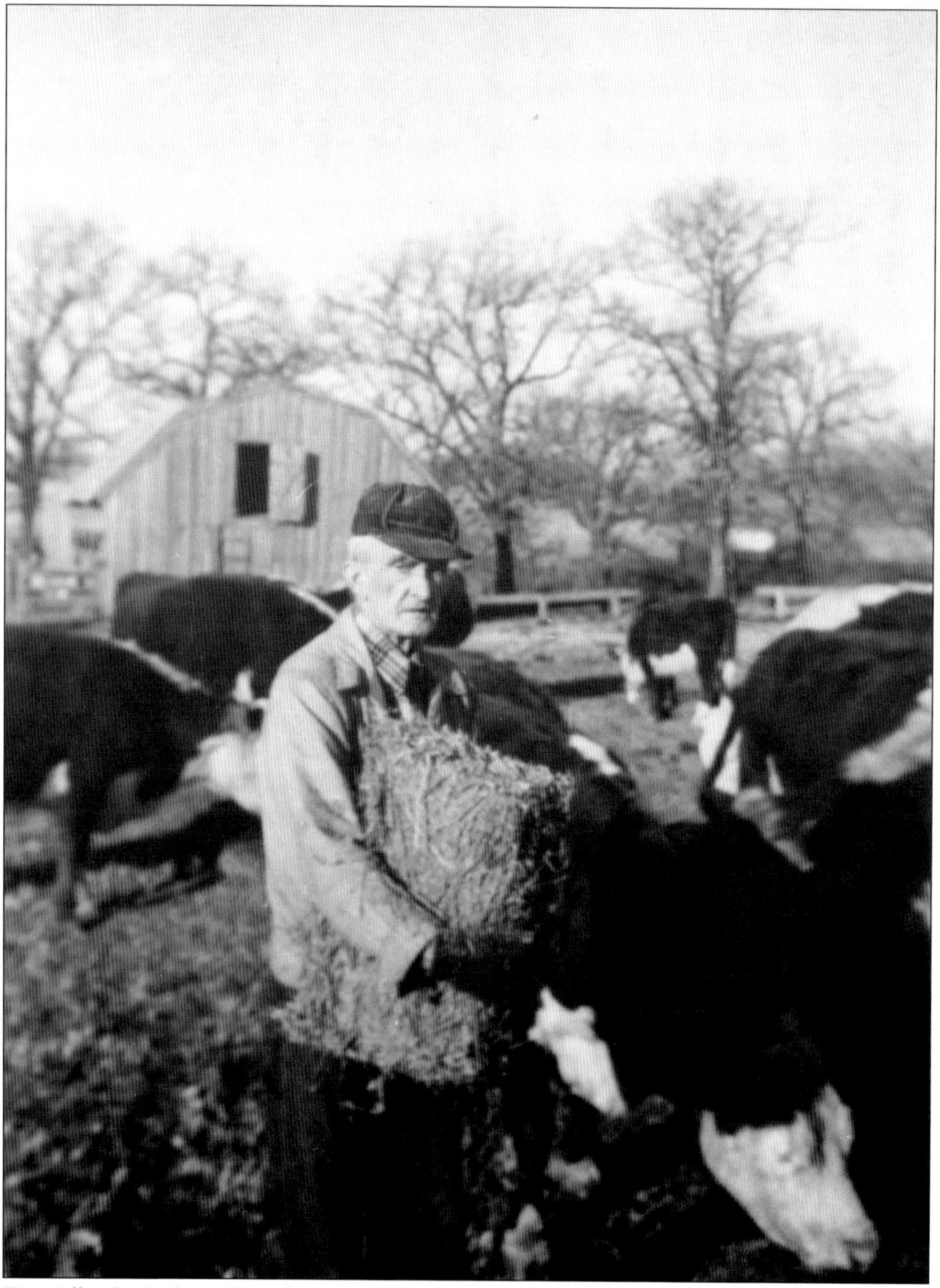

Tom Albright feeds cattle in this 1964 photograph. Albright was very proud of his eight children and their successful careers. Clyde owned a steel company, Tommy was the mechanical engineer working with Clyde, and brother Ray worked in the steel company as well. Dan was a veterinarian, Irene and Kirby were in real estate businesses, Nadine worked with General Electric in Dallas, and Joe had a 50-year career with the US Department of Agriculture and a law degree that he earned by attending night school.

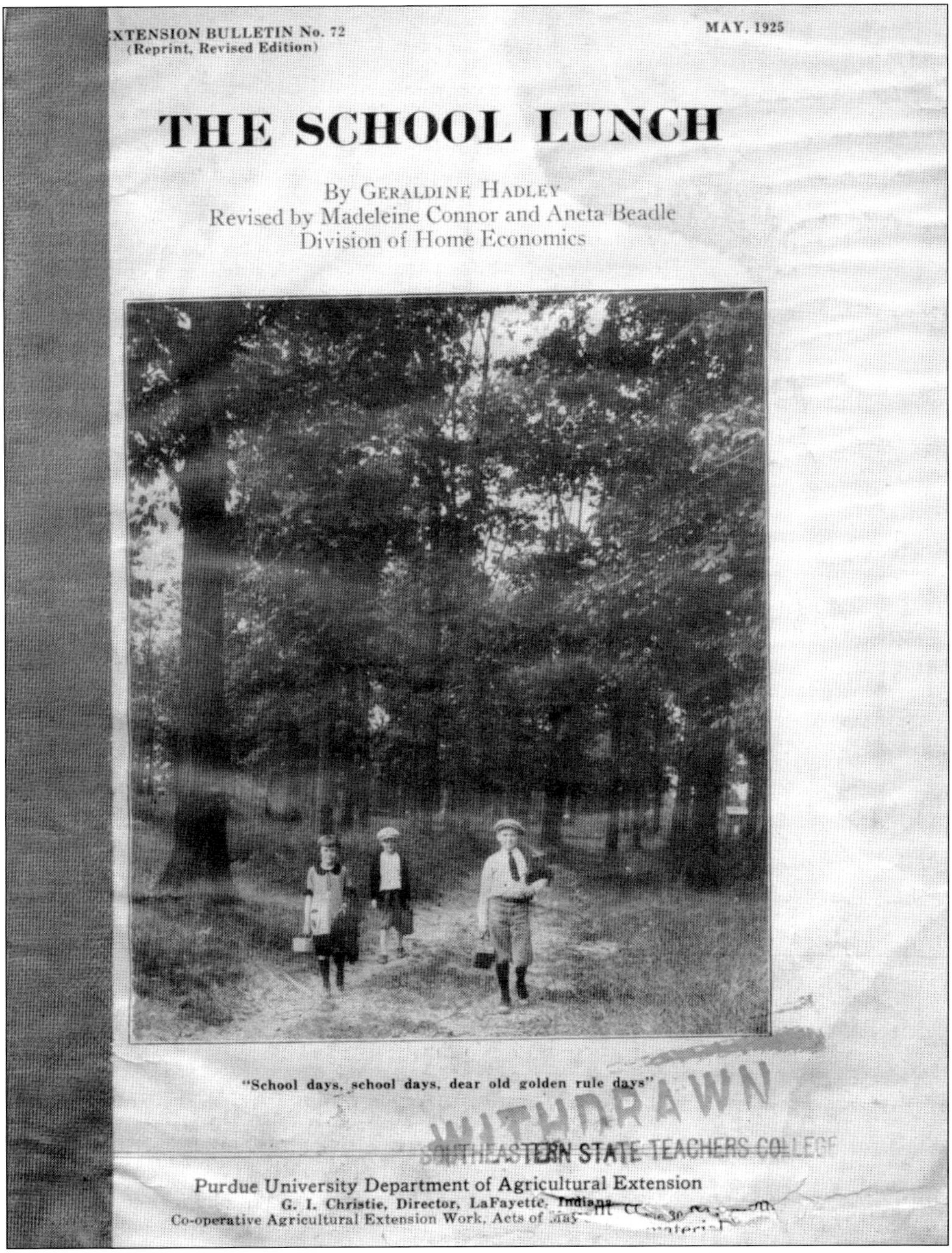
XTENSION BULLETIN No. 72
(Reprint, Revised Edition)

MAY, 1925

THE SCHOOL LUNCH

By GERALDINE HADLEY
Revised by Madeleine Connor and Aneta Beadle
Division of Home Economics

"School days, school days, dear old golden rule days"

Purdue University Department of Agricultural Extension
G. I. Christie, Director, LaFayette, Indiana
Co-operative Agricultural Extension Work, Acts of May

Here is the school lunch in a 1925 *Extension Bulletin*. The opening of the bulletin introduces lunch at school with the following opening paragraph: "A serious problem presents itself when we consider the great number of workers and school children who depend on the lunch box for one-third of their food supply. Too often food materials left over from breakfast, such as fried meat, fried eggs, crackers or biscuit, are wrapped in a newspaper, placed in a coat pocket or school bag and given to the children as they hurry to catch the school wagon. Food wrapped in newspapers, carried in this manner has every opportunity for germ infection, from the newspaper the cloak hall garments, the air in schoolroom and the dirty hands of the consumer."

5

Advantages of Hot Lunch:

To Pupils—Increases vitality and scholarship.
Trains in food preparation, food value, food habits, serving, table manners, discipline, business.
Insures more time for eating.
Improves character of lunch brought from home.

To School—Makes discipline easier, improves attendance and punctuality.

To Home—Carries study of food into the home.
Becomes another link between home and school.
Dignifies cooking, housework and home industry.

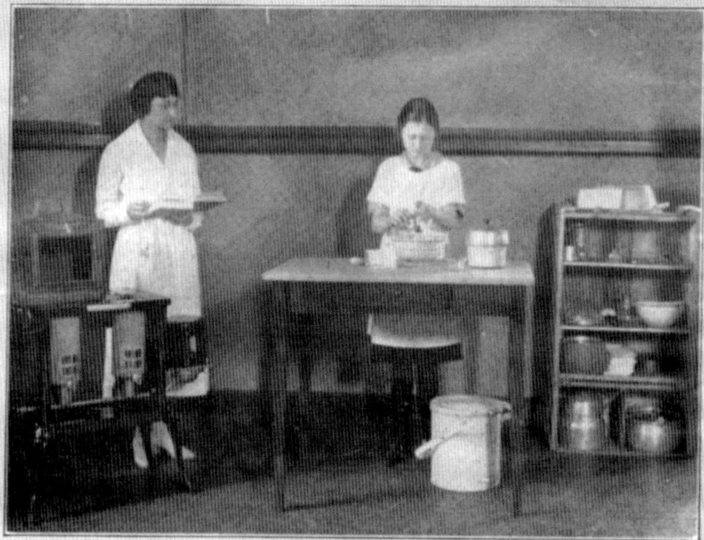

Fig. 4. Equipment for Serving Hot School Lunch.

How to Finance a Hot Lunch

As it is necessary to secure a certain amount of equipment, the following are ways suggested to obtain funds:

1. Trustees might buy equipment.
2. Given by some local organization.
3. Give entertainments to secure funds.

Necessary Equipment

The equipment needed will vary in different localities, and with the extensiveness of the lunch served. The following list is the minimum needed by every school.

1. Stove.
2. Double boiler.
3. Large kettle.
4. Paring knife.
5. Carving knife.
6. Long-handled spoon.
7. Tablespoon.
8. Two dish pans, dish cloths and towels.
9. Paper napkins.

The 1925 *Extension Bulletin* introduced a new idea—hot lunches—for public schools. The bulletin statements include the following quotes: "The hot lunch should be correlated with the subjects studied in school. In the arithmetic class the pupils may keep account of the cost of food needed for lunch, figuring quantities of supplies, and in changing quantities in recipes to meet the needs of the school. In the geography class, a study of production and transportation of the food used in the hot dish. Many interesting and attractive posters may be made in the art class using such subjects as 'Preparing Lunch,' 'Etiquette at the Table,' 'To Set the Table,' and 'To Wash Dishes.'"

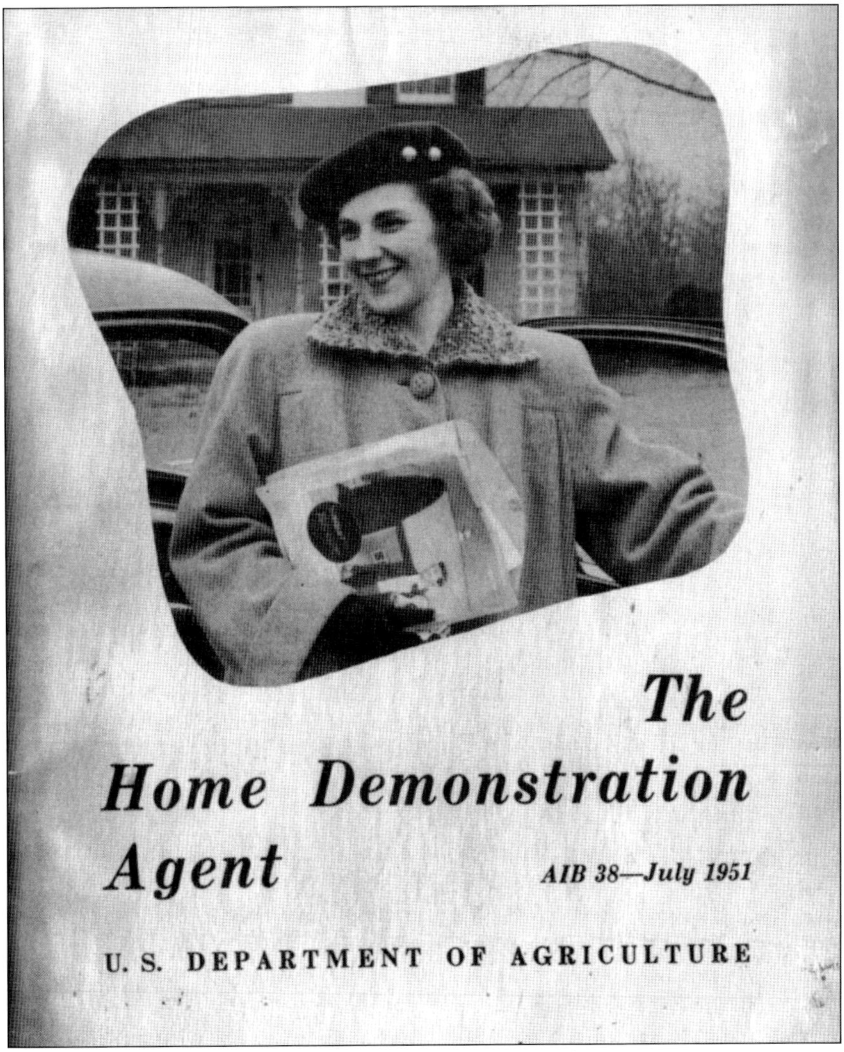

The Home Demonstration Agent's Objectives:

- To give to rural people, in a form in which they can use it at a time when they need it, information that will enable them to become better citizens in a democracy.
- To help rural families obtain and manage an income—both money and nonmoney—that will contribute to better living for the family.
- To develop leadership abilities in rural women and girls.
- To develop an awareness of the need of improved facilities for medical care and of improved nutrition practices and other preventive measures in promoting improved health among all rural families.
- To assist families in planning and making housing improvements in rural homes.
- To develop an appreciation of the importance of recreating in rural homes and communities.
- To develop in rural women and girls competence in using their human and material resources in ways that will contribute to better rural living, these ways based on the findings of research and the experience of homemakers.
- To stimulate in rural people an awareness of the part they can play in making their communities more wholesome and attractive places in which to live.

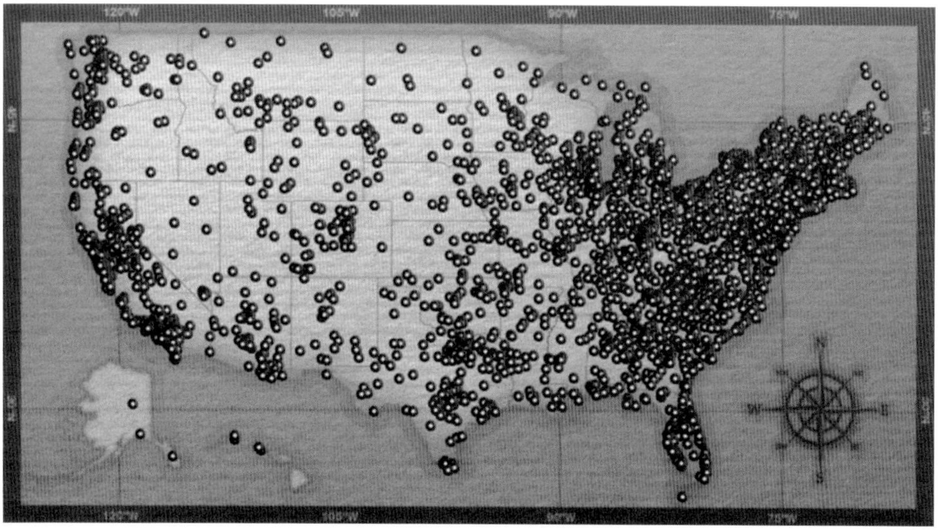